Walking By Faith

God's Progressive Will In My Life

Loretta Bray

To my family so precious, my seven children, my seventeen grandchildren, and my seventeen and growing great grandchildren, whom God has so wonderfully blessed us with. My husband already gone home, my family and his family, all my friends and brothers and sisters in the Lord.

I especially want to thank my son Alan who has helped me so much in getting this book written.
I know he has spent hours and hours getting it ready.

I love you all

© 2019 Loretta Bray, All Rights Reserved.

Scriptures marked KJV are taken from the KING JAMES VERSION (KJV): KING JAMES VERSION, public domain.

Cover photo credit: Logan Bray

ISBN: 978-0-578-48702-1 (hardback)
       978-0-578-48706-9 (paperback)
       978-0-578-48762-5 (epub)
       978-1-09-095736-8 (pbk/Amazon)

Contents

Introduction 14
With God Nothing Shall be Impossible 16
Answered Prayer 17
The Altar is Important 18
Convictions 19
Confession is Good for the Soul 20
We All Like Sheep, Have Gone Astray 21
A Dream from God 22
Something is Missing 23
My First Conviction 25
Becoming Aware 27
Forgiveness 28
The Drawing of God's Spirit 29
If You Love Jesus, Raise Your Hand 30
Seeking Him 31
Another Step Closer to God 32
Mt. Zion Church of God 34
Time to Pray 35
The Visit From Pastor Henry 36
Jesus and Me 37
The Whole World Looked Clean and New 39
How Do I Know He Lives? 40
The First Thanksgiving 41
Come, I Say Come 43
The Darkness Departs as Jesus Comes In 44
With Him, We Have Everything We Need 45
The Purpose of the Church 46
We Never Walk Alone 47
Deliverance From Fear 48
Be an Overcomer 49
Trust God 50
The Battle Is The Lord's 51
This Battle Is The Lord's 52
So Sincere 53
The Cleft Of The Rock 54
A Note To Soul Winners 55
Personal Contact 56-58
Am I My Brothers' Keeper? 60-62

Strong Faith 63
Influence..64-65
Influence.. 65
His Ways Are Not Our Ways 66
The Face Of Jesus 67
If We're Going To Shine 68
Wisdom From Above, The Need 71
Children Are A Blessing 72
Blessed Moments 73
Eyes To Behold... 74
Daddy, Are You Going With Us? 75
Happy Father's Day, Paul 76
Bible Stories On The Radio 77
Memories.. 78
Stepping Stones 79
Miracles Still Happen... 80
Ask And Ye Shall Receive 81
Disappointments Bring Growth............................... 82
Needs Met 83
Continue In The Christian Life 84
Blessing Returned.. 85
There Must Be A Desire 87
Abide In Christ... 89
Know By Experience 90
A Healing.. 92
Just Ask.. 93
Walking By Faith 94
Seeking God's Will.. 95
Nellie Bray 96
Who Will Stand In The Gap?.................................. 97
Jesus Is The Source Of All Revelation.......................... 98
Truth And Freedom 99
A New World.. 100
One And Only True God..................................... 101
Amazing Grace.. 102
1961.. 103
Follow Me 105
A Relationship, Not Just A Name..................... 106-109
The Lord Will Provide 110-111
God Hears Our Cry.. 112
It's Going To Take Faith 113
Having Abundant Life 115

Your Source Of Authority.................................116
Knowing God's Nature And His Will....................117
God's Commands Are For Your Good 118
God Is All Knowing..............................119-121
God Reveals Himself To You 122
Give No Place To The Devil............................123
To Any Daddy...125
Sanctification...126
New Life..127
Let There Be Light....................................128
A Set Time 129
He Will Be Our Shield.................................130
Battle For The Quiet Time........................131-132
Joseph..133
Clothed In His Righteousness 134
We Can Rest In Him..................................135
Beneath God's Brightest Star 136
The Eyes..137
Faith Is Believing In His Love..........................138
A Place Of Love 139
A Place Of Love: A Place Of Sharing 140
A Place Of Love: My Secret Place......................142
Storing Up Our Treasures........................143-145
The Straight Gate................................146-147
God's Purpose For Our Lives....................148-152
Hold Them Up To God 153
Parable Of The Talents 154
Set Your Affections On Things Above, Not On Things
Of The Earth 156
Schooling By The Great Teacher.................158-162
Confidence In The Cleansing Power 168
The Key To Power..............................169-174
Building A Wall Of Faith..............................175
The Just Shall Live By Faith 177
Keep Your Joy..178
What Is The Difference Between Spiritual "Milk" and "Solid Food"?....179
Fasting And Prayer...................................180
The Safe Place..181
God Send A Great Awakening: In Him Is No Darkness....182-183
Developing Faith................................184-185
Jesus Told Us 187
The Meaning 189

Leaders, Be Strong And Of Good Courage; Go After It	196
Going Into Battle	198-200
Keep Your Eye On Jesus	201
The Teachers Inventory Sheet; To Be Checked Daily	202
Jesus Wants Us To Know Him, Not Just Know About Him	203
Anointed To Share The Burden	204
Putting First Things First	205
Living In The Present	208
Let The Word Be Made Flesh	209-210
Grace	211
The Word	212
The Path To Greatness Is Goodness	213
What Causes Lukewarmness?	214
Praying God's Word	221
The Call Of Wisdom	222
In Jesus' Name	224
Open Eyes	225-227
Trusting In Ourselves	228
Genuine Love	229
Ask; Seek; Knock	236
There Must Be A Desire To Know Him	237
My First Fast	238
Blind Man's Bluff	239
What Is Speaking In Tongues?	240
Heavenly Breezes	242-244
We Are Not Alone	245
A Safe Place	246-248
Garden Times	249
Lean Thou On Me	250
God Is Truth	251
God's People Are A Special People	252
An Encouraging Word	253
Special Moments	254
Be Focused	255
Who Are You Pleasing?	256
Our Prayer Closet	257-259
The Miracle Of Prayer	260
Spiritual Application To Salvation	261-262
The Church	263
Five Senses	264-265
My Heart Is Fixed	266
Daily	267

Do We Truly Know Him?	268-269
Dwelling Place	270
Discipline	274
It Is The Humbled Soul That Has Power With God	275
The Key	277
Up On The Mount	278-280
The Family Fortune	282-283
Trusting In The Lord	285
Being More Aware	286
Jesus Came To Do His Father's Will	288
Our Testimony Is Important	289
Consider The Lilies	290-291
Words Giving Rest	292
My Special Place	293-295
A Commission And A Revelation	296
Temptation And Sin	297
The Cross	298
God Always Keeps His Promise	299
Special Times With Little Ones	301
A Separate People	302
Waiting For God's Time And Revelation	304
It Is God's Will For Us To Praise Him And His Works	305
Conduct	307
Reflections	308
Old Things Are Past Away	309
I Am Not Ashamed	310
Sitting At Jesus' Feet	311
The Spirit Of The World And The Spirit Of God	312
By What Power Do You Do This?	313
The Anointed Savior Is Worthy Of All Praise!	315
The Search For Happiness	316-318
A Prayer Was Prayed; God Heard	319
The Meaning Of Meekness	320
Symbols Of The Word Of God	321-322
Seven Steps In Obtaining Help	324
When Thou Hast Shut The Door	327
Build The Home	329
Faith – Believing - Doing	331
Her Name Is Ruth	332
Repentance	333
Being Made Ready	337-339
Light Overcomes Darkness	341

We Need a Set Time for Prayer. 342
We Are Laborers Together With Him. 346
Baptism In The Word. 348
Strength For Each Day. 349
God Has Absolute Power 350
My Mother's Stories 351
Having Your Feet Shod. 355
Encounters With God 356
Behind Closed Doors 357
Listen To His Voice. 358
Christ In You: The Hope Of Glory 359
Soul Winners 360
Four Simple Rules 361
Only One Way. 362
Refusing To Bow 363
Think On These Things 364
The Desires Of Our Heart 365
Divine Protection 367
The Disciple Whom Jesus Loved 369
Omnipotent; Omniscient; Omnipresent 370
Daily Grace 371
What Separates God's People From All Others On Earth? 373
God's Set Time 374
Do Our Words Fit Who We Are? 375
Starting Young 376
Words Of Life 379
God's Word – Our Road Map 380
Jesus Equal With God In Nature 381
Jesus Equal With God In Power. 382
Jesus Equal With God In Authority 383
First Love 384
We Too Must Wait 385
Seeking Treasure 386
For A Purpose. 387
Submission To God's Will 389
Wealth That Doesn't Pass Away 390
Singers And Singing In Worship 391
The War Between The Flesh And Spirit 392
Obedience 393
Spiritual Warfare – The Whole Armor of God. 394
Pray In The Spirit. 395
Be Not Afraid; Only Believe. 396

Christian Growth	397
Be Not Anxious	398
Trust And Depend On God	399
What Is Self-Denial	400
Justification	401
No Need To Worry; Have Faith	402
Baptism In The Holy Spirit	403
Jesus Our Intercessor	404
In Him	406
Confidence In His Word	407
God Always Has A People	408
Thankful For The Lessons	409
The Anointing Of The Holy Spirit	410
What A Wonderful Comforter He Is	411
For God So Loved The World	412
WORKS CITED	413

Introduction

As I look back over my life, I'm so thankful for God's love toward us. I can see Him watching over us all through the years. There have been special times, when He has shown me His greatness and His love. At times, I've suffered His correction and chastisement, known His comfort, and felt His presence with me. He is Wonderful, and I am so thankful to Him for His love and all that He is to me. He is the Living Water.

Have you ever heard of an Artesian Well? I don't think I had ever heard of an Artesian Well until we moved to Indiana around 1969. These wells were on the properties of the small housing addition we ended up settling into, where I still live today, almost 50 years gone by. After we'd lived there for some time, I found out many of the houses had these wells. Some people actually used them instead of the city water service. The water was so pure; it was always good and cold; it was so refreshing. Others had their wells capped off, simply because of the constant flow of water. The wells could often overflow, and water would stand in the yard at times.

As I remembered the wells, I was reminded how the Holy Spirit works. In the first book of the Old Testament, the creation of the world is described. Genesis 1:2 reminds me of the condition I was in before God began drawing me to Him. The verse says, *"And the earth was without form and void; and darkness was upon the face of the deep. And the Spirit of God moved upon the face of the waters."* I was in darkness, separated from God because of sin, empty within, yet not knowing I was in such a terrible condition.

The Holy Spirit began to move and hover over me and let me begin to realize my need for God. In the New Testament, we see the Holy Spirit, after Jesus ascended, abiding in the chosen ones of God. He filled them to overflowing.

Christ reveals the Living Water. He said in John 7:38, *"He that believeth on me, as the scripture hath said, out of his belly shall flow rivers of living water….."*

We, as vessels, are to be emptied of self and filled with God's Holy Spirit; always ready and willing to do God's will. Don't cap off the flow of the Holy Spirit and what He wants to do in your life. He is a well in us. There is Life in Him. What He does in our lives will bless and bring life to those in need. As He overflows in our lives, He will receive the glory.

He is the Living Water!
He is my God and a Wonderful Father!

With God Nothing Shall be Impossible

I thought, "I could never write a book."
But out of my life's precious moments I took,
And put them together for hearts so dear.
For it's my desire for them to hear,
Of how wonderful our Father's love is toward us.
Who sought us and brought us to Him who is so precious.
How He's led us and drawn us by His spirit so dear,
Until we came to the place, His voice we could hear.

"Is anything too hard for the Lord? At the time appointed I will return unto thee, according to the time of life, and Sarah shall have a son."— Genesis 18:14

"Ah Lord God! Behold, thou hast made the heaven and the earth by thy great power and stretched out arm, and there is nothing too hard for thee."— Jeremiah 32:17

Answered Prayer

It was somewhere around 1945; I was about 8 years old. Even as a little girl, God had begun developing real faith in me. I remember one occasion, my mom was very sick, and dad sat at her bedside. I can recall dad crying. I went into another room and knelt to pray. I asked God, "Please don't let my mommy die." Then I remembered to say, "If it is your will." The experience that I had at that moment was so very real. I felt God's presence come down over me with such a sweet peace and faith so bright. I knew in my heart that she was going to be okay. I knew God had heard my prayer. I knew He was near, and He really does care. I told my dad, "She will be alright." Everything to me was now so bright.

As I write this today, my mother will soon be ninety-seven years old. The peace that came over me that day and spoke to my heart still resides with me. God is so real and Wonderful and hears every sincere prayer and heart's cry. No child goes unnoticed when in faith he or she looks to Him.

He is so Wonderful!

"And this is the confidence that we have in him, that, if we ask anything according to his will, he heareth us: And if we know that he hear us, whatsoever we ask, we know that we have the petitions that we desired of him."— I John 5:14,15

The Altar is Important

I was young; I can't remember exactly how old I was when some people began to stop by to take us to Sunday School and church. Sadly, I can't even remember their names, but I realize now what a blessing it was from above. I began to learn more about God and His great love.

It was at this age that I began to go to the altar and pray. I'd go there and kneel and for a long time I'd stay. I recall, there was a change that took place in my young life. Now, instead of fears and loneliness, faith began to replace it all. Now I could rest in His precious love, knowing that He was ever watching His children from above.

"And they brought young children to him, that he should touch them: and his disciples rebuked those that brought them. But when Jesus saw it, he was much displeased, and said unto them, Suffer the little children to come unto me, and forbid them not: for of such is the kingdom of God. Verily I say unto you, Whosoever shall not receive the kingdom of God as a little child, he shall not enter therein. And he took them up in his arms, put his hands upon them, and blessed them."— Mark 10:13-16

Convictions

The convictions of God are great and so real. Some of the convictions that I had from childhood, I remember still. "Goodnight everybody. Say your prayers," were my last words each night, as our family laid down at bedtime. I would never forget, because as soon as I laid down, the convicting thoughts came to me, "I need to say my prayers."

I remember, sometimes when it was cold, I would dread so badly getting out of the bed to kneel on the cold floor, so I'd start to say my prayers in the bed. I would pull the covers up over my head enjoying the warmth. Then, I would think, "No, it's just not right!" I'd quickly get out of the bed and down on my knees to say my prayers. I was so young, but I still could sense that God was pleased with me, as I reverenced Him there.

"God is greatly to be feared in the assembly of the saints, and to be had in reverence of all them that are about Him."— Psalm 89:7

*Reverence - A feeling of deep respect, love, awe, and esteem.

Confession is Good for the Soul

When I was a child of only about eight, deep in my heart I knew God was great. Often at night I couldn't sleep, and if I had done wrong, I would lay awake and weep. I'd think, "Oh, if I die, I know it won't be well. I'll go to that place, that awful place called hell." I remember one night after I'd done something wrong that the feeling of fear and guilt were so strong that I could not sleep. I got out of bed to find my mom who was still awake quilting. I told my mom of my terrible guilt. I told her I was so sorry for what I had done. And through her love and understanding, the battle was won.

As my confession was made, I felt completely forgiven. I could go to sleep now.

I always thank God for the lesson He gave me!

"If we confess our sins, he is faithful and just to forgive us our sins, and to cleanse us from all unrighteousness."— I John 1:9

We All Like Sheep, Have Gone Astray

I was aware of God, even at an early age. I recall a real and distinct hunger for Him. There was an emptiness that only He could fill. As I began to pray and look to Him, and acknowledge Him, my Faith began to grow.

Then the years passed, and I started growing into a young woman. We weren't part of a church and no longer attended Sunday School. My awareness of God grew dim. I don't even remember thinking about God, as when I was younger. It was almost as if I had blocked out some of those years. Now, I was busy with school, friends, and the everyday life of a young lady. At 16 years and one week old, I now had become a wife. First one thing, then another, soon I forgot to pray, and I became one of those little sheep who had gone astray.

Life tends to occupy every minute of time that we'll give up to business. When He calls our name, may we never neglect that time with the Master.

"All we like sheep have gone astray; we have turned everyone to his own way; and the Lord hath laid on Him the iniquity of us all."— Isaiah 53:6

A Dream from God

It was somewhere around 1953 or 1954 when God gave me the dream. Paul and I hadn't been married very long. Friends of ours, a couple who had grown up with Paul, were in the hospital expecting the arrival of their first baby. I decided to visit them in the hospital. As I walked up the stairs of the Catholic hospital, I admired the Holy statues that had been placed on each floor. A feeling of reverence overcame me as I looked upon each one.

That night, God gave me a dream that stirred my heart.

In the dream, I stood at the bottom of a hill covered with statues. At the very top of the hill, stood the living Jesus. His white robe was blowing in the breeze. A wonderful, joy filled my heart, like I'd never felt before. I was so excited; I wanted to tell someone. I wanted everyone to see Him before He went away. I knew in the dream that if I was prepared, when He does return, that I would have a joy and happiness that could never be explained. I recall in the dream that I ran to get my mother, so she could see him. I was singing and telling others to sing, "Jesus is coming again."

When we find something so good that it completely changes our lives, we have no choice but to share it with others.

"Whom having not seen, ye love; in whom, though now ye see him not, yet believing, ye rejoice with joy unspeakable and full of glory."— I Peter 1:8

Something is Missing

It was somewhere around 1960. My husband and I had moved to Tampa Florida, and I had come to a place in my life that I could sense something was missing. I told my husband Paul one night, "I should be the happiest person in the world. We have two healthy little girls and our little home. We are happy, but something is missing; I don't know what it is." I had no sooner said those words than I knew in my heart what it was. It was God.

I hadn't been to church in years, but now I wanted to go. There just happened to be a revival going on at a little church near where we lived. I decided to go. I'm sure this was no coincidence. God was drawing me, and He had brought me to that place in my life where I realized that I needed Him.

We find ourselves living our lives every day according to *our* plans. Every day doing whatever we want. We become accustomed to our lives.

Then: Things change. We find ourselves feeling that something is wrong; something is missing.

It reminds me now of the children of Israel in Egypt, in the Book of Exodus. They had everything good in Egypt; they were happy and content. Then things began to change. Joseph died, and a king arose that didn't know Joseph. The children of Israel didn't have any thoughts of returning to their home land (the land of Canaan) God had given them. They had grown comfortable with their lives in Egypt…until things changed. God has a set time for all things. He heard their cries because of the hard task masters. God had been preparing Moses for years to bring his people out of Egypt.

Like the Israelites in Egyptian bondage, many of us are in bondage to the taskmaster of Satan. Satan would like to keep us standing afar from God and the blessings He has for our lives. God knows exactly where we are and the trials we are facing today. He even knows our names. He begins to draw us back to Him and out of "Egypt."

"For we have not an high priest which cannot be touched with the feeling of our infirmities; but was in all points tempted like as we are, yet without sin. Let us therefore come boldly unto the throne of grace, that we may obtain mercy, and find grace to help in time of need." — Hebrews 4:15-16

My First Conviction

The best goal I know is the desire to live a life that will please God. He is the best guide and protector there is. He is the only Savior.

I sure am thankful that He drew me to Him and saved me. He began to give me knowledge to know that there had to be more to life than I was experiencing. He put a desire in my heart to seek Him. I knew the Bible was important, and if I went to church, maybe I could find Him. I hadn't been to church since I was a little girl, but I knew that God was there. My first memory of church was as I was leaving the church building. There was a crying out in my heart; a longing. I thought, "Oh, how I would love to live a life that would please God." The words that came to me next were not from my thoughts, but the Spirit of God directing me. The words that I heard were, "But you'd have to quit smoking." I didn't think on this long; I guess I just excused it from my mind. I had never even thought of there being anything wrong with smoking. Anyway, I went back to church's revival the next night. The same thoughts and feelings were stirred within me that night. I had the same desire in my heart to live a life that pleased God, and again the same words came to me. That night, when I got home and put the children to bed, I knelt to pray. My prayer was, "God, I want to live to please you. If you don't want me to smoke, I don't want to do anything you don't want me to do. I ask you to take all desire away that I will never want another cigarette.

When I got up the next morning, I saw my cigarettes on the television. I passed by them and never even thought to stop to get one. The whole day went by, and I never even wanted one. I suddenly realized what had happened. I have gone all these years and never wanted another cigarette.

I praise Him for all He has done for me. That has been many, many years ago. So many other miracles He has done in my life.

He is Wonderful! He sets us free.

"Doth not wisdom cry? And understanding put forth her voice? She standeth in the top of high places, by the way in the places of the paths. She crieth at the gates, at the entry of the city; at the coming in at doors. Unto you, O men, I call: and my voice is to the sons of man. O ye simple, understand wisdom: and, ye fools, be ye of an understanding heart. Here; for I will speak of excellent things; and the opening of my lips shall be right things."—Proverbs 8:1-6

Becoming Aware

One day I thought, "Oh, how I wish I could start my life all over again and never do anything wrong. This was the life of sin and the heaviness that comes along with it. It is a separation from God.

But, I thank Him for sending His Holy Spirit to work conviction in my heart to let me feel the emptiness inside.

**Only His Holy Spirit can make us aware of the emptiness!
Only His Holy Spirit can fill it!**

"And when he is come, he will reprove the world of sin, and of righteousness, and of judgment."—John 16:8

Forgiveness

If I am blinded by an unforgiving spirit toward my brother, how can I see God? There is blessedness for the pure in heart, for they shall see God. Forgiveness is the ultimate proof of love, both of God's love and of our love to one another. Love goes into action to make the first move. Love does not wait for the other person to take the blame and reach out first.

These are the ways of love.

"Therefore I say unto you, what things soever ye desire, when ye pray, believe that ye receive them, and ye shall have them. And when ye stand praying, forgive, if ye have ought against any: that your Father also which is in heaven may forgive you your trespasses. But if ye do not forgive, neither will your Father which is in heaven forgive your trespasses."—Mark 11:24-26

The Drawing of God's Spirit

God's working in my life didn't start with the new birth experience. My new birth experience was the beginning of living in this new life with Him. The drawing of God's Spirit began about three years before my new birth.

It reminds me of what Jesus said in John 6:44 *"No man can come to me, except the Father which hath sent me draw him: and I will raise him up at the last day."*

Before God started dealing with me, my life had been going on pretty much the same as it had been for years. I was busy with everyday tasks, working, doing whatever I wanted or needed to do.

Then suddenly, things began to change. I began to feel like there had to be more to life than what I had been experiencing.

"Blessed are they which do hunger and thirst after righteousness: for they shall be filled."— Matthew 5:6

**I thank God for the hunger and thirst
he placed in my heart for Him!**

If You Love Jesus, Raise Your Hand

I went back the third night of revival. During the service, the preacher said, "If you love Jesus, raise your hand." I started to raise my hand, then I stopped and thought, "I can't raise my hand; I'm not like these people." The preacher repeated his statement. "If you love Jesus, raise your hand." I had another opportunity. Oh, how I wanted to raise my hand, but my thoughts continued to war, "I'm not like these people; I can't. Then, if I don't, Jesus will think I don't love Him."

At that thought, I raised my hand! I immediately felt something wonderful that I'd never felt before; Jesus touched me! A clean, pure feeling traveled from my hand throughout my body. That touch changed my life! I began to hunger after Him, losing the desires for the things of the world.

So many things were happening in my life, but I was learning to trust God. He was teaching me to take one step at a time, trusting and looking to Him, as I did. Little by little, He would bring me to maturity.

"When he was come down from the mountain, great multitudes followed him. And, behold, there came a leper and worshipped him, saying, Lord, if thou wilt, thou canst make me clean. And Jesus put forth his hand, and touched him saying, I will; be thou clean. And immediately his leprosy was cleansed."—Matthew 8:1-3

Seeking Him

After these meetings at God's house, a lot of things began to change. We had bought a very nice, little house. It was the first time we'd had our own home. Unfortunately, our financial circumstances changed, and we needed a job. So, we planned to leave our little house and go North in hopes of finding work. We talked to the man from whom we had bought the house. Fortunately, he was a very nice person, and when we let him know our plans, he told us we could just sign the house back over to him. He then gave us an unexpected blessing by giving our down payment of $500 back. That was a lot of money back then. He gave far more than he knew in his words to us. He said, "You will not find what you are searching for unless you find Jesus Christ."

Thank God for His people, who speak His Words. These words stuck with me. I thought on these words, day after day. My experience when I had gone to the church revival was also still with me every day.

We were expecting our third child now, and it was a lot colder in the North than we were used to. Things didn't go well; there was no work to be found. We returned to Florida where Paul continued his search for work. Things were hard, but I kept my hope in God. When the bottom fell out of one hope, God gave me another. I didn't know that He was teaching me to trust Him. One day at a time. One step at a time.

At the time, I didn't know of the Scripture in Jeremiah 29:13 *"And ye shall seek me, and find me, when ye shall search for me with all your heart."*

I was following Him. He was drawing me and teaching me to follow His Spirit.

I am so thankful for God's goodness and His love!

Another Step Closer to God

About two years passed before we moved back to Kentucky. We had three children now, aged eight, four, and one year old.

I ask you a question: Has God placed you somewhere away from friends, family, and acquaintances, where you seem very alone?

We must always remember, there is a purpose and a plan in the journey God has for you, and there are no mistakes, when it comes to God.

That's the way it was in the winter of 1963. It was a cold winter. We lived in the back three rooms of a store house in Kentucky. The store had long been closed; the only thing that remained were the shelves and counters and a big empty storage room attached. I didn't realize the wonderful things that God had in His plan for me and my family of five at the time.

We picked up the little pieces of coal from the empty coal pile outside in an effort to stay warm. When all the little pieces of coal were gone, we burned paper to keep a fire going and a source of heat for those three little rooms.

It was our job, as part of our rent, to keep the ice broken on the pond for the cows in the field beside the old storehouse. It was also our responsibility to feed them. The hay was stored in the loft of the barn there on the property. I was afraid of the cows. Not having been raised on a farm, they seemed so big to me. But realizing they were hungry and thirsty, I knew I had to overcome the fear of them.

Yes, it was a very trying time, but all this time, God was very near. He was bringing me to the end of myself and to the beginning with Him. I needed Him.

Our wonderful Father and Savior knows and plans our lives. His plans for us are good.

"For I know the thoughts that I think toward you, saith the Lord, thoughts of peace, and not of evil, to give you an expected end. Then shall ye call upon me, and ye shall go and pray unto me, and I will hearken unto you. And ye shall seek me, and find me, when ye shall search for me with all your heart."—Jeremiah 29:11-13

Mt. Zion Church of God

There was a little country church just down the hill from the store house where we lived. Paul's uncle, Henry Bray, was pastor there. On Sunday Mornings we could hear the church bell ringing from our house. It was such a special sound. One beautiful, spring Sunday morning the children and I decided to go.

When it was time for church to start, some of the people gathered up front with their hymnals and began to sing. I remember the beautiful hymn they sang, A Beautiful Life. The words filled the church, "Each day I'll do a golden deed, by helping those who are in need. My life on earth is but a span, and so I'll do the best I can."

As they sang, I began to feel something I didn't understand. I wanted to cry and turned my face towards the window, so no one could see the tears.

They sang "Let my life be a light, shining out through the night."

**God pulls on the strings of our heart,
and He waits for us to respond.**

"As the hart panteth after the water brooks, so panteth my soul after thee, O God. My soul thirsteth for God, for the living God: when shall I come and appear before God? —Psalm 42: 1,2

Time to Pray

I noticed hanging on the church wall a large thorn. Hung there, I'm sure, as a reminder of Christ's suffering. As I thought of Jesus with the crown of thorns on His head, I was filled with such a sad feeling that I didn't quite understand.

It was time to pray, as the Christians all gathered around the altar and at the front row of seats. Pastor Bray began to pray, and I'll never forget the words he prayed. "Oh God, save that lost man, that lost woman, that lost boy and girl, that they won't have to go down under the frowns of the vengeance of God."

I knew I was one of those people he was praying for. Such misery and despair, I had never felt before. Soon Sunday School was over, and we walked our way back up the hill toward the house. I didn't know it then, but we were being exposed to the most precious things in the world, God's Holy Spirit. He was hovering over our little family, convicting us of sin, righteousness, and judgment. How precious His love and His goodness are to us.

The Father gave His very best for us, that we might have a relationship with Him, and find the joy in our lives that He truly wants us to experience. It's our decision, nonetheless.

"O the depth of the riches both of the wisdom and knowledge of God! How unsearchable are his judgements, and his ways past finding out!"— Romans 11:33

The Visit From Pastor Henry

A few days passed when there was a knock at the door. Paul's Uncle Henry had come by to invite us to church. It was Friday; the night reserved for our mid-week, prayer meeting. We decided we would go. My first thought was, "I don't have real nice clothes to wear". I pushed away that thought. "It doesn't matter, as long as they're clean." That settled it. We got the children all ready and went that Friday night, March 29th, 1963.

A lot of people were there. Although I didn't know many of them, I guess Paul knew most of them. Service opened with prayer followed by the singing and preaching. Near the end of the service, Brother Bray announced that he felt like having an old-time hand shake. All the people began to move around shaking hands with one another, as they sang Kneel at the Cross.

Suddenly, I was overcome with feeling and wanted to cry. As one of the older women shook hands with me, she asked, "Would you like to come up and let us pray with you?"

I just stood there silently, as she went on her way, continuing to shake more hands.

What power is found in the cross of Christ! Through and by the Cross, we, who were once so far away from God, strangers to Him, have become part of the household of God.

"For all have sinned, and come short of the glory of God."
— Romans 3:23

Jesus and Me

Then, it was like there was no one else in the room but me and Jesus. The congregation continued to sing, "Kneel at the Cross. Christ will meet you there. Come while He waits for you." It was like He stood at the altar with His arms outstretched to me, saying "Come."

About that time another sister shook my hand, asking if I wanted to pray.

This time, I moved toward the altar. I knelt down. I said, "All things I thought were so important are not important at all." I wanted Him more than anything! I could hear Brother Henry praying as he said. "Lord you said, that all that come unto you, you will in no wise cast them out."

I believed His Word; I entered in; I entered into a new life.

What happened then was a miracle. When I arose from that altar, I had been born again! Born from above! I had had a spiritual birth. I was so full of Love, joy, and peace. It was wonderful. I hugged my mother-in-law and others.

Pastor Henry with a big smile on his face asked, "How do you feel?"

I answered, "I feel wonderful!"

The greatest miracle of all, is that moment in time when we receive Salvation. We pass from death unto life…a new life, fresh and glorious.

"There was a man of the Pharisees, named Nicodemus, a ruler of the Jews: The same came to Jesus by night, and said unto him, Rabbi, we know that thou art a teacher come from God: for

no man can do these miracles that thou doest, except God be with him. Jesus answered and said unto him, Verily, verily I say unto thee, except a man be born again, he cannot see the kingdom of God. Nicodemus saith unto him, how can a man be born when he is old? Can he enter the second time into his mother's womb, and be born? Jesus answered, Verily, verily, I say unto thee, except a man be born of water and of the Spirit, he cannot enter into the kingdom of God. That which is born of the flesh is flesh; and that which is born of the Spirit is spirit. Marvel not that I said unto thee, ye must be born again. The wind bloweth where it listeth, and thou hearest the sound thereof, but canst not tell whence it cometh, and whither it goeth: so is every one that is born of the Spirit."— John 3:1-8

The Whole World Looked Clean and New

As we left church that night, I felt like the whole world was clean and new. The stars were brighter; it seemed there was praise just ringing in the sky.

The next morning I remember so well. Oh, it was a beautiful spring day. The window was open, and a breeze was blowing through the window; it felt so pure and good. I could hear the birds singing, I don't remember ever hearing them sing like this before. My heart seemed to be singing along with these birds, singing praises to the Lord. The trees looked greener; the sky looked bluer; the clouds so beautiful. I loved my family more than ever before.

This is how I know, He is alive; He gave me Life! Once I was dead, separated from God because of my sins, but in just one second that separation was no more!

> *"Therefore if any man be in Christ, he is a new creature: old things are passed away; behold, all things are become new."*— II Corinthians 5:17

How Do I Know He Lives?

God gave His Son to buy our pardon and pay the price for our sins, so we could have life. He arose from the dead. Now, He waits to impart that new life to all that will come to Him.

How do I know He lives? How do I know He arose from the dead and ascended back to the Father?

I know because He gave me new life and He said that He would not leave us comfortless. When He ascended, He sent the "comforter" from the Father. When He is come, He will reprove (convict) the world of sin, of righteousness, and of judgment. His spirit is in the world today just like He said. He came and worked this miracle in my heart, drawing me to Him.

He lives, and He is coming again!

"Nevertheless I tell you the truth; it is expedient for you that I go away: for if I go not away, the Comforter will not come unto you; but if I depart, I will send him unto you. And when he is come, he will reprove the world of sin, and of righteousness, and of judgment: Of sin, because they believe not on me; Of righteousness, because I go to my Father, and ye see me no more; Of judgment because the prince of this world is judged."— John 16:7-11

Now, we have His great and precious promises.

The First Thanksgiving

It was getting close to Thanksgiving, 1963. Such a joyous time for this family of five, because since March 29th, a great change had taken place. This mother had found what she had longed and searched for, all her life…..Jesus. I was living now as a child of God, and the children knew something wonderful had taken place. They could see that their home was a happier place since Jesus lived there, too.

One Sunday morning, we awoke, got out of bed, and got ready for church. This was different, too, since that day in March. They were so happy and excited about this new life. We all got ready, ate our breakfast of gravy, biscuits, and eggs, and headed off to church. The children all enjoyed Sunday School at our little country church.

After church as we started toward the car, we saw Grandma Bray headed our way. She said, "I always give the young'uns some garden and canned stuff, and I have y'alls in the car." I thanked her as we put sweet potatoes, a big jar of canned apples, and some green beans in our car and headed home.

As we turned up the lane that led to our house, our neighbor came out to the road to flag us down. He (our neighbor) said "Cordillie and me were expecting company for Thanksgiving but found out they're not coming after all. We had gone to the store and bought two chickens. We'd never be able to eat two. Could you all use one of them"? I said we could and I thanked him as we went on down the road home.

Soon dinner was ready. We had chicken and dumplings, green beans, sweet potatoes, and fried apple pies. We all seated ourselves around the table and bowed our heads in thanksgiving to our heavenly Father for His provision. His presence filled the room that day, as we sat together around that table, enjoying the blessing of God.

I, of course, hadn't let the children know, but when we left for church that morning, we had eaten the very last of our food, except for some shortening and some flour.

I hadn't told anyone about the need, so no one knew. But our heavenly Father knew all about it.

He is so wonderful. Thank you, Father!

"Therefore I say unto you, take no thought for your life, what ye shall eat, or what ye shall drink; nor yet for your body, what ye shall put on. Is not the life more than meat, and the body than raiment? Behold the fowls of the air: for they sow not, neither do they reap, nor gather into barns; yet your heavenly Father feedeth them. Are ye not much better than they? Which of you by taking thought can add one cubit unto his stature? And why take ye thought for raiment? Consider the lilies of the field, how they grow; they toil not, neither do they spin: and yet I say unto you, that even Solomon in all his glory was not arrayed like one of these. Wherefore, if God so clothe the grass of the field, which today is, and tomorrow is cast into the oven, shall he not much more clothe you, O ye of little faith? Therefore take no thought, saying, what shall we eat? Or, what shall we drink? Or, wherewithal shall we be clothed? (For after all these things do the Gentiles seek) for your heavenly Father knoweth that ye have need of all these things. But seek ye first the kingdom of God, and his righteousness; and all these things shall be added unto you."— Matthew 6:25-33

Come, I Say Come

When Jesus says, "Come", it's an invitation. We can't come on our own. He must invite us. He says, "Come. Enter in." Then, it's left up to us. He opens the door, but we must walk through that door to enter the place God has for us.

How do we do this? We move forward. When He says, "Come," His words will give us the power to do so.

I questioned myself. How exactly is "come" defined? It means to approach or draw near.

God told Noah to come into the ark. There was a reason for it. There was safety there, and God wanted to establish His covenant with Noah.

God is constantly inviting us to "Come. Enter in" to that ark of safety.

We struggle all our lives, trying to do the right thing every time, when all we must do is turn everything over to Him. He is inviting us to come and bring all our cares to him.

"Come unto me, all ye that labor and are heavy laden, and I will give you rest. Take my yoke upon you and learn of me; for I am meek and lowly in heart: and ye shall find rest unto your souls."— Matthew 11:28,29

The Darkness Departs as Jesus Comes In

Like a blind person who walks in darkness, never seeing the light, so it is in our walk in darkness, separated from God. Our sins separate us. Then, the Spirit of God comes and begins to woo us toward a place we follow in the path of the just. One day we come to a place where we must make a decision. We must take a step of faith toward Him, bow in His presence and accept Him into our heart.

The darkness goes out, as He comes in. He (Jesus) is the Light, and He lights our world.

We can See! We can See!

"In him was life; and the life was the light of men."— John 1: 4

"But the path of the just is as the shining light, that shineth more and more unto the perfect day."— Proverbs 4:18

With Him, We Have Everything We Need

I remembered a time when we were living in Kentucky. I had been saved for some time. I came through the house one day feeling sorry for myself, I guess. I thought, "I don't have this, or I don't have that." As I passed by my bedroom, I felt a drawing to pray. I went in the bedroom and knelt. Before my knees touched the floor, a word of scripture came to my mind. His word said, "Be content with such things as you have, for have I not said I will never leave you nor forsake you."

I was ashamed and filled with joy at the same time. I asked for His forgiveness and thanked Him for His Words. I left my bedroom with a different thought and a different desire.

He is so Wonderful! He makes His Word very real to us. Let us fill our heart with His Word.

With Him, we have everything we need!

"Let your conversation be without covetousness; and be content with such things as ye have: for he hath said, I will never leave thee, nor forsake thee."— Hebrews 13:5

The Purpose of the Church

Our daily living as Christians should be to live a separated and sanctified life. Our lives should be a life set apart from the world; set apart for God's use. When we come into His house, we come to worship Him, in song, in testimony, and in hearing His Word. As we live that daily life, that pleases God, and as we come to His house to worship Him, His house is filled with His glory. He pours out His blessings; our cup runs over.

One purpose of the church is so sinners will come, God will draw them to Him and conviction will be worked in their hearts as they hear, see, and feel our love for God. His presence is there.

We must be a people that truly love and worship Him if we are to be a witness for Him.

"He that hath my commandments, and keepeth them, he it is that loveth me: and he that loveth me shall be loved of my Father, and I will love him, and will manifest myself to him."— John 14:21

We Never Walk Alone

Often, it appears that we are walking all alone. I have found in my experience that those are the times God is very near, and we can hear His voice in a loving tone.

Some years ago, when I had a new son, I wanted to dedicate him to God. There were two other couples, also with new baby boys, who too wanted to give them to God. As we went forward in the service that night, the enemy of our souls put up a fight. He insisted, "It's not proper for you to go alone without your husband by your side." As I walked, I heard the sweetest voice one could ever hear. As Jesus spoke to me and said, "You're not alone, for I am here."

On we went, so thankful.
We three…Jesus, Danny, and me.

"And he that sent me is with me: the Father hath not left me alone; for I do always those things that please him."— John 8:29

Deliverance From Fear

When I was a little girl, maybe seven or eight years old, I always awoke very early in the mornings, before anyone else in the family. I would feel so alone and found myself hoping that someone else was awake, so I wouldn't be so alone. More than once, during this lonely, early time, something would happen. Suddenly, I would feel so tiny, in the center of a large place or room. It seemed as if the world was so very large, and I was a tiny dot in this place. I realized, I guess, in this huge place, God knew I was there. I never knew why I felt like that, and I never told anyone. I knew in my heart, God was aware of me and where I was.

Years later, when I was saved and reading the Bible, I would read about David in a large place. The experience that I had as a little girl would always come back to me, and I was reminded of the feelings I had so many years ago.

I'm still not sure about the significance or connection, but I'm still encouraged to think of God's wonderful love and watchful care of us young or old. He hears our hearts cry, and nothing can keep him from hearing our voice. He is faithful to let us know that He is aware of us and comforts us.

> He delivered me from fear and loneliness,
> because my thoughts were upon Him.

What a wonderful Father!

"What time I am afraid, I will trust in thee."—Psalm 56:3

Be an Overcomer

Are you troubled with some need? Do you have a way, an attitude, maybe a habit that you know is not pleasing to the Lord? Maybe, it seems like you're having such a problem with it, it's on your mind so much, and so big, that it's all you can think about right now.

Now, let's look on past that to our Father's need for us to overcome, so we are free to do His will. There is a lot to be done, so many people needing our help. Let us ask God to fill our hearts with His love, the love so great that it caused Him to send His own son to be the sacrifice for mankind; the same Love that Jesus has, that caused Him to be willing to suffer and give His life. Remember Jesus' words, "Love one another, as I have loved you."

We ask Him for grace to help us to do His will. As we begin to see His love so real and great, we get our eyes off our need and soon we discover that we have overcome our own need. It's by His great love that we also get Faith.

"For whatsoever is born of God overcometh the world: and this is the victory that overcometh the world, even our faith."— I John 5:4

Trust God

To be free from fear, we must learn to trust God. David gives us such a great example of the mental position we must take against the enemy.

"In my distress I called upon the Lord, and cried unto my God: he heard my voice out of his temple, and my cry came before him even into his ears."—Psalm 18:6

God in all His mighty power in heaven and in earth, showed Himself strong in my behalf.

"He brought me forth also into a large place; he delivered me, because he delighted in me."—Psalm 18:19

"I called upon the Lord in distress: the Lord answered me, and set me in a large place."—Psalm 118:5

He also said in Psalm 32: 7 & 8 "*Thou art my hiding place; thou shalt preserve me from trouble; thou shalt compass me about with songs of deliverance. Selah.*" "*I will instruct thee and teach thee in the way which thou shalt go: I will guide thee with mine eye.*"

If we can put our faith in Him and Trust in Him, we don't have to be held captive to fear.

"There is no fear in love; but perfect love casteth out fear: because fear hath torment. He that feareth is not made perfect in love. We love him, because he first loved us."— I John 4:18,19

The Battle Is The Lord's

We read in Joshua chapter 6 of the battle of Jericho. In verse 2, the Lord tells Joshua, *"I have given into thine hand Jericho, and the King thereof, and the mighty men of valour."*

In the previous chapter, Joshua was given both instruction and assurance when the "Captain of the host of the Lord" visited him. This was the Lord's battle. Joshua fell on his face and worshiped. The unseen host will fight for Israel! What a relief for Joshua.

If it be true that there were hosts of light, it is certainly true there are hosts of darkness.

Does the Church face these foes? Our Lord Jesus did. All throughout His ministry our Lord encountered dark powers that opposed Him through the victims they possessed. The life and death of Jesus Christ turned the tide. He arose and ascended far above all rule and authority and power and dominion, and every name that is named.

He is more than a conqueror and this victory was not just for Jesus only but for us. His people. The Church. He will also fight our battles.

He is with us!

"So the Lord was with Joshua; and his fame was noised throughout all the country."—Joshua 6:27

This Battle Is The Lord's

I remember going through a battle so great, facing the enemy on every hand. I decided to go to Kentucky. I wanted to go to the little church where I had been saved, and the enemy was fighting me all the way. As I packed up, I'm sure the children didn't know or see the unseen host of darkness warring against me. We had a visit, we prayed, and headed back home to Indiana. It was raining as we left London, Kentucky and headed north on I-75. I felt so alone. But God was getting ready to fight my battle.

The powers of darkness fought hard against me telling me, "You're all alone; no one cares; you're such a failure." Suddenly, I felt a Holy presence enter our car; I simply prayed, "Father, watch over us and keep us safe." In seconds, the hood of the car came loose covering the windshield, blocking my vision. Miraculously, I was able to guide the car to the side of the road.

There was a calmness; no fear; no excitement. Only peace. The Captain of my Salvation was present. He tore down those walls, as they crumbled.

I was NOT alone! He was with me, ever present.

My children and I sat there on the side of the road and thanked and praised Him. There were two men from the county, in a yellow truck, that stopped and tore the hood off the car and threw it over in the ditch.

My God had conquered the enemy once again that day in my battle. The battle is the Lords!

I realized that He was there all the time, as we drove home happy and safe.

"God is our refuge and strength, a very present help in trouble."
—Psalm 46: 1

So Sincere

When we are very young in the Lord, I guess we sound very odd or our testimonies very strange to some others, but to us, all is so sincere.

I remember one time as I went to the bedroom to pray during the time I had set aside, I was distracted by things I saw out of place. I stopped along the way to pick up first one thing and then another; a shoe in the middle of the floor; a random piece of clothing. When I got to my place of prayer and knelt, there was a stillness as I came before the Lord. It was like I could hear Him say; "What took you so long?" I was so hurt that I put all those trivial things before my time with Him. Weeping, I got up and went to the closet, got the piece of clothing out and threw it back in the floor. The other things I had picked up, I also put back where I had found them. Sobbing like a child, I hurried back to pray. I told Him how sorry I was.

Our meeting with Him should be the most important time of our day.

Do we still have those most sincere convictions?

Is our love for that special time with Him as it should be?

He is Wonderful!

"Nevertheless I have somewhat against thee, because thou hast left thy first love. Remember therefore from whence thou art fallen, and repent, and do thy first works; or else I will come unto thee quickly, and will remove thy candlestick out of his place, except thou repent."—Revelation 2:4,5

Have we left our first love?
Remember, repent, and do!

The Cleft Of The Rock

Like a mighty mountain, with a cleft in the side,
Our loving savior is our safety and a place where we can hide.
And oh the beauty we behold, and the peace we find inside.
This is the place we desire to enter and abide.
There are times of great danger, when some would do us harm,
but there is a shield that God has placed around us.
We are safe in the shelter of His arms.

"I will love thee, O Lord, my strength. The Lord is my rock, and my fortress, and my deliverer; my God, my strength, in whom I will trust; my buckler, and the horn of my salvation, and my high tower. I will call upon the Lord, who is worthy to by praised: so shall I be saved from mine enemies."— Psalm 18: 1-3

A Note To Soul Winners

There are so many children in the world with fears; ready for God to mold them; ready for His Word to be sown in their hearts. Maybe the parents at this moment, don't even realize their need for God or His Word.

It is so important that we reach out to them, take the time to pick them up, and bring them to God's house. We may never see the results of this labor of love in our life time, but we can be sure there will be results. These "Little Ones" need our help and our time.

I often stop to Thank God for those who took time for me.

Somewhere around 1947 when we lived on Ft. Wayne Avenue in Richmond, Indiana, there were some people who would come by and take us children to Sunday School. We began to learn more about God and His great Love for us. We started praying at the altar, realizing our need for Him in our lives. His Word was sown in our hearts as young children.

May we look to Jesus as our example.
He had time for the little ones.
Oh, let us have this same love and concern.

"And let us not be weary in well doing: for in due season we shall reap, if we faint not." — Galatians 6:9

Personal Contact

As I read today in Charles Spurgeon's book Joy in Christ's Presence, I was impacted by the chapter that discussed real contact with Jesus. As he talked about Jesus being in the midst of a crowd teaching and preaching, multitudes followed but few converts were found. Jesus was aware of everybody that touched Him. Luke 8:46 gives us the account, Jesus said *"Somebody hath touched me."*

Spurgeon described how that, just as the ocean leaves very little behind when it has reached full tide and recedes again to deeper waters, so the vast multitude around the savior left only this one precious deposit, one "somebody" who had touched Him and had received miraculous power with Him. On Sunday mornings, the crowds pour into the churches, like a mighty ocean, and then they all withdraw again. Here and there a "somebody" is left, weeping for sin, a "somebody" is left rejoicing in Christ, a "somebody" is left who can say, "I have touched the hem of His garment, and I have been made whole."

We should gather insight from this encounter with Jesus:

We should never be satisfied unless we get into personal contact with Christ, so that we touch him as this woman touched His garment.

If we can get into such personal contact, we will have a blessing. Jesus said, "I perceive that virtue is gone out of me."

If we do get a blessing, Christ will know it, and He will have us make it known to others. He will speak and ask the questions that will draw us out and manifest us to the world.

"And Jesus said, Somebody hath touched me: for I perceive that virtue is gone out of me. And when the woman saw that she was not hid, she came trembling, and falling down before him, she declared unto him before all the people for what cause she had touched him, and how she was healed immediately. And Jesus said unto her "Daughter, be of good comfort: thy faith hath made thee whole; go in peace."— Luke 8:46,47

Personal Contact

I thought of the time I went to church in search of Him, not knowing anyone in the crowd. During the preaching the preacher said to the congregation, "If you love Jesus, raise your hand." When I finally did raise my hand, He touched me. Joy filled my soul from the tips of my fingers to the souls of my feet. It was a feeling that I could never describe, but it left me with a hunger to be touched again.

I've often thought back to that moment, and like the ocean described at full tide and the Sunday service crowd, that Charles Spurgeon referred to in yesterday's devotion. All those people that day didn't even know what a wonderful thing happened to me when I received this "personal contact" with the Savior of this world. Nevertheless, He touched me, and oh the joy that filled my soul.

"And a woman having an issue of blood twelve years, which had spent all her living upon physicians, neither could be healed of any, Came behind him and touched the border of his garment; and immediately her issue of blood stanched."— Luke 8:43,44

Resumé

Loretta Bray
Richmond, Indiana
Age: 57

Personal Goal:
   To be a laborer together with God and help point souls to Him, that they might believe and be saved.

Education:
   Attending School of Prayer and God's Word. I'm being taught by the Holy Ghost. (Still being taught, still schooling, still learning)

Personal Reference:
   I am a seed of Abraham and God is my Father. Jesus Christ, God's Son is my Savior, Redeemer, and Brother. The Holy Ghost is my Teacher and Guide. I have many brothers and sisters.
   "For both he that sanctifieth and they who are sanctified are all of one: for which cause he is not ashamed to call them brethren."— Hebrews 2:11

Experience:
   I was born again on March 29th, 1963, as Jesus described in John 3. That was the beginning of my new life with God. I have been blessed to teach classes of all ages. I have been blessed with songs at times. God has anointed me to write letters. Every job is a great joy and blessing. My responsibilities have included raising a family. Having Faith in God and depending on His help have brought me this far and will never fail. I praise Him for the great joy and peace He has allowed me to find in Him.

   "Would to God ye could bear with me a little in my folly: and indeed bear with me."— II Corinthians 11: 1

Am I My Brothers' Keeper?

The answer is yes! It's God's will for us to care for one another. God cares for you, and I do too. So, I'd like to share some good news with you.

We know from God's word, *"For all have sinned and come short of the glory of God."* (Romans 3:33) We also know that we must all stand before the judgment seat of Christ and give an account of ourselves to God. II Corinthians 5:10 says *"For we must all appear before the judgement seat of Christ; That everyone may receive the things done in his body, according to that he hath done, whether it be good or bad."*

We will each stand before Him.

Here's the wonderful news! We don't have to stand there alone and guilty before Him. He made a way for our escape.

"For God so loved the world, that He gave His only begotten son that whosoever believeth in Him should not perish but have everlasting life."—John 3:16

Am I My Brothers' Keeper?

Jesus took our sins upon himself and paid our debt on the cross of Calvary, so you could be free and have life. What Jesus did for us is real and wonderful, but it will only become real and wonderful to us as we accept His great love and what He has done for us. When we can see what our sins have done and the suffering it brought to the sinless Son of God, we begin to see how great the love of God is.

**Jesus arose and is alive for evermore,
and He is praying for you!**

"Wherefore he is able also to save them to the uttermost that come unto God by Him, seeing He ever liveth to make intercession for them."— Hebrews 7:25

Am I My Brothers' Keeper?

Without Jesus, there is no escape. We would stand before God in our sins and be judged, condemned, and forever lost without hope. It's not God's will that any should perish, but that all come to repentance. The Word of God tells us that "...*Except ye repent, ye shall all likewise perish.*" (Luke 3:3) He also tells us that if we confess our sins, He is faithful and just to forgive us our sins and to cleanse us from all unrighteousness. (I John 1:9)

He is Wonderful!

Are you prepared to stand before God on that day?

Remember, God loves you, and gave His Son to die for you. Have you believed in Him and accepted what He's done for you?

I'd like to encourage you today, to read God's Word and hear what He has to say to you. If you have already received Him, and you've been born again, I know you've never been sorry that you made Him your choice.

I really felt like sharing this wonderful news with you. With Jesus, we have hope. Talk with Him today about your soul.

A friend who cares, wants to share.

"*And as it is appointed unto men once to die, but after this the judgment.*"— Hebrews 9:27

Strong Faith

The Bible says that faith cometh by hearing and hearing by the Word of God. As we feed upon the Word of God, we are acquainting ourselves with God Himself, who is revealed there. He is the God who made the promises on which faith rests. As we become acquainted with God, it's easy to trust and have faith in Him, putting our confidence in Him. Over time, He becomes our closest friend.

It's like the process of forming friendships with those around us. If a person lives close to us, we may casually speak to them every day, but we don't know them personally. If we have a problem, we won't take it to that person because we don't really know them, and don't really feel like they would in interested in hearing our troubles. We just won't tell a stranger our secrets or important things. We're not acquainted with them. On the other hand, the person we are well acquainted with, we find it quite easy to discuss our troubles with, in confidence. We believe that they will help us all they can.

We are to cast our cares upon Him – our Father and Friend. He cares for us, and He can help us more than we know. I really believe He desires for us to feel like He is our best and closest friend. He wants our trust and confidence.

Almost every home has a Bible there. Maybe it's on a table or on a shelf. It's often overlooked, and we fail to pick it up to read. We even dust around it. But, remember, we become acquainted with Him through reading His Word. It's inside the covers that we become acquainted with the Savior of the world.

He is that Wonderful person to put our faith in.

"That Christ may dwell in your hearts by faith; that ye, being rooted and grounded in love, may be able to comprehend with all saints what is the breadth, and length, and depth, and height; and to know the love of Christ, which passeth knowledge that ye might be filled with all the fullness of God."— Ephesians 3:17-19

Influence

When my children were small, they were so sweet and innocent; so easy to influence with God's goodness. As they grew older and started school, they were exposed to the world more. The influence of the world is so strong; it's easy for young people to drift off and fall into so many traps that the enemy has set for them.

Not just the youth; all throughout our lifetime we must be aware that we are apt to fall behind or take the wrong path. Without God's guidance we may not see things as clearly as we should. We need a clear vision, so we do God's will and not our own.

In Revelation 3:18, eye salve is mentioned. *"I counsel thee to buy of me gold tried in the fire, that thou mayest be rich; and white raiment, that thou mayest be clothed, and that the shame of thy nakedness do not appear; and anoint thine eyes with eye salve, that thou mayest see."*

I believe this eye salve is the word of God and prayer. Focusing on God's remedies will keep us on the right path throughout this life. The Word of God will be a positive influence on our lives and keep us focused.

His Word is Wonderful!

Influence

While I was studying this morning, in Exodus, God began putting into my thoughts things about influence. I looked up the word in the dictionary.

Influence:
1. Power of persons or things to act on others.
2. Have power over.
3. Persons or things that have power.

As I thought about the literal definitions, I considered Moses' influence over the Israelites. Moses' Godly influence kept the children of Israel clean from things while his presence was with them, even though they wanted to return to Egypt when things went wrong. These people had no doubt been greatly influenced by their many years in Egypt. They had been slaves there and lived under bondage to the Egyptians for 400 years. I guess that's why they wanted a god they could see, like the Egyptians

Aaron, who was left in charge during Moses' absence, was weak in character. Instead of being a positive, strong leader, he was a bad influence. He could have just said "NO". Instead, he just drifted along with them, farther away from God. He could have resisted and stood against the evil of making the golden calf.

I wondered about our influence. I considered the fact that we need more of God in our lives, as we raise our families and the influence of the world grows stronger in their lives.

"And the Lord said unto Moses, Go, get thee down; for thy people, which thou broughtest out of the land of Egypt, have corrupted themselves: They have turned aside quickly out of the way which I commanded them: they have made them a molten calf, and have worshipped it, and have sacrificed thereunto, and said, These be thy gods, O Israel, which have brought thee up out of the land of Egypt."— Exodus 32:7,8

His Ways Are Not Our Ways

We don't understand God's working in our lives so many times. We must remind ourselves and let the Spirit of God remind us. All is in God's hands. Sometimes hard things come, and those things are through the hands of man. We get our eyes on those trials, and we tend to forget, God is in Control. Even though we don't understand it, we are told in God's Word, "Lean not unto your own understanding. In all your ways acknowledge Him." We have a promise of His direction.

It's so important for us to remember that His ways are not our ways nor His thoughts our thoughts.

He knows what He's doing. He has all knowledge and perfect wisdom.

Are we yielded trustfully in His hands?

Father, help us to be more like your Son, who fully trusted in your will for His life. We know that you love us, and you know what is best for us. You know just what we need. Help us and teach us, to fully trust you.

"Trust in the Lord with all thine heart; and lean not unto thine own understanding. In all thy ways acknowledge him, and he shall direct thy paths."— Proverbs 3:5,6

The Face Of Jesus

After completing this morning's devotional reading by Ray Stedman, my thoughts were...

**Where do you find the light of the glory of God?
In the Face of Jesus Christ.**

**Where do you find the Face of Jesus Christ?
In the scriptures.**

As you read the scriptures, and let the Spirit of God interpret them, the "Face of Jesus Christ" becomes clearer and clearer. That's how light comes into a darkened heart.

I remembered a little card that I had seen one time. It had some little marks on it. It didn't really look like anything special, but, I was told to hold it and stare at the small marks for so many seconds, and then look at the wall. To my surprise, when I looked at the wall, I could see the face of Jesus there on the wall. It was an image like the pictures we see of Him today.

I was reminded this morning, with this scripture that it's because we stare at, and look steadfastly into the face of Christ, in the Word of God, that we are able to see Him.

"For we preach not ourselves, but Christ Jesus the Lord; and ourselves your servants for Jesus' sake. For God, who commanded the light to shine out of darkness, hath shined in our hearts, to give the light of the knowledge of the glory of God in the face of Jesus Christ."— II Corinthians 4:5-6

If We're Going To Shine

As a child, you may have held a mirror and with it, threw sunlight at a certain spot. You had to bring the mirror into such a relationship with the sun, that the sun came fully onto it. Then, you could turn the mirror in a direction so that it reflected the light. If we are going to shine, we will need to bring our heart into such a relationship with God that the light of His countenance will shine directly into our heart.

It was that way with Moses. Remember, he spent forty days on Mount Sinai in the presence of God. When he came down and moved among the people, his face shone so brightly that they couldn't look at him. He had to take a veil and cover his face to be able to move among the people, and he didn't even realize the glow.

"Neither do men light a candle, and put it under a bushel, but on a candlestick; and it giveth light unto all that are in the house. Let your light so shine before men, that they may see your good works, and glorify your Father which is in heaven."—Matthew 5:15-16

Treasures From My Grandchildren

My Grandmother

You guys may not know how fun or funny Grandma can be. We have shared so many good times and a few sad and serious times as well. I really don't like to cry, so I'm just going to tell you some of the fun times. Many of you know that Grandma use to have a graphic (newspaper) route. It was a large route that had to be delivered by car. The good ol' graphic. Well, Eric and I loved to go with Grandma to deliver the papers. She always let us go even though I think it was more work for her. I mean come on you have two, not one, but two kids that are like six or seven years old going to deliver the paper. First, she had to stack some of the papers in the seat, so we could reach the boxes. If we heard a dog, we'd just drop it (missing the box) and tell her, "Go, Grandma, Go!" In the meantime, the other kid, who wasn't putting papers in boxes, would be making themselves look like a warrior, painting up our faces with good ol' graphic ink. And after the job was done, she would take us to Hardees or to get an ice cream cone. She never made us wash our faces before we went in anywhere, so we looked like a couple kids who hadn't taken baths in weeks. I think she knew how we liked looking like we had just come from work. It was like she was letting us feel all grown up. She didn't care because she knew how important it made us feel.

Many fun times with Grandma were at her home. I smile when I think of all the memories in the kitchen....the Nerf basketball tournaments, and the electric football games. The best was watching Grandma chase Stephen around the table, after he'd lit a pack of Black Cat Firecrackers in Kathy's back pocket in the kitchen. I don't know if Grandma really wanted to spank him or just laugh hysterically at him, but there they went, another round around the kitchen table.

Then there was missing the school bus. I think Eric and I missed the school bus more than we actually caught it. We thought we were cool riding to school with Grandma.

I really believe I spent more time over at Grandma's house growing up than I did at my own house.

So, I just want to say, "Thank you." Thank you for the laughs, thank you for all the good times, and most of all, thank you for being you. And, of course, for all the patience you had with us all.

"I love you, Grandma!"
Written by Melissa, to her Grandma
on Grandma's 70th birthday.

July 23rd, 2007

Wisdom From Above, The Need

One day after being asked many times by her children, "Go to church with us. Please, mom!" The answer they were looking for finally came. "Yes, I will go", she said. The children were so happy; their hearts all aglow. Unfortunately, the meeting that was to be so good turned out not to be so. The others there that day may not have been aware of the sadness going on inside of these young hearts and this mother so dear. Their hearts cried as their hopes faded for the young mother to place her hope in the Lord. They had hoped for a message from above; a message that would tell the sinner of God's great love.

Let us not mock the sinner but let us show the sinner God's love for them. He will cleanse them and make them whole. Let us ask Him for words and wisdom and love. May we tell them of the love the Father has, who sent His son to die for us. As He reveals to them their own sins, they will see the reason why One had to take their place. That One, who did no sin, sacrificed himself that they could be cleansed and really be born again.

"The fruit of the righteous is a tree of life; and he that winneth souls is wise."—Proverbs 11:30

Children Are A Blessing

Sometimes I'll sit and think of days gone by.
My heart will fill with joy, and sometimes I cry.
God blessed us with seven precious gifts that mean so much.
Joy fills my heart with their smiles or a tender touch.
There have been times in their growing
when things went wrong for a while.
Then all would be fine, and again we could smile.
We learned a lot together, I guess you might say.
One of the most important things
is how there is always a need to pray.
We can't make the journey through this life alone.
For all our mistakes, there's only one whose blood can atone.
So, as we journey on with those whom we love,
Let us always strive to please our Father up above.
We'll be happy, joyful and a blessing to each other.

To my children, I want you to know,
I'm thankful and pleased to be your mother.
I love you so very much!

What a blessing it is for us to remember how precious our children are. It's no wonder that they are such a blessing to us; they are the heritage of the Lord. They belong to the Lord and everything He has for us is wonderful. Our children are such a blessing!

"Lo, children are an heritage of the Lord: and the fruit of the womb is his reward. As arrows are in the hand of a mighty man; so are children of the youth."—Psalm 127: 3,4

Blessed Moments

I sat with my youngest son, Stephen. We talked of Abraham facing a test and about how Abraham offered Isaac as a sacrifice. We talked of God giving His best for us, and how He didn't stop his accusers as Jesus took our place at Calvary.

I could see the joy and love as tears ran down Stephen's face. Moments with God's Word are so very precious, as we can feel His presence all around us. These are the blessed moments that will mold us and make us and hold us together.

God is Love!

Mark 10:15 *"Verily I say unto you, Whosoever shall not receive the kingdom of God as a little child, he shall not enter therein."*

Eyes To Behold

Well the first snow is here, and as beautiful as can be
So pretty and white, oh you should just see.
It's on every fence post and branch of every tree.
How God can make such beauty, I never could see.
It looks so pure as it falls from the sky.
Sometimes it's such a sight to behold, I get a feeling to cry.
I thank God for my eyes, so I can behold
The beauty of His creation, the half cannot be told.

"For he saith to the snow, Be thou on the earth; likewise to the small rain, and to the great rain of his strength."— Job 37:6

Daddy, Are You Going With Us?

As years go by, I often recall
Moments so precious, of one so small.
We would sit side by side, in the quiet of day,
And read from the Bible to hear what God would say.
We would read of Jesus coming in the clouds
She would go outside to see if He is coming now
Her faith so pure; of His return she was sure.
When her dad came home for lunch one day,
She ran to meet him, and these words she did say.
"Daddy, are you going with us when Jesus comes?"
She was so anxious and happy, and she let him know
That was her desire, she wanted him to go.
She's been a great blessing down through the years,
She's written me poems that touched me with tears.
Sometimes we have trials down here,
But they keep us ready, we don't have to fear.
Jesus is coming; we can be sure!
Just keep watching, so you will be pure.

I'm thankful for August 11th, 1972, when God blessed us with a little girl.

Kathy, I love you!

"And then shall they see the Son of man coming in the clouds with great power and glory."—Mark 13:26

Happy Father's Day, Paul

Often, I'd like to say things that are in my heart.
I'd like for you to know my love for you,
but don't know just how to start
Many years have passed since we first met.
The joy of those young and sharing years I'll never forget
Oh, there were bad times as well as good,
But I guess what helps most is remembering
just what we should.
God has been so good to us from the start.
When I think of the many ways He's blessed, joy fills my heart.
He's blessed us with healthy, wonderful children, even seven.
Now my desire is that we'd all meet again someday in heaven.
I know we can make it, all the way through.
As we look to Him, He is the way, and I know His Word is true.
So, as we walk on through this life,
I want you to know I desire to be a better wife
And for this, I will pray.

I love you, Dad.
Happy Father's Day!

"That they may teach the young women to be sober, to love their husbands, to love their children."—Titus 2:4

Bible Stories On The Radio

When we were little children, we would listen to Bible stories on the radio. We would be playing and then we would hear that song, "As you left your room this morning, did you think to pray? Did you come before the Savior, did you ask for loving favor as a shield today?" When we heard this song, we all came running and sat down on the couch to hear the Bible story that was coming on. We learned about baby Moses and so many others in the Bible. Our heavenly Father was teaching us even then of His Word. He was molding our young hearts to one day receive Him.

"And all thy children shall be taught of the Lord; and great shall be the peace of thy children."—Isaiah 54: 13

"It is written in the prophets, And they shall be all taught of God. Every man therefore that hath heard, and hath learned of the Father, cometh unto me."—John 6:45

Parents, teach your children of God's great love. Read His precious, powerful Word to them. The rewards are great.

Memories

God has given us so many family memories in years gone by.
Some make us laugh, and some make us cry.
He has blessed us so greatly in our family.
There's my Dad and Mom, four sisters, and me.
If our blessings we tried to count,
It would be like the stars, too great an amount.
Some blessings are in disguise.
In a trial, it came hidden from our eyes.
As we walk by faith, putting our trust in Him,
we grow stronger and become more like Him.
But, once we've come through the trial, we could see plain,
another blessing for which we could praise His name.
He is always near and ready to hear,
As we lift our voice to Him.

**He is wonderful; He is our Savior
and for our family I thank Him!**

"Yet setteth he the poor on high from affliction, and maketh him families like a flock."—Psalm 107:41

Stepping Stones

Early in my coming to the Lord, I experienced some terrible trials, struggles, and seemingly hopeless times. Sometimes it seemed that there was no way, then suddenly, there was what seemed like a stepping stone that would appear in front of me. A way. There it was, time and again. With each trial, a way. Another trial, another stone (way). I learned to trust in the Lord.

Years later, maybe 56 years later, I read in F.B. Myers book Great Verses, "He went out not knowing whether it was what a man calls a venture, but as he stepped out on what seemed a void, he found it a rock beneath his feet. Day by day a track appeared across the desert and all his needs were met, till he reaches the place of blessing."

**God was teaching me a great lesson,
to trust in Him one step at a time.**

"Jesus saith unto him, I am the way, the truth, and the life: no man cometh unto the Father, but by me."—John 14:6

Miracles Still Happen

I was to speak to the young people in youth service one Sunday night, so I had been preparing all week. Sunday night came, and I had this terrible headache from sinuses. My face was so sore I could hardly stand to touch it; it even hurt to talk. I went to the prayer room as soon as I got to church. As I began to pray, I bowed my throbbing head. It felt like the top of my head would just burst. I prayed, "Father, it even hurts to talk. Would you just take this all away"? As soon as I said this, I felt the pain lift from me, and it was all gone. I was so thankful, and I praised my wonderful heavenly Father. This was a miracle! As I spoke to the people that night, it was wonderful to share this experience.

Yes, miracles still happen. We must ask and believe. Jesus still hears and answers.

He is Wonderful!

That experience was years ago, and I've never had a sinus problem again of any kind.

I praise Him!

"Jesus answered and said unto them, Verily I say unto you, If ye have faith, and doubt not, ye shall not only do this which is done to the fig tree, but also if ye shall say unto this mountain, Be thou removed, and be thou cast into the sea; it shall be done. And all things, whatsoever ye shall ask in prayer, believing, ye shall receive."—Matthew 21:21, 22

Ask And Ye Shall Receive

I had been praying for some time that I could find a place or way that I could get Bibles for our people in the church. We needed good study Bibles. We were not able to pay the high price in the Bible book stores.

After I had prayed sincerely, I heard a man on the radio, the same day, say, "If you want to be a Bible Distributor…..," and he gave a phone number. So, I called. He came from Ohio, and I began ordering the Bibles. They were the best study Bibles at a reasonable cost! I think everyone in the church bought these Bibles. In some cases, both husbands and wives ordered one. I guess we bought over 100 Bibles in all, over time.

God is so Good to us!

"And this is the confidence that we have in him, that, if we ask any thing according to his will, he heareth us: And if we know that he hear us, whatsoever we ask, we know that we have the petitions that we desired of him."—I John 5:14,15

Disappointments Bring Growth

Once when we were living in Kentucky, we had planned to go to church, but for no cause of our own, we were not going to get to go. I was broken hearted, because I had really wanted to go. So, I went to pray. In prayer, the Lord encouraged me so much. He brought His Word to me through the scriptures where Joseph was put into prison for no fault of his, and the Bible says more than one time. "But the Lord was with Him." I was so blessed.

"But the Lord was with Joseph, and shewed him mercy, and gave him favor in the sight of the keeper of the prison." "The keeper of the prison looked not to anything that was under his hand; because the Lord was with him, and that which he did, the Lord made it to prosper."—Genesis 39: 21,23

Sometimes we don't understand when things go against us, but God uses it all as a God ordained test and a lesson he wants to make real to us.

He is a wonderful teacher, and each lesson matures us a little more.

Jesus is Wonderful!

A big disappointment turned out to be a wonderful blessing.

"Until the time that his word came: the word of the Lord tried him.— Psalm 105:19

Needs Met

We were living in Florida when my children were small. I sewed clothes for my two girls, but I didn't quite know how to make shirts for my two boys. My boys needed some new shirts, and I wondered how I could get some for them. I thought about our church friend, Sister Bartee, who worked at a shirt factory. She was very familiar with making boy's shirts. The same day that I was thinking about my boys, three and five years old, so badly needing shirts, Sister Bartee knocked at my door. She had brought a bag of left over pieces of shirt material to share with me. It was enough to make small boys' shirts. She asked me if I knew how to make the short sleeved double cuff. I, of course, told her "No, I don't." So, she showed me how. God's timing was perfect. He sent Sister Bartee right on time.

Our Father knows our every thought and need before we ask.

Thank you, Father!

"Be not ye therefore like unto them: for your Father knoweth what things ye have need of, before ye ask him."—Matthew 6:8

Continue In The Christian Life

A little girl fell out of bed one night and when asked about it the next morning, she replied, "I must have stayed too close to where I got in." It's a serious thing to quit and not continue growing in our Christian life. We must move forward, follow Him, and believe with all our hearts that He is able to finish what He has started in us.

Search your heart and make sure you started right. Did you start because you realized you were lost and needed a Savior? You knew you were a sinner? Then you started right. Just continue following, moving forward, and don't stop. Keep praying, reading God's Word, going where He leads you. Go to God's house and worship Him. He will never lead us wrong.

"Let us therefore fear, lest, a promise being left us of entering into his rest, any of you should seem to come short of it."— Hebrews 4:1

Blessing Returned

It was a cold and windy day as I went to pick up Brenda and Heather (my daughter and granddaughter) from work. Before we came home, we ran by Springwood Park to get water from the springs. While we were getting our water, we saw a little lady, using a cane, who had just finished filling her four small bottles with water. She was having a real struggle getting everything together since she could hardly climb the steps coming up from the spring. So, I approached her to ask if I could help carry her water bottles to her car. When we had the water loaded, she thanked me from her heart, and said "God bless you."

We got our water loaded and went back to the drug store where we'd dropped some prescriptions off. While there, we noticed a tire was going flat on my car. After getting Heather's medicine, we pulled across the street to a gas station to put air in the tire. Unfortunately, it was just going flat, and putting air in the tire did not help.

Heather worked to get the jack and donut tire from the trunk of my car, but had a hard time getting the jack placed under the car. Seeing our struggle, an older man getting gas in his truck came over and asked if we needed help. It was extremely cold, so we were all thankful with the man's gracious offer to change the tire.

A young man then walked up to us with a cell phone, calling possible places to fix our tire. After finishing the calls, he had us follow him to Walmart where he went inside to get what he needed to fix the flat tire. He then told us to follow him to Studebaker Buick where he worked, and he said he'd fix the tire. He did fix the tire and refused to take any money for his efforts.

He was a blessing. We were so thankful.

God did bless greatly that day, and I thank him!

As I testified about my day later in church, I thought "Lord, let us help others, and be a blessing to someone else." I thought of the little lady in the park getting her water that day and what a joy it was to help someone else.

The Blessing was returned.

"And as ye would that men should do to you, do ye also to them likewise."—Luke 6:31

There Must Be A Desire

As we desire deeper things of God,
we will find great hindrances.

We must be determined!

I was desiring the things of God when I had a dream or a vision. In the dream, there was a great, tall giant. He was standing in front of the door that I had to enter. He stood with his arms folded across his chest, as if to say, "You're not coming in here." With a longing, a desire and a determination to enter that room, nothing was going to stop me. The giant disappeared. I could see him no more. In my dream, I could see that there was one other thing that had to be done to enter this door. There was a hasp lock on the door. Instead of there being a lock in the hasp, there was a piece of bread through the hasp.

This is how we enter into the things of God. We must eat of that Bread of Life to unlock the doors that He wants to open in our lives. It was so clear to me that eating this bread was how we enter into the things of God.

It's by the Word of God that we enter the door into the deep things of God.

Don't look at the giant, look to God.

"Then said Jesus unto them again, Verily, verily, I say unto you, I am the door of the sheep. All that ever came before me are thieves and robbers: but the sheep did not hear them. I

am the door: by me if any man enter in, he shall be saved, and shall go in and out and find pasture. The thief cometh not, but for to steal, and to kill, and to destroy: I am come that they might have life, and that they might have it more abundantly. I am the good shepherd: the good shepherd giveth his life for the sheep."—John 10:7-11

Abide In Christ

When we stare at the sun, it is so bright that when we look away, we can't see anything else. Everything stays bright and blocks out the things around that brightness. In prayer, we are looking into that brightness, as we look toward heaven where the Father and the Son are. The Spirit of God is our helper in prayer. He is that One here on earth that directs us toward God. He helps us to pray. As we pray, we are in that brightness with a glow around us. When we come out of prayer, we still see that brightness and the things around us are blocked out except for seeing them through this glow.

We need to abide in Him and stay in that spirit of prayer in Him. This is the only way that we can avoid walking in our own ways and fulfilling our own lusts - going where we want to go, doing what we want to do, and getting things our own way. We don't even see these things if we abide in Him and His brightness.

"If ye abide in me, and my words abide in you, ye shall ask what ye will, and it shall be done unto you."—John 15:7

Know By Experience

I read where John the Baptist sent his disciples to question Jesus about whether He was the "sent one" or were they to look for another. Jesus told them to go tell John the things they had seen, how the blind see, the lame walk, the deaf hear, the dead are raised up, and the poor have the good news preached to them.

This passage reminded me of a time a couple of weeks after I got saved on March 29th, 1963, when I had a visitor. She was of another religious belief and began to ask me what my church believed about some subject. I don't even remember now what it was. Then she asked another question, and another. I simply replied, "I don't really know about all these things." She said, "If you don't know these things, how do you know that you have found the right thing or the right way?"

I answered her, "Because I found it in God's Word."

I only knew that I had been born again, His Word was my evidence, and my foundation. Jesus led me in the scriptures in John. I didn't doubt because there was my experience. He had opened my blinded eyes; I could see His Word. He healed me; a complete cure from sin. He had cleansed me from every spirit unlike Him. Nothing could make me doubt what I had found, when I had entered that place with Him.

His presence is Wonderful!

It was a life changing experience…
                         …from old to new.

"Now when John had heard in the prison the works of Christ, he sent two of his disciples, And said unto him, Art thou he that should come, or do we look for another? Jesus answered and said unto them, Go and shew John again those things which ye do hear and see: the blind receive their sight, and the lame walk, the lepers are cleansed, and the deaf hear, the dead are raised up and the poor have the gospel preached to them. And blessed is he, whosoever shall not be offended in me."—Matthew 11:2-6

A Healing

My son, Alan, had a high fever one night when he was about five years old. I kept putting cool cloths on his head and the bends of his arms and legs to keep the fever down some. I prayed all night as I kept the cool cloths on him.

It was about dawn when I fell asleep. Alan woke me up soon and told me, "Mommy, Jesus just now touched me." It was true. His fever was gone, and he wanted to get ready to go to Sunday School that morning.

**The Lord is so good! I am so thankful
that He hears and answers when we pray.
I thank Him for touching Alan.**

"And when Jesus was come into Peter's house, he saw his wife's mother laid, and sick of a fever. And he touched her hand, and the fever left her: and she arose, and ministered unto them."—Matthew 8: 14,15

Just Ask

This was the first miracle I experienced, after the miracle of my New Birth. We were visiting with my sister, Wanda in Alabama. Alan, my son, had a bad ear ache and was crying in pain. At the time, he was around 18 months old. He wasn't even able to talk in sentences yet. As I worried about how to help my baby, God's Word came to my heart so clearly. Jesus said "Ask". It was so real and clear to me. I told my mom and dad who were also there. I said, "Let's pray for him." As we prayed for him, Alan instantly stopped crying. He put his finger in his ear, pulled it out, and smiled.

Jesus had touched him!
This was the first miracle I had ever witnessed.

I thank God for His compassion, for His love, and for being the same today.

"Jesus Christ the same yesterday, and today, and forever."
—Hebrews 13:8

Our Wonderful Savior never changes.
He loves us and wants to do miraculous things for us.

Walking By Faith

Just as when a baby begins to learn to walk, we must learn to walk by faith not by sight. My children, when learning to walk, would be at complete ease, as long as they could feel my hand on their backs. When I saw that they were walking on their own, I would ease my hand away. As soon as they noticed and couldn't feel my hand, they became scared and would usually fall. After a while, as I assured them, "I am right here; it's alright; I'm right here," they began to walk by faith.

We, too, must learn to walk by faith. Faith pleases God.

Abraham walked by faith, and it was accounted to him for righteousness.
"Even as Abraham believed God, and it was accounted to him for righteousness." (Galatians 3:6) He believed God.

Having faith, he obeyed God.

"By faith, Abraham, when he was called to go out into a place which he should after receive for an inheritance, obeyed; and he went out, not knowing whither he went."—Hebrews 11:8

"Now the just shall live by faith: but if any man draw back, my soul shall have no pleasure in him."—Hebrews 10:38

I think of Jesus' disciples and how they had to learn to walk by faith, too. They were so used to Jesus being right there with them. To walk on their own, faith had to grow.

Seeking God's Will

We must seek God to know His will. So many times, God shows us things. We may not understand those things at the time and what it is that He is trying to say to us. If we will seek Him, He will reveal Himself to us.

He said in Isaiah 55:8 *"For my thoughts are not your thoughts, neither are your ways my ways, saith the Lord."*

We must live in a close fellowship, with Him. Moses talked with God face to face, (Exodus 33:11). We never read where Moses was interested in pleasing himself. Neither did Jesus, who was a greater prophet than Moses. Jesus' will was to please the Father who sent Him.

"Then said I, Lo, I come (in the volume of the book it is written of me,) to do thy will, O God."—Hebrews 10:7

"Then said I, Lo, I come: in the volume of the book it is written of me, I delight to do thy will, O my God: yea, thy law is within my heart."—Psalm 40:7,8

Jesus said unto them, *"And he that sent me is with me: the Father hath not left me alone; for I do always those things that please him."*—John 8:29

If we are to do His will, hear His voice, and understand the Words He speaks to us, we must live a life of denying "self".

Jesus came to seek and to save the lost and gave His life a ransom for many. We must be willing to give our lives for others and deny ourselves. Let your light so shine so that those that are blind and walk in darkness, can see.

Nellie Bray

My mother-in-law was the first Christian I ever knew. Although I didn't know what made her so different at the time, her light truly shined. She was so kind and patient, never getting upset, even when others tried hard to upset her with things they said to her. Even I occasionally thought to myself, "Why doesn't she just tell them off?" (I wasn't saved at the time.)

But when Jesus came into my heart, not too many years after that, I remembered how I had seen that light in her. It was then that I was able to understand exactly what it was that I had seen in her. It was clear to me now what it was that made her that shining light. It was His presence in her.

**I am so thankful for my mother-in-law.
She was and is so precious to me.**

"Ye are the salt of the earth: but if the salt have lost his savour, wherewith shall it be salted? It is thenceforth good for nothing, but to be cast out, and to be trodden under foot of men. Ye are the light of the world. A city that is set on an hill cannot be hid. Neither do men light a candle, and put it under a bushel, but on a candlestick; and it giveth light unto all that are in the house. Let your light so shine before men, that they may see your good works, and glorify your Father which is in heaven."—Matthew 5:13-16

Who Will Stand In The Gap?

"Behold, the Lord's hand is not shortened, that it cannot save; neither his ear heavy, that it cannot hear."—Isaiah 59:1

"And he saw that there was no man, and wondered that there was no intercessor: therefore his arm brought salvation unto him; and his righteousness, it sustained him."—Isaiah 59:16

"And I sought for a man among them, that should make up the hedge, and stand in the gap before me for the land, that I should not destroy it: but I found none."—Ezekiel 22:30

"Therefore he said that he would destroy them, had not Moses his chosen stood before him in the breach, to turn away his wrath, lest he should destroy them."—Psalm 106:23

**Let us be faithful to stand in the gap
and pray for those who are still lost.**

Jesus Is The Source Of All Revelation

"But the Comforter, which is the Holy Ghost, whom the Father will send in my name, he shall teach you all things, and bring all things to your remembrance, whatsoever I have said unto you."—John 14:26

Those that teach the things of God must first be taught of God. This is the Holy Spirit's work.

David prays earnestly, that God, Himself, would be his teacher. He had prophets, wise men, and priests all around him. David himself was well instructed in the law, yet, he begs to be taught of God. He knew that none could teach like Him.

In Psalm 86:11, David prays, *"Teach me thy way, O Lord; I will walk in thy truth: unite my heart to fear thy name."*

David wanted singleness of heart and to have reverential awe for God's name, His statues and His ways.

We too, must have that hunger to be taught of God.

"And the things that thou hast heard of me among many witnesses, the same commit thou to faithful men, who shall be able to teach others also."— II Timothy 2:2

Truth And Freedom

"The Spirit of the Lord God is upon me; because the Lord hath anointed me to preach good tidings unto the meek; he hath sent me to bind up the brokenhearted, to proclaim liberty to the captives, and the opening of the prison to them that are bound;"—Isaiah 61:1

As I read this scripture, my focus was drawn to the words that explain to us that Jesus was sent and anointed to "proclaim liberty to the captives and freedom to prisoners." Prisoners, those are people who the judge sends to prison. Captives are the people who have been captured in battle and are now being held as prisoners of war. These people do not have unforgiveness in their hearts but instead are bound by what they have believed.

Jesus said, we need a revelation of "truth" of God, so we can escape to freedom.

"And ye shall know the truth, and the truth shall make you free."—John 8:32

Satan blinded man and held him captive until Jesus came. Then, as Isaiah 61:1 and Luke 4:18 say, Jesus set us free!

A New World

God gave us sounds and sights to behold.
They are precious to us, yes more precious than gold.
To hear the wind rushing through the trees,
And to hear a bird's song and feel the gentle breeze.
We have so much to be thankful for,
He gave us all these things and oh so much more.
He gave us families and let us feel love.
It's not of this world; it came from above.
I am so thankful to Him, that is true.
And one day we'll rejoice, together with Him,
in a world that is new.

"And God saw everything that he had made, and behold, it was very good. And the evening and the morning were the sixth day."
— Genesis 1:31

One And Only True God

Not everyone in our lives and families are going to realize that we can have a "personal relationship" with God in a very "personal" way. They may not realize that God hears and answers our prayer. I thought of Naomi and Ruth as I prayed today, February 19, 2013. I remembered that Ruth was from Moab where they worshipped other gods and not the only true living God. Ruth married one of Naomi's sons, while Naomi and her family were living in Moab. Naomi worshipped the one and only true God. Ruth could see a light in Naomi that she had never known before. Naomi's husband and both of her sons died, and Naomi was returning home to her own country.

Ruth insisted on going with Naomi, back to Naomi's country. Ruth said to Naomi (Ruth 1:16) *"Intreat me not to leave thee, or to return from following after thee: for whither thou goest, I will go; and where thou lodgest, I will lodge: thy people shall be my people, and thy God my God."*

Ruth now knew and believed in the one and only true God, because she had been with Naomi. Even a person who has not been brought up to believe in the one true God and His living word can be a believer and have faith in God. It's our assignment to keep praying for those friends and family, and let Jesus live His life in us, in front of them. They will come as God makes Himself real to them and their Faith in Him begins to mature.

"Ye are the light of the world. A city that is set on a hill cannot be hid. Neither do men light a candle, and put it under a bushel, but on a candlestick; and it giveth light unto all that are in the house. Let your light so shine before men, that they may see your good works, and glorify your Father which is in heaven."—Matthew 5:14-16

Amazing Grace

The hour I first believed. I was in a deep, dark, miry pit, sinking. Then the words were spoken to me. "His blood cleanses; it washes away all sin." In that instant, I believed! I knew! It was not because of what I had done, but because of what He had done.

At that moment, it was His Amazing Grace that lifted me out of that pit.

Oh, Praise His Wonderful name!
Jesus, I love you! I praise you for life, for even a life new!

> Amazing Grace, how sweet the sound,
> that saved a wretch like me.

My Prayer: Father, make me a witness of your love and mercy, to witness to others who need your amazing grace. In your wonderful son's name, Jesus, I pray.

"I waited patiently for the Lord; and he inclined unto me, and heard my cry. He brought me up also out of an horrible pit, out of the miry clay, and set my feet upon a rock, and established my goings. And he hath put a new song in my mouth, even praise unto our God: many shall see it, and fear, and shall trust in the Lord."—Psalm 40:1-3

1961

It was in the year of nineteen hundred sixty-one.
My experience with God had not long begun.
I believe it was June or there about.
I found I was with child, and there was no doubt.
So, I prayed to God who I knew to be true,
"Give me a son, and I'll give him back to you.
If this is your will, I know it will be".
And when the time came, I knew He had answered me.
There in the delivery room,
I thanked Him and praised His name.
The nurse spoke up and said, "Everyone should do the same."
As the days passed, and I'd look at this baby so pure,
He belonged to God and of this I was sure.
As I'd pass by his bed so many times a day,
A feeling so humble, I'd feel that I wanted to pray.
And as I would look in his eyes of love,
It seemed they would talk to me;
they brought a message from above.
For his eyes always said, "God is Love!"

These precious moments, I'll always remember.

A message to Alan

March 23, 1982

Alan, God has a purpose and plan for your life.
His blessings are precious as you can see in your wife.
So, as you live absorbed in His love,
His blessings will always come down from above.

"And we have known and believed the love that God hath to us. God is love; and he that dwelleth in love dwelleth in God, and God in him."—I John 4:16

Follow Me

At a time when Jesus saw the hunger in my heart, I cried out, "Oh, how I would love to live a life that would please God."

Jesus said to me, "Follow me, but you'll have to cast aside some things."

It was so clear to me that I would need to read His word and do the things He requires. I realized that we don't make ourselves. It is He who makes us. If we are to follow Him, it's okay to begin by taking baby steps.

What made Phillip so sure when he talked to Nathanael in John 1:46? Phillip didn't argue when Nathanael asked him, "Can anything good come out of Nazareth?"

Phillip simply replied, **"Come and see."**

Jesus knows our heart.
When He speaks to us, we know it is Him.

"Know ye that the Lord, He is God: it is He that hath made us, and not we ourselves; we are His people and the sheep of His pasture."—Psalm 100:3

A Relationship, Not Just A Name

God reveals Himself with purpose. He created you for a loving relationship with Himself. When He reveals Himself to you, He is allowing you to come to know Him by experience.

"If ye love me, keep my commandments. And I will pray the Father, and he shall give you another Comforter, that he may abide with you forever; Even the Spirit of truth; whom the world cannot receive, because it seeth him not, neither knoweth him: but ye know him; for he dwelleth with you, and shall be in you. I will not leave you comfortless: I will come to you. Yet a little while, and the world seeth me no more; but ye see me: because I live, ye shall live also. At that day ye shall know that I am in my Father, and ye in me, and I in you. He that hath my commandments, and keepeth them, he it is that loveth me; and he that loveth me shall be loved of my Father, and I will love him, and will manifest myself to him."—John 14:15-21

A Relationship, Not Just A Name

If you have a love relationship with God, you have come to know God through experience. He has worked in and around your life.

For instance, you could not know God as the "Comforter in sorrow" unless you had experienced His comfort, during a time of grief or sorrow.

You come to know God when He reveals Himself to you.
You come to know God when you experience Him.
His Word is the true foundation to base all experiences.

"But whoso keepeth His word, in Him verily is the love of God perfected: hereby know we that we are in Him."—I John 2:5

"And we know that the Son of God is come, and hath given us an understanding, that we may know him that is true, and we are in him that is true, even in his Son Jesus Christ. This is the true God, and eternal life."—I John 5:20

A Relationship, Not Just A Name

In Hebrew custom, the Hebrew name described a person's character or nature. The name was closely associated with the person and his presence. Thus, to call on one's name, was to seek his presence.

God's name is majestic and worthy of our praise. Acknowledging God's name amounts to recognizing God for who He is. Calling on His name indicates you are seeking His presence.

Praising His name is praising Him.
God's name in scripture can become a call to worship for you.

The psalmist said in Psalm 89:15-16, *"Blessed* is *the people that know the joyful sound: they shall walk, O LORD, in the light of thy countenance. In thy name shall they rejoice all the day, and in thy righteousness shall they be exalted."*

A Relationship, Not Just A Name

To worship is to reverence and honor God; to acknowledge Him as worthy of your praise.

Watch for times throughout your day today to worship God, through His names. To focus your attention on His name is to focus attention on the God of the name.

Remember, His name represents His presence.

"For unto us a child is born, unto us a son is given; and the government shall be upon His shoulder: and His name shall be called Wonderful, Counselor, The mighty God, The everlasting Father, The Prince of Peace."— Isaiah 9:6

The Lord Will Provide

In Genesis 22: 1-18, God was in the process of developing Abraham's character to be the father of a nation.

Abraham's faith and obedience were put to the test. Up to this point, Abraham had known God only by experience, as "God Almighty." God had provided Abraham and Sarah with a son when they were both beyond the human limits of childbearing.

In verse 8, God was now requiring Abraham to walk by faith.

Abraham acted on his belief that God was his provider.

Abraham named the place after the God he had just come to know by experience. He had come to an intimate knowledge of God that day, through the experience of God as his provider.

> "And Abraham called the name of that place Jehovah-jireh: as it is said to this day, in the mount of the Lord it shall be seen."
> —Genesis 22:14

The Lord Will Provide

We come to know God as we experience Him. God reveals Himself to us through our experience of Him at work in our lives.

We can come to know about God as a provider as we read of Abraham. But we really come to know God as our Provider as we experience Him providing something for our lives.

It's our choice; we can know and read about God and His power, or we can know and experience God Himself in a personal way, by a personal experience.

God is asking for our obedience.

"That in blessing I will bless thee, and in multiplying I will multiply thy seed as the stars of the heaven, and as the sand which is upon the sea shore; and thy seed shall possess the gate of his enemies."—Genesis 22:17

All our experiences must have God's Word as their foundation.

God Hears Our Cry

The children of Israel had been in Egyptian bondage for some 400 years. We read in Exodus, chapter three, that God heard the cry of the people, saw their affliction, and knew their sorrows.

Verse seven reads: *"And the Lord said, I have surely seen the affliction of my people which are in Egypt and have heard their cry by reason of their taskmasters, for I know their sorrows."*

Egypt symbolizes a type of the world for us today. The time comes for us to come to God, out from the world, out from the bondage we've been in for many years.

Just like Moses led the children of Israel out of bondage, God's Spirit begins to lead us out.

"He found him in a desert land, and in the waste howling wilderness; he led him about, he instructed him, he kept him as the apple of his eye. As an eagle stirreth up her nest, fluttereth over her young, spreadeth abroad her wings, taketh them, beareth them on her wings: So the Lord alone did lead him, and there was no strange god with him."—Deuteronomy 32:10-12

It's Going To Take Faith

As God was teaching Moses to depend on Him. He told Moses to do all those wonders before Pharaoh, but God was going to harden Pharaoh's heart that he would not let God's people go. Moses was going to have to have faith in what God had told him. He would have to believe that God was going to do what He'd told Moses He was going to do. It was going to take Faith when Pharaoh made things even harder for the Israelite people.

"And the tale of the bricks, which they did make heretofore, ye shall lay upon them; ye shall not diminish ought thereof: for they be idle; therefore they cry, saying, Let us go and sacrifice to our God. Let there more work be laid upon the men, that they may labour therein; and let them not regard vain words."—Exodus 5:8,9

Moses did question God in Exodus 5:22,23; asking God, "Why?"

"And Moses returned unto the Lord, and said, Lord, wherefore hast thou so evil entreated this people? Why is it that thou hast sent me? For since I came to Pharaoh to speak in thy name, he hath done evil to this people; neither hast thou delivered thy people at all."—Exodus 5:22,23

Moses didn't remember what God had told him in Exodus 4:21. *"And the Lord said unto Moses, when thou goest to return into Egypt, see that thou do all those wonders before Pharaoh, which I have put in thine hand: but I will harden his heart, that he shall not let the people go."*

We must remember, things don't always work out overnight. It doesn't mean that God can't see the situation we are facing. He is faithful; His promises are true. We just need to remember to take it all to Him in prayer.

God will fight our fight for us, and He will lead us day and night. We must be filled with faith, knowing that it is through much tribulation that we will enter the kingdom of God.

"Confirming the souls of the disciples, and exhorting them to continue in the faith, and that we must through much tribulation enter into the kingdom of God."—Acts 14:22

Having Abundant Life

As you follow Jesus, one day at a time, He will keep you in the center of God's will. Knowing God doesn't come through a program or a method but through a loving relationship with Him.

Jesus wants us to experience life to the fullest. He has more in store for your life than just to do something for Him. He wants you to experience a love relationship with Him that is real and personal.

We read in John 14:26 that Jesus wants to be your teacher.

He will teach you all things.
God is looking for an intimate relationship!

"The thief cometh not, but for to steal, and to kill, and to destroy: I am come that they might have life, and that they might have it more abundantly."—John 10:10

Your Source Of Authority

The Bible is God's Word to you; your source of authority. You cannot depend on traditions, your experiences or others' experiences as accurate authorities on God's will and ways. Experience and traditions must always be examined against the teaching of Scripture.

In John 17:3, Jesus said, *"And this is life eternal, that they might know thee the only true God, and Jesus Christ, whom thou hast sent."*

Knowing God's Nature And His Will

**God is love: His will is always best.
God is all knowing: His directions are always right.
God is all powerful: He can enable you
to accomplish His will.**

God's very nature is Love. God does bring discipline, judgment and wrath on those who continue in sin and rebellion, but even His discipline is based on love. His Word tells us in Hebrews 12:6 *"For whom the Lord loveth he chasteneth, and scourgeth every son whom he receiveth."*

Your trust in God's love is all important. Always remember the cross. No matter what the circumstances are His love never changes. Look at everything through the backdrop of the cross. Every experience is an expression of His love for you.

"For God so loved the world, that he gave his only begotten Son, that whosoever believeth in him should not perish, but have everlasting life."—John 3:16

God's Commands Are For Your Good

When you trust God, you obey Him. I John 5:3 says *"For this is the love of God, that we keep his commandments: and his commandments are not grievous."*

It's because of His love for us that He gives us guidelines to follow through life. Life is full of dangers, so we need those guidelines.

I thought of the landmines that were once, and maybe even today buried in foreign lands. Stay close to the person who knows where they are all hidden.

A good example: Having a spouse is wonderful. Then God gives the command, "Thou shalt not commit adultery." Is that command to limit and restrict you? No, it is to protect and free you to experience love at its human best. What happens if this command is broken? The love relationship is broken, trust is gone, and the pain comes.

His commands are designed to guide you to life's very best.

If you love Him, you will trust and obey Him.

"And now, Israel, what doth the Lord thy God require of thee, but to fear the Lord thy God, to walk in all his ways, and to love him, and to serve the Lord thy God with all thy heart and with all thy soul, to keep the commandments of the Lord and his statutes, which I command thee this day for thy good?"—Deuteronomy 10: 12, 13

God Is All Knowing

God's directions are always right. By nature, He is omniscient or all knowing. He possesses all knowledge, past, present, and future. Therefore, His direction is always right. What about God's knowledge about me and what is best for my life?

He absolutely knows what is best for me!

"Be not ye therefore like unto them: for your Father knoweth what things ye have need of, before ye ask him."—Matthew 6:8

"Them" in this verse refers to the Gentiles, or heathen, or the ones not knowing the One True God; all those in other nations who worshipped other gods.

"(For after all these things do the Gentiles seek:) for your heavenly Father knoweth that ye have need of all these things."
—Matthew 6:32

God Is All Powerful

God is omnipotent; He is all powerful!
He **can enable** you to accomplish His will.

* God enabled Noah and his sons to build the ark to save their lives as we are told in Genesis, chapters six through nine.
* In Judges, chapters seven and eight, God enabled Gideon and three hundred men to defeat an army of one hundred and twenty thousand.
* In Matthew, chapter 10, Jesus Christ enabled his twelve disciples to heal people and cast out demons.
* God enabled Paul to carry the Gospel to the Gentiles and establish churches throughout Asia Minor and all the way to Rome.

**Even when it doesn't make sense to us,
God's direction is always right, and He is all Powerful!
He is able!**

"What man is he that feareth the Lord? Him shall he teach in the way that he shall choose."—Psalm 25:12

God Is All Knowing

There was an elderly sister in the Lord, Sister Miller, who was also a teacher in the church we attended in Florida, who told this story not long after I was saved. She said that when she first got saved, she loved the Lord so much and she was so faithful to God's house and His Word that her husband didn't understand. He was so upset with her that he told her he was going to leave if she continued these actions. They had two small children, and he was so upset that he told her that he would take the bigger one and she could keep the baby. She went upstairs and laid across the bed and wept, talking to the Lord. She knew she couldn't give up on the Lord, she loved Him far too much. The Lord spoke to her and told her to tell her husband to take both the children. Her heart was broken, but she did as the Lord told her. Her husband stormed out of the house. He returned a little while later, and never mentioned it again.

God knows, and He's always right!

"For the Lord giveth wisdom: out of his mouth cometh knowledge and understanding."—Proverbs 2:6

God Reveals Himself To You

The names of God in Scripture reveal something of His nature, activity and character. You come to know God by experience at His initiative, (as He reveals Himself to you). As you experience God, you come to know Him more intimately and personally. As you come to know Him, you will want to express your praise, gratitude, and worship to Him.

Some of the names God has revealed to me personally are:

Wonderful, Provider, and Savior.

"Beloved, let us love one another: for love is of God; and every one that loveth is born of God, and knoweth God. He that loveth not knoweth not God; for God is love."—I John 4: 7, 8

Give No Place To The Devil

I remember a message that I heard that came at a time that I needed it and was such a blessing to me. I'm so thankful to God for the message and the young man who brought it. The message text was taken from Ephesians 4:17-27 and focused on verse 27. *"Neither give place to the devil."* As he preached the message, it was like I could see so many places where I had been giving place to the devil - in my life; in my home; in my place in the church.

I thought, in my everyday life, if I don't read and pray as I should, I'm giving that place to the devil to get something in. In our homes, if we let things go on that are not right like talk, activities, entertainment, these things give place to the devil. This will weaken our faith. Our absence from church gives the devil a place to work on others from our empty place. I don't want the devil to have place in my heart, home, or my church.

After the message was preached, and the altar call was made, I knelt at my seat to pray. My heart was filled with thanksgiving for the message and the speaker. I remember thanking God for this young man preaching the message that I needed so badly. The Spirit began to unfold something very real to me. I prayed, "Thank you for my brother." My mind went back to when I was a very young girl and I first thought how good it would have been to have a brother. There were five of us girls. I would often think how it would be to have a big brother to watch over me and protect me. It was so real as the Holy Spirit unfolded this thought to me. Jesus, through this young man, was doing just that. He could see where there was danger. He was giving the protection we needed as he watched over us. I thank Him for that. There was such a peace that night and a calm in my heart as I came home from church. A great victory had been won.

As we work to keep from giving room for the devil, he has no place to work on us or others concerning us. Every time he works it's because we've given him place.

I thought of the scripture in John 14:30, 31 where Jesus said, *"Hereafter I will not talk much with you: for the prince of this world cometh, and hath nothing in me. But that the world may know that I love the Father; and as the Father gave me commandment, even so I do. Arise, let us go hence."*

To Any Daddy

(June – Father's Day)

There are little eyes upon you,
And they're watching night and day.
There are little ears that quickly,
Take in every word you say.

There are little hands all eager,
To do anything you do.
And a little boy who's dreaming,
Of the day he'll be like you.

You're the little fellow's idol.
You're the wisest of the wise.
In his little mind about you,
No suspicions ever rise.

He believes in you devoutly.
Holds that all you say and do.
He will say and do in your way,
When he's grown up like you.

There's a wide eyed little fellow.
He believes you're always right.
And his ears are always open,
And he watches you day and night.

You are setting an example,
Every day in all you do.
For the little boy who's watching,
To grow up to be like you.

By: Ken Clasper (by permission)

Sanctification

Holiness is in contrast to worldliness. Worldliness is living, acting, and desiring according to the standard of the world. Worldliness is human activity with God left out. Two great truths are involved in sanctification. The first truth is consecration or a true relationship with God that conveys the truth of separation. We are redeemed in order to be set apart. The second truth is purification or a true condition before God. The presence of God by the Holy Spirit in our hearts and lives will purify our thought life bringing our desires and motives into subjection to God's will.

"If a man therefore purge himself from these, he shall be a vessel unto honour, sanctified, and meet for the master's use, and prepared unto every good work."—II Timothy 2:21

"But if we walk in the light, as he is in the light, we have fellowship one with another, and the blood of Jesus Christ His son cleanseth us from all sin."—I John 1:7

New Life

John the Baptist first prepared the way for the Lord Jesus Christ by causing people to recognize and confess their sins and desire deliverance from their sins.

Then John pointed them to Jesus.

John said, *"I indeed baptize you with water unto repentance: but he that cometh after me is mightier than I, whose shoes I am not worthy to bear: he shall baptize you with the Holy Ghost and with fire."* (Matthew 3:11)

Then again in John 1:29 *"The next day John seeth Jesus coming unto him, and saith, Behold the Lamb of God, which taketh away the sin of the world."*

John said that he could not enable people to receive the Holy Spirit or to be baptized by the Holy Ghost, only Christ could do this.

The Holy Spirit is the one who creates spiritual life within the believer.

In Hebrew, the word for Spirit is ruach, which also means "breath". The promise of the Holy Spirit is the promise of "New Life". The Hebrew word, ruach, also means "wind", and wind speaks of power. Jesus compared the Holy Spirit to wind.

The Holy Spirit dwells in our hearts; His power transforms our lives.

"That which is born of the flesh is flesh; and that which is born of the Spirit is Spirit. Marvel not that I said unto thee, Ye must be born again. The wind bloweth where it listeth, and thou hearest the sound thereof, but canst not tell whence it cometh, and whither it goeth: so is every one that is born of the Spirit."—John 3:6-8

Let There Be Light

God said, "Let there be light", and there was light.

As light began to stream into my life, I became aware of a need in my life. Something was missing; I knew it was God. My life was empty of God's presence and His light. I got out of bed in the morning, went to work, doing everything day by day. Every day my routine was the same. I was living my life as I pleased. Then as God began to draw me by His Spirit and that Light began to appear, I became aware, "There must be more to life than this."

I am so thankful for God's goodness and mercies to us. The light reveals the former darkness. We know something is missing in this old life.

Let there be "Light"!

"In Him was life; and the life was the light of men. And the light shineth in darkness; and the darkness comprehended it not."
—John 1:4, 5

A Set Time

What a great blessing is granted to us when God chooses to draw us by His Spirit and calls us unto Himself. He has a pattern and time set. He begins to draw us and knows exactly how and when to draw us to Him and to His house.

When God drew me to Him and brought me out of darkness and sin into a new life in Him, it wasn't by might nor by power but by His spirit.

It was His Spirit that let me know that I needed Him.
It was His Spirit that let me know
and desire a new beginning.
It was His Spirit that led me to go to church.

I knew that it was His house, and I was seeking Him. I remember thinking, "Oh, how I wish I could start my life all over again and never do anything wrong." I desired a new beginning.

"Then he answered and spake unto me, saying, This is the word of the Lord unto Zerubbabel, saying, Not by might, nor by power, but by my spirit, saith the Lord of hosts."—Zechariah 4:6

He Will Be Our Shield

There was a little song we learned to sing as children:

> As you left your room this morning,
> Did you think to pray?
> Did you meet the loving Savior?
> Did you ask His loving favor as a shield today?

We need spiritual strength to stand against all the temptations; we need humbleness when faced with hard attitudes; we need boldness to make our stand for God. We need wisdom, understanding, and guidance in all our decisions.

**We must put our faith in God
when we are faced with fears.**

Abraham was not a warrior. His only battle recorded in the Bible was to rescue Lot when he'd been captured during the battle of the Kings. The Bible said that after these things, Abraham began to think on these things and maybe he began to fear. But God visited him in a vision. Genesis 15:1 says, *"After these things the word of the Lord came unto Abram in a vision, saying, Fear not, Abram: I am thy shield, and thy exceeding great reward."*

**We do not have to fear;
God will be our shield.
Just ask Him.
He will give us loving favor as a shield today!**

Battle For The Quiet Time

The battle for the quiet time is never over. We are not alone in our striving to keep a quiet time. But is it worth the struggle?

So many Christians don't keep a quiet time with the Lord. They manage to get along. But they become struggling Christians; Christians with no testimony. Sometimes they become a Christian that the world looks at and says, "If he/she is a Christian, I don't care to be one." The Christian who doesn't keep quiet time isn't prepared when trouble comes. Physical health and spiritual health are much alike. It is easier to fight a cold if you are healthy, and it is easier to have courage if you are spiritually up to par. The way to keep spiritually fit is to have that daily session of Bible reading and prayer. The Christian who fails to keep quiet time, falls prey to confusion and frustration. He can turn from one thing to another in search of spiritual peace. Only when returning to the quiet time, does the victory come. Now when he allows other things to come first, he begins to doubt and fear again. It is very easy to not keep a quiet time. If you are convinced that without a quiet time you will lose your peace of mind and a measure of your reward, then the battle begins.

It seems to me that the best time to have devotions is the first thing in the morning. You may complain that you don't have time. But that is not the real issue. One may get up at the last minute, gulp a cup of coffee, and rush from the house. The other may get up leisurely, take his time with breakfast, read the paper, then calmly stroll off to work. Neither one keeps a quiet time. So, it is not time that counts, it is discipline.

Beware of saying, "I have no time to read my Bible and pray," but instead, say, "I have not bothered to discipline myself to do these things."

Battle For The Quiet Time

Let's say that you have set your quiet time; the next thing or problem to overcome is people. The important thing in winning this part of the battle is to get alone. If you attempt your quiet time in the presence of others, you are almost sure to miss the real spiritual benefit of close communion with your Lord.

The third enemy to overcome is the pull of your work. People are motor minded, and the urge to keep on the move is terrific. Yet, we must realize that only as we have fellowship with the Lord in our quiet time, can we expect to be blessed in our work for Him.

We must also realize that we are the biggest enemy of all. Most people find it hard to pray because there is so little in common with God. The great interest is in the world instead of in the Kingdom of God. It takes a complete about face in our desires and motives to enjoy spending time with the Lord.

We often lose the battle of the quiet time because whether we admit it or not, we don't really want to win it! There are two ways in which a Christian wins this battle. Some go down into the valley of the shadow of death, face the awful fact of final judgment and then become determined to keep a regular time of devotion with the Lord. Others learn the better way; they fall in love with the Lord Jesus. Like earthly love, this love for Him does not come the same way to all. With some it is love at first sight, others grow slowly into knowing and adoring Him. Whether this love rushes or creeps into our souls, nothing can keep us from the quiet time and from the joy of being alone with God when the true Love comes! Ever increasing love for Him is the secret to winning the battle for the quiet time.

Author unknown

Joseph

It means so much to commit your future into the hands of God, to say yes to the will of God on the mountain top or in the valley. Joseph was loved by his father, hated by his brethren, sold into slavery, accused and cast into prison; yet, he was faithful to his God. He believed in seeking first the kingdom of God.

God is looking for men today who will put Him first in their lives. By Joseph's faithfulness, he was able to save many souls, including his family. It is the plan of God to use men to save men. An angel cannot preach this gospel. In our trials and tests, we may feel that God has forsaken us and that evil doers abound, but God is going to have a tried people: it is His plan. When all of our days, both evil and good have come to a close and are weighed before God, then we will know how much good we have done. The soil of the human heart will produce either good or evil. If God then, permits anything hard in our lives, let it be understood that the real peril, the real trouble, is that we should lose, and our witness be lost if we flinch or rebel.

"But seek ye first the kingdom of God, and His righteousness; and all these things shall be added unto you."—Matthew 6:33

Clothed In His Righteousness

I can remember as a little girl how my sisters and I often had to wear old and mended clothing. One thing my mom was always sure of was that even though it may be old and mended, it was always clean.

As children of the King, we have authority! Without His righteousness, we have no authority. Jesus could touch the sick or lame or even be touched and the work was done. We read many times in the new testament where Jesus was wearing a white raiment, symbolizing His righteousness. If we will live and be clothed in Him, in His righteousness, we too can see miracles.

**Have we laid aside this garment, to be clothed
in our own garment of self-righteousness?
There is no power nor authority in any garment
but the robe of righteousness, that He clothes us in.**

We are tempted to judge people by the way they dress. People high in society dress in expensive attire. We, as children of the King, also have a most beautiful garment and the most expensive by far. We can be clothed in His righteousness.

We are often tempted to hold to our old clothing, or our self-life. Everyone can see what we are wearing; all people must do is look and observe. What is it that they see?

Remember, our Father owns the best; it's up to each one of us to put it on. There is clothing provided for God's children today; there is power and authority in this garment.

"And that ye put on the new man, which after God is created in righteousness and true holiness."— Ephesians 4:24

We Can Rest In Him

This morning I awoke early, before dawn. I arose to read God's Word and study for this Sunday's lesson. It was such a good feeling as I could hear the birds singing outside greeting the new day. I, too, thanked God for the new day, so clean and fresh. I thought, only with His guidance and help, can I say at the end of the day, "It was good", like God was able to say at the end of each day of creation.

He is wonderful!

I don't know the temptations or pain this day may hold, but with Him by my side, I know each step will be made wisely and victoriously. He will keep me from the evil. At the day's end, I can rest in Him.

Just a little while later I could hear the rain and thunder, but the birds sang on. The rain fell gently and made such a calming sound. God knows our everyday needs. He is in control of all the universe. We can rest in Him.

"He hath made everything beautiful in his time: also he hath set the world in their heart, so that no man can find out the work that God maketh from the beginning to the end."—Ecclesiastes 3:11

Beneath God's Brightest Star

As Mary gazed down at her babe,
That night so long ago.
Perhaps she touched his hands and crooned,
In tender voice and low.

His hands would one day heal the sick.
Five thousand men would feed;
Would flex in pain upon the cross,
And, pierced with nails, would bleed.

I think she might have kissed his feet.
Adored his baby ways.
So soon her child would walk for God.
The Christians' pathway blaze.

Perhaps she touched with finger tips,
The brow which thorns would mar.
All this within a humble shed,
Beneath God's brightest star.

Although Christ died, praise God He rose!
Such love no force could bar;
Divinely planned, this holy birth.
Beneath God's brightest star.

Author unknown

The Eyes

When the physical eye is in an unhealthy condition, the image is doubled or blurred and not accurate. What we see affects our desires and our actions. We purchase something because we see it and it looks good to us, as we desire it, and our heart is affected by what our eyes see.

The Lord is telling us in Matthew 6:22, we are to look straight forward and have an eye, "single for his glory."

We are to look away from every other attraction and look to Jesus. Our eyes affect our hearts. Therefore, we are to let only those things enter our minds and hearts through the eye gates that will bring glory to God and blessing to us and others.

The single eye is to focus on Him!

"The light of the body is the eye: if therefore thine eye be single, thy whole body shall be full of light."—Matthew 6:22

Faith Is Believing In His Love

We believe and are sure of God's love, even though things happen that make it seem that He's not taking notice. Heartache comes, along with pain, disappointments, and discouragements, but we know all He has done for us in the past. He gave His only begotten son to die for our sins, so we could have life. His love was proven at Calvary. Jesus died, proving His great love. He freed us from the power that satan held over us. We are free; redeemed by His blood. And now, no matter what comes we know He loves us. Even when situations arise, we look to His word and remember, we know that all things work together for good to them that love God, to them, who are the called according to His purpose. We don't doubt God's love every time something goes wrong or He seems far away. No, we have faith, in His Love.

"For whatsoever is born of God, overcometh the world: and this is the victory that overcometh the world, even our faith."—I John 5:4

A Place Of Love

There is a place of love; a place to adore and worship Him. Have we gotten away from that place? There are so many hindrances, and often we are too busy to get away to that place. Maybe, we go there, but we find we're in such a hurry that we don't have the time to dwell there.

There is a time to REMEMBER, REPENT, and DO.

Jesus told the church at Ephesus in Revelation 2:2-5, "*I know thy works, and thy labour, and thy patience, and how thou canst not bear them which are evil: and thou hast tried them which say they are apostles, and are not, and hast found them liars: And hast borne, and hast patience, and for my name's sake hast laboured, and hast not fainted. Nevertheless, I have somewhat against thee, because thou hast left thy first love. Remember therefore from whence thou art fallen and repent, and do the first works; or else I will come unto thee quickly, and will remove thy candlestick out of his place, except thou repent.*"

A Place Of Love:
A Place Of Sharing

He wants to share with me precious things. Jesus said in John 15:15, *"Henceforth, I call you not servants; for the servant knoweth not what his lord doeth: but I have called you friends; for all things that I have heard of my Father I have made known unto you."*

Not too long ago, the Spirit of God spoke to me .His message overwhelmed me, so I did as David did in Psalm 61:2, *"From the end of the earth will I cry unto thee, when my heart is overwhelmed: lead me to the rock that is higher than I."* That is where He met me and had Words for me. He spoke, "There is a place by Me." As I felt His love and comfort there, I thought on these things.

"And Moses said unto the Lord, see thou sayest unto me, Bring up this people: and thou hast not let me know whom thou wilt send with me. Yet thou hast said, I know thee by name, and thou hast also found grace in my sight. Now therefore, I pray thee, if I have found grace in thy sight, shew me now thy way, that I might know thee, that I may find grace in thy sight: and consider that this nation is thy people. And he said, My presence shall go with thee, and I will give thee rest. And he said unto him, If thy presence go not with me, carry us not up hence. For wherein shall it be known here that I and thy people have found grace in thy sight? Is it not in that thou goest with us? So shall we be separated, I and thy

people, from all the people that are upon the face of the earth. And the Lord said unto Moses, I will do this thing also that thou hast spoken: for thou hast found grace in my sight, and I know thee by name. And he said, I beseech thee, shew me thy glory. And he said I will make all my goodness pass before thee, and I will proclaim the name of the Lord before thee; and will be gracious to whom I will be gracious, and will shew mercy on whom I will shew mercy. And he said, Thou canst not see my face: for there shall no man see me and live. And the Lord said, Behold, there is a place by me, and thou shalt stand upon a rock: And it shall come to pass, while my glory passeth by, that I will put thee in a clift of the rock, and will cover thee with my hand while I pass by; And I will take away mine hand, and thou shalt see my back parts: but my face shall not be seen."—Exodus 33:12-23

Going into the trial, we may not see. When we've come through it, we see God's Glory! After He passes by. He is Wonderful!

A Place Of Love: My Secret Place

In the Spring of 1963, we moved back to Keavy, Kentucky looking for work and found a place to rent. We rented three rooms in the back of an old store house building that had closed some years before. I had just gotten saved and had started my new life. There was a room that had once been used for storage. The door to the room was all barred up; not even a crack of light could see its way through. Without even a window, it was truly the darkest place I had ever seen.

In the day time it was pitch black dark; no light from anywhere. This storage room became my secret place of prayer, away from all else. I had an old foot stool in the center of the room that was my altar. When I entered the room and shut the door, I had to feel with my feet across the room until I came to the stool, and there I knelt. As I worshiped and talked with the Lord, His presence was so bright and glorious. It was wonderful. I was amazed when our visit was over, and I opened my eyes and saw the darkness once again. I felt my way back to the door. I didn't mind at all, because I was full of joy and love from being in His presence.

"Glory and honour are in his presence; strength and gladness are in his place. Give unto the Lord, ye kindreds of the people, give unto the Lord glory and strength. Give unto the Lord the glory due unto his name: bring an offering, and come before him: worship the Lord in the beauty of holiness. Fear before him, all the earth: the world also shall be stable, that it be not moved. Let the heavens be glad, and let the earth rejoice: and let men say among the nations, The Lord reigneth. Let the sea roar, and the fulness thereof: let the fields rejoice, and all that is therein. Then shall the trees of the wood sing out at the presence of the Lord, because he cometh to judge the earth. O give thanks unto the Lord; for he is good; for his mercy endureth forever."—I Chronicles 16:27-34

Storing Up Our Treasures

We had been studying in Genesis for some time when I had some thoughts on our treasures and where it is that we have stored them. One example is found in Genesis thirteen. The Bible says that Abraham was very rich in cattle, in silver, and in gold. He left Egypt and went to the place of the altar. We can see where Abrams affections were. We can see that it didn't matter to Abram which part of the land Lot took in verse nine, because Abrams affections were not set on things on the earth. His affections were set on God and where He was taking him.

"By faith, Abraham, when he was called to go out into a place which he should after receive for an inheritance, obeyed: and he went out, not knowing whither he went. By faith he sojourned in the land of promise, as in a strange country, dwelling in tabernacles with Isaac and Jacob, the heirs with him of the same promise: For he looked for a city which hath foundations, whose builder and maker is God."—Hebrews 11:8-10

Storing Up Our Treasures

What are we seeking after? When I ask myself this question, there is a scripture that comes to my mind.

"Therefore take no thought, saying What shall we eat? Or, what shall we drink? Or, Wherewithal shall we be clothed? (For after all these things do the Gentiles seek.) For your heavenly Father knoweth that ye have need of all these things. But seek ye first the kingdom of God, and his righteousness; and all these things shall be added unto you."—Matthew 6:31-33

The Gentiles didn't know the one true God. Look around us! We can easily see what people are concerned about today.

Jesus said, "For your heavenly Father knoweth that ye have need of all these things." Again, in verse 31, "Take no thought".

When all these thoughts came to me, I was driving along, pretty discouraged. I was uncertain about the future, financially. That's when God reminded me of a "sale" sign I had seen many years ago. "Your Choice $3.00" I remembered the dress. I began to cry, and said, "Thank you, Father", as I remembered the blessing He was reminding me of. This is a treasure indeed and comforts us. The Holy Ghost uses what is stored up in us.

God is so good to us.
He is Wonderful!
The blessings our Heavenly Father gives us are truly treasures.
Always remember His Word!

Storing Up Our Treasures

Are we storing up some treasures? Are we setting our affections on things above? As we seek God and His Kingdom, Blessings come. Everything else is taken care of.

My prayer is that our Father will help us to not seek the things of the world, but instead be like David when he said in Psalm 42:1, 2 *"As the hart panteth after the water brooks, so panteth my soul after thee, O God. My soul thirsteth for God, for the living God: when shall I come and appear before God?"*

"In the last day, that great day of the feast, Jesus stood and cried, saying, If any man thirst, let him come unto me, and drink. He that believeth on me, as the scripture hath said, out of his belly shall flow rivers of living water. (But this spake he of the Spirit, which they that believe on him should receive: for the Holy Ghost was not yet given; because that Jesus was not yet glorified.)"— John 7:37-39

The Straight Gate

Because of our "Adam" nature, we're stubborn and self-willed, wanting our way. It's difficult for our stubborn heart to repent or change. Even the world teaches us the wrong way in most all things. We must choose between the two.

Jesus said, "Enter ye in at the straight gate". It's more difficult because God's way and His will are so different from what we would choose, or even our desire to have our way. God gives grace which makes it possible for us to choose to go the right way. We can walk in this straight and narrow way but only with the help of the Lord Jesus. We should remember that all things are possible with God. We must ask for His help, as we obey and follow Jesus, humbling ourselves before Him.

"Lord, give us grace."

"Enter ye in at the strait gate: for wide is the gate, and broad is the way, that leadeth to destruction, and many there be which go in thereat: Because strait is the gate, and narrow is the way, which leadeth unto life, and few there be that find it."—Matthew 7: 13-14

The Straight Gate

There are advantages to the straight way. We don't travel alone; Jesus is here with us. There are blessings unspeakable that we can find only on this narrow way. There are things that God has for us, spiritual things. He reveals unto us spiritual truths in His Word as we travel on this road. At the end of this road is eternal life. We cannot even imagine these blessings, unless we enter. As behind a closed door, we can't see what is waiting on the other side without entering.

"Strive (to try hard, labor, struggle) to enter in at the strait gate: for many, I say unto you, will seek to enter in, and shall not be able."—Luke 13:24

The natural man is not able to see the kingdom, until he be born again. It requires a regeneration; a new birth.

"Jesus answered and said unto him, Verily, verily, I say unto thee, Except a man be born again, he cannot see the kingdom of God."—John 3:3

Jesus said for us to deny ourselves, take up our cross, and follow Him.

"Then said Jesus unto his disciples, If any man will come after me, let him deny himself, and take up his cross, and follow me. For whosoever will save his life shall lose it: and whosoever will lose his life for my sake shall find it."—Matthew 16:24

God's Purpose For Our Lives

To Know Him – The Father

First, I want us to look at the Greatness of God. There are so many wonderful words to describe God, and all of them are good, holy and perfect.

David wrote in Psalm 8: 1-4, 9 *"O Lord our Lord, how excellent is thy name in all the earth! Who has set thy glory above the heavens. Out of the mouth of babes and sucklings hast thou ordained strength because of thine enemies, that thou mightest still the enemy and the avenger. When I consider thy heavens, the work of thy fingers, the moon and the stars, which thou has ordained: What is man, that thou art mindful of him? And the son of man, that thou visitest him? O Lord our Lord, how excellent is thy name in all the earth!"*

Moses desired to see the Glory of God. God told Moses that he couldn't see his face: *"For there shall no man see me and live."* But He told Moses in Exodus 33:21-23 *"...Behold, there is a place by me, and thou shalt stand upon a rock: And it shall come to pass, while my glory passeth by, that I will put thee in a clift of the rock, and will cover thee with my hand while I pass by: And I will take away mine hand, and thou shalt see my back parts: but my face shall not be seen."*

Jesus is the rock today. Being hidden (placed) in Him, God shows us His Glory, through Christ.

"Now unto the King eternal, immortal, invisible, the only wise God, be honour and glory for ever and ever, Amen."—I Timothy 1:17

Anything invisible cannot be seen, so God sent His son.

"Which in his times he shall shew, who is the blessed and only Potentate, the King of kings, and Lord of lords; Who only hath immortality, dwelling in the light which no man can approach unto; whom no man hath seen, nor can see: too whom be honour and power everlasting, Amen."— I Timothy 6:15, 16

**Jesus came to show us the Father,
and God's will is for us to know Him.**

God's Purpose For Our Lives

To Know Him – The Son

We cannot know God, His love, His ways, and His holiness, without Jesus, His Son. He hath declared Him. Jesus is the visible representation and manifestation of God to us.

"Jesus saith unto him, Have I been so long time with you, and yet hast thou not known me, Philip? He that hath seen me hath seen the Father, and how sayest thou then, Shew us the Father?"—John 14:9

"No man hath seen God at any time; the only begotten Son, which is in the bosom of the Father, he hath declared (to make known in word and deed) him."—John 1:18

Jesus was in the bosom of the Father. The word bosom is derived from the fond and intimate union of children and parents. I'm so thankful for Christ, the Son, in the bosom of the Father, who came forth to be the revealer of the Father.

"In the beginning was the Word, and the Word was with God, and the Word was God."—John 1:1

"And the word was made flesh, and dwelt among us, (and we beheld his glory, the glory as of the only begotten of the Father), full of grace and truth."—John 1:14

God's Purpose For Our Lives

To Know Him – The Word

Today, I want to talk about "The Word." Word is an expression of an invisible thought. It brings a thought out. As words utter thoughts, so does Christ utter God. For example, someone may be troubled. You know something is wrong, but you don't know what it is until they speak or tell you. Maybe you want someone to do something, but they don't understand until you speak to let them know by your words.

Look at the things Jesus spoke to us, and the things He did. His Words show us the way of life that pleases God. He points out the things that are wrong in our lives. He has shown us God's will for sickness and disease. Jesus went about doing good and healing all manner of sickness. It is God's will for us to be well in spirit, in soul, and in body. He brought Salvation. He made us whole, and He is the same yesterday, today, and forever.

"And the very God of peace sanctify you wholly; and I pray God your whole spirit and soul and body be preserved blameless unto the coming of our Lord Jesus Christ."—I Thessalonians 5:23

God's Purpose For Our Lives

What About Me?

What does all this mean in terms of God's purpose for my life? It's God's will that we be "One" with Him.

When Jesus prayed in John 17:11, 20 *"And now I am no more in the world, but these are in the world, and I come to thee. Holy Father, keep through thine own name those whom thou hast given me, that they may be one, as we are. Neither pray I for these alone, but for them also which shall believe on me through their word;"*
His will is for a closeness between us and Jesus, that the world may believe that God and Jesus are one, and we are one with Him. To be made perfect as "one."

"Then said Jesus to them again, Peace be unto you: as my Father hath sent me, even so send I you. And when he had said this, he breathed on them, and saith unto them, Receive ye the Holy Ghost."—John 20: 21,22

The Holy Ghost reveals Him to us, and we are to reveal Him to others by the light we shine in the world. We are to show forth His love, we are to be filled with His Spirit, and bear the fruit of His Spirit.

Others will see and come to Him as we show Him to the world.

Hold Them Up To God

Is someone on your heart today?
Hold him up to God.
He'll know just what that person needs.
Your part is that you intercede.
His name before our Heavenly Father plead.
Hold him up to God.
Has someone been unkind to you?
Hold him up to God.
Let God his troubled heart embrace.
Hold him up to God.
Then patience He will give and grace,
To love through every trial you face.
Hold him up to God.
Is someone ill and in distress?
Hold him up to God.
The Great Physician Christ became,
For all who call upon His name.
Why not His healing promise claim?
Hold him up to God.
So many need our faithful prayers.
Hold them up to God.
Friends, neighbors, husbands, wives,
Our nation's leaders as they strive.
Pray down God's blessings for their lives.

Hold them up to God!

—Author unknown

Parable Of The Talents

For our devotion today, I'd like for us to just read this passage of scripture and focus on this fact. The key of this parable is not the five, or two, or even the one talent. The key is faithfulness in each case. Faithfulness, not the amount, is what links the talent to the joy of the Lord. The amount of ability is not the first thing for us to consider; it is our faithful use of whatever ability we have.

**God wants to be able to trust us
with whatever He gives us to do.**

"For the kingdom of heaven is as a man traveling into a far country, who called his own servants, and delivered unto them his goods. And unto one he gave five talents, to another two, and to another one; to every man according to his several ability; and straightway took his journey. Then he that had received the five talents went and traded with the same, and made them other five talents. And likewise he that had received two, he also gained other two. But he that had received one went and digged in the earth, and hid his lord's money. After a long time the lord of those servants cometh, and reckoneth with them. And so he that had received five talents came and brought other five talents, saying, Lord, thou deliveredst unto me five talents: behold I have gained beside them five talents more. His lord said unto him, Well done, thou good and faithful servant: thou hast been faithful over a few things, I will make thee ruler over many things: enter thou into the joy of thy lord. He also

that had received two talents came and said, Lord, thou deliveredst unto me two talents: behold I have gained two other talents beside them. His lord said unto him, Well done, good and faithful servant; thou has been faithful over a few things, I will make thee ruler over many things: enter thou into the joy of thy lord. Then he which had received the one talent came and said, Lord, I knew thee that thou art an hard man, reaping where thou hast not sown, and gathering where thou hast not strawed: And I was afraid, and went and hid thy talent in the earth; lo, there thou hast that is thine. His lord answered and said unto him, Thou wicked and slothful servant, thou knewest that I reap where I sowed not, and gather where I have not strawed: Thou oughtest therefore to have put my money to the exchangers, and then at my coming I should have received mine own with usury. Take therefore the talent from him, and give it unto him which hath ten talents. For unto everyone that hath shall be given, and he shall have abundance: but from him that hath not shall be taken away even that which he hath. And cast ye the unprofitable servant into outer darkness: there shall be weeping and gnashing of teeth."—Matthew 25: 14-30

Set Your Affections On Things Above, Not On Things Of The Earth

I was driving down the road the other day, with some thoughts on my mind that troubled me. Discouraging thoughts. Things looked uncertain for me. As the Holy Ghost began to draw things from my memory, I began thinking in a different direction. Oh, what a blessing as I thought about storing up our treasures!

All the blessings our Heavenly Father gives us are treasures, valuable things, riches, we store up.

Jesus said in Matthew 6:19-21 *"Lay not up for yourselves treasures upon earth, where moth and rust doth corrupt, and where thieves break through and steal: But lay up for yourselves treasures in heaven, where neither moth nor rust doth corrupt, and where thieves do not break through nor steal. For where your treasure is, there will your heart be also."*

I began to think what are we seeking? For about three weeks, part of a scripture has kept coming to me. It is found in Matthew 6, verse 32, *"For after all these things do the Gentiles seek:"*

Now read Matthew 6: 31-33 *"Therefore take no thought, saying, What shall we eat? Or, What shall we drink? Or, Wherewithal shall we be clothed? (For after all these things do the Gentiles seek): for your heavenly Father knoweth that ye have need of all these things. But seek ye first the kingdom of God, and his righteousness; and all these things shall be added unto you."*

I could see that I was doing exactly what Jesus was referring to here in scripture.

I am so thankful for God's Word, and His Spirit!

As I continued driving down the road, He began to remind me of one of the greatest blessings I had ever known.

That blessing I want to share with you.

Schooling By The Great Teacher

Children begin school around the age of five years old. They advance to first grade and move on up through their school years. This education prepares them for the years ahead, when they will have to face the world on their own. As you can see, the growth is in body (outward) as well as in knowledge (inward).

They have text books according to their ability to receive that knowledge. A kindergartener doesn't have the same test as a 12th grader, because they must grow gradually to these harder things. Faithfulness in attendance is very important. And, who learns the most? Is it the one who is faithful to school or the one who is absent a lot? If we miss the lessons, when the test is given, we will fail the test!

After grade school, junior high, and senior High School, then comes graduation. It's the big day! It's a great honor and a special time. Students are becoming men and women, ready to receive jobs. They all dress in their graduation gowns, attend the commencement ceremonies, and receive their diplomas. There's great joy in the achievement.

If the graduating student has a desire to be of special service, there's even more training to become a doctor, a lawyer, a teacher, or other specific field. In college if one studies to become a doctor, the special training may give an opportunity to even go into the surgery room and watch a surgery being performed. A new teacher studies under veteran teachers. After finishing college, the student can continue higher education to receive a masters' degree, to be highly qualified to do the work of a teacher, doctor, or other professional area.

The definition of degree is a rank or title given by a college to a student whose work fulfills requirements, or to a noted person as an honor. With his masters' degree, the student enters the field for which he has been trained.

"And when they had performed all things according to the law of the Lord, they returned into Galilee, to their own city Nazareth. And the child grew, and waxed strong in spirit, filled with wisdom: and the grace of God was upon him." — Luke 2:39-40

Schooling By The Great Teacher

Spiritual Schooling

The spiritual man also needs schooling. When we first become a Christian, we begin like a kindergartener. That's okay. We know very little about the spiritual life, so, we take our text book (The Bible) and start. We begin growing, outwardly and inwardly. Others can see our growth.

"And the child grew and waxed strong in spirit, filled with wisdom: and the grace of God was upon him."—Luke 2:40

Something special happened with Jesus when, at the age of twelve, he attended the customary Hebrew feast at Jerusalem – the grace of God was upon him.

Maybe there was a time in your experience when your spiritual experience was deepened. Maybe, the first time you felt the spirit of God and the desire for His word was stirred.

"And he said unto them, How is it that ye sought me? Wist ye not that I must be about my Father's business?"—Luke 2:49

Even as a boy, Jesus desired to stay where He was being filled with wisdom. He didn't understand why his family would look elsewhere for him, but He left with them. There was more learning and more growing to be done.

"And Jesus increased in wisdom and stature, and in favour with God and man."—Luke 2:52

God sees every heart and sees something in us. He puts a desire there and puts a call there. As we have a desire and feel the call, we must go on with this special training. We realize we need more wisdom. We enter the chamber of His presence; the place of this special training. We are taught by the Great Teacher from the Great Text Book - God's Word. We do it all for one purpose. To know Him and to obey Him.

Jesus said, *"Go ye into all the world."* We are the church today. We need this special training to help us and help others.

Schooling By The Great Teacher

In the Old Testament, we read about customs of the age. It was a Hebrew custom for the pupil to sit at the feet of his teacher.

Deuteronomy 33:3 *"Yea, he loved the people; all his saints are in thy hand: and they sat down at thy feet; everyone shall receive of thy words."*

Mary sat at Jesus' feet in Luke 10:39, *"And she had a sister called Mary, which also sat at Jesus' feet, and heard his word."*

Paul sat at the feet of Gamaliel in Acts 22:3 *"I am verily a man which am a Jew born in Tarsus, a city in Cilicia, yet brought up in this city at the feet of Gamaliel, and taught according to the perfect manner of the law of the fathers, and was zealous toward God, as ye all are this day."*

"My son, if thou wilt receive my words, and hide my commandments with thee; So that thou incline thine ear unto wisdom, and apply thine heart to understanding; Yea, if thou criest after knowledge, and liftest up thy voice for understanding; If thou seekest her as silver, and searchest for her as for hid treasures; Then shalt thou understand the fear of the Lord, and find the knowledge of God. For the Lord giveth wisdom; out of his mouth cometh knowledge and understanding. He layeth up sound wisdom for the righteous: he is a buckler to them that walk uprightly."—Proverbs 2:1-7

Schooling By The Great Teacher

Results

Being taught and being willing to learn gives us boldness. If a teacher asks a question and you know the answer, you're not afraid to raise your hand and give the answer. Boldness comes with knowledge.

Peter had been with Jesus and had been taught by Him. He preached by the Power of the Holy Ghost those things he had witnessed.

We read in Acts 2:38-41 *"Then Peter said unto them, Repent, and be baptized every one of you in the name of Jesus Christ for the remission of sins, and ye shall receive the gift of the Holy Ghost. For the promise is unto you, and to your children, and to all that are afar off, even as many as the Lord our God shall call. And with many other words did he testify and exhort saying, Save yourselves from this untoward generation. Then they that gladly received his word were baptized: and the same day there were added unto them about three thousand souls."*

Schooling by the Great Teacher will bring results.

Schooling By The Great Teacher

The Presence Chamber

The door to this presence chamber is closed on the world and all unbelief. Some never enter that chamber. Why?

Jesus said, "Knock, and it shall be opened unto you." Inside is revelation. He reveals His Word to us.

In Exodus 20:18, Moses entered the cloud on the mountain to receive God's word. Some of the people saw the thundering and lightning, the noise of the trumpet and the mountain smoking. When the people saw it, they removed and stood afar off.

That didn't stop Moses!

We read in verse 21, *"And the people stood afar off, and Moses drew near unto the thick darkness where God was."*

Moses received God's Word to give to His people. There were great things to be seen here. Genesis 22:14 *"…In the mount of the Lord it shall be seen."*

So, we sit at the feet of Jesus until one day He calls us out of class and commissions us to "Go"!

Schooling By The Great Teacher

Disciples and Apostles

Just like in college, the teacher takes the class of future surgeons to an operating room to watch an operation. A future teacher sits under a teacher and observes the teaching process in the classroom.

The call of Jesus is, "Come follow me, and I'll make you to become fishers of men." He didn't say, come, you are now fishermen. He said, "Come, follow me, and I will make you to become, fishers of men." There is much training to be done first. The Word, the teacher, the sincere pupil, and the altar are all necessary for learning to take place.

The disciples (learners) who walked with Jesus, later were called apostles. Apostles, in the Greek means "to send off." The disciples had to attend "class" with the Great Teacher before they were ready to send. Jesus sent them forth to share the Words they had learned.

"And he goeth up into a mountain, and calleth unto him whom he would: and they came unto him. And he ordained twelve, that they should be with him, and that he might send them forth to preach, And to have power to heal sicknesses, and to cast out devils."—Mark 3:13-15

We must be disciples (learners) before we can be apostles (those sent). As the Father sent the Master, so the Master sends us.

Schooling By The Great Teacher

Our Mission

God is still sending forth today! Our mission is threefold. To bear him company, to perform His errands, and to cast out devils. We must sit at the feet of Jesus until someday He calls you from the class and commissions you to the world.

"And He ordained twelve, that they should be with him, and that he might send them forth to preach, and to have power to heal sickness, and to cast out devils."—Mark 3:14, 15

Notice the threefold work of the church:
1. That they should be with Him. The Master dearly loves our company. Let us seek Him more, not just praying or praising or learning, but just sitting quietly with Him.

2. That He might send them forth to preach. Since Jesus is not physically on the earth to preach the message, He is now raising up voices, witnesses, lips, which He teaches how to speak and touches with His live coals.

3. That they might have authority over demons. The power of satan is strong. It mastered Adam, but it met more than its match in the Christ nature, in Matthew, chapter four. If that nature is in you, you too will have power over all power of the enemy. Nothing shall by any means hurt you, and you will be able to deliver others who have long been held captive.

As the Father sent the Master, so the Master sends us.

Schooling By The Great Teacher

The Sheep Becomes A Shepherd

As Jesus reveals more and more of His ways to us in the presence chamber, the door begins closing on the world and all unbelief.

"As thou hast sent me into the world, even so have I also sent them into the world."—John 17:18

"Then said Jesus to them again, Peace be unto you: as my Father hath sent me, even so send I you. And when he had said this, he breathed on them, and saith unto them, Receive ye the Holy Ghost."—John 20:21, 22

One thing yet that He knew we would need;
"Receive ye the Holy Ghost."

"But he that entereth in by the door is the shepherd of the sheep."
—John 10:2

"I am the door: by me if any man enter in, he shall be saved, and shall go in and out, and find pasture."—John 10:9

We forever have access!
We come in for fellowship, we go out for service.
Do you desire to be sent?
Hear His voice say, "Go ye."

In Luke 10:2, Jesus said, *"The harvest truly is great, but the laborers are few. Pray ye therefore the Lord of the harvest, that He would send forth laborers into His harvest."*

Confidence In
The Cleansing Power

**Charles Spurgeon wrote:
"What we say we must prove by our actions."**

I had a dream several years ago. In this dream, I was at my house when some men came to do some sort of lab testing. There was a life-sized dummy lying on a cot in the same room. As I lay without moving, the men put wires on my head like a brain test of some kind. It seemed that the purpose of all this was to determine my truthfulness like a lie detector test. As they asked me questions, the dummy was to react to my true feelings based on my reactions to the questions they asked me.

They began to ask questions like, "Have you sinned and done this and that?" My answer was consistently, "Yes, but Jesus cleansed me by His blood."

The dummy on the cot just lay there still with no reaction.

I had a peace and assurance in my heart.

"Thank You Jesus, for cleansing me from all unrighteousness!"

The Key To Power

Around 1964 my family and I moved back to Florida. We found a little Church of God in Drew Park, Tampa, Florida. By now I had experienced the New Birth, and one of my sisters had also been saved. God had been dealing with her heart all the while He had been dealing with me. My sister, her husband and their oldest daughter, Linda, had all come to Christ at the same little Mont Zion Church of God we had gone to in Kentucky. They, too, had moved back to Tampa, Florida and began attending the same church there in Drew Park.

There was another family who had moved from "up North" and came to the church there at Drew Park about the same time. They'd moved from Hamilton, Ohio. I can see now looking back that God sent them there because we needed the spiritual leadership they brought to our lives. There were actually two families who had a positive influence on my life while we lived in Florida. The mother, Sister Ruth Miller, was a Bible teacher. Sister Miller's daughter, Sister Leah Herd and her family were also wonderful influences. Sister Herd was also a Bible teacher and had other callings on her life. Both were wonderful children of God.

My mom and Dad began coming to church here too, and God wonderfully saved them at this church. God was leading, and we were all following in this new life He had given us. We had so many wonderful experiences as He led us in this way.

> *"But grow in grace and in the knowledge of our Lord and Savior Jesus Christ. To him be glory both now and forever. Amen."*
> —II Peter 3:18

The Key To Power

At Drew Park Church of God in Tampa, Florida, Sister Miller was our adult Sunday School teacher. She was such a light to us. I remember the first Sunday School picnic we had; I was so hungry to know all about my Savior. I overheard Sister Miller telling some people about her experience. I wanted to hear, so I got just as close as I could. That was the food I hungered for not the natural food.

God is so good, and He knows all things. As we yield our lives to Him, and follow where He leads, we will grow and mature in Him.

"Blessed are they which do hunger and thirst after righteousness: for they shall be filled."—Matthew 5:6

The Key To Power

Some Time Later

One day after service, Sister Miller came to me and asked me if I would speak at our youth program, Young People's Endeavor service. I had learned by now that when God's Spirit leads you to do something, whether it's to sing, to testify, or anything else that He gives you to do, you have a silent still feeling and you obey. It was like that when she asked me, so I said, "Yes." I'm sure I had a look of concern on my face that showed I wasn't sure what to do from there. She said, "It can be on something like, "a key" for instance." That was all she said. I had two weeks to prepare.

"Trust in the Lord, and do good: so shalt thou dwell in the land, and verily, thou shalt be fed. Delight thyself also in the Lord: and he shall give thee the desires of thine heart. Commit thy way unto the Lord: trust also in him: and he shall bring it to pass. And he shall bring forth thy righteousness as the light, and thy judgement as the noonday."—Psalm 37:3-6

The Key To Power

Preparing to teach the lesson for the youth program was another wonderful experience for me. I started studying; oh, it was wonderful. I found there were only a few scriptures that had the word "key" in them, but I kept studying. The Holy Spirit was taking me on a journey through the Word. During this study time, it occurred to me that I would like to have something special to wear. It wasn't that I just wanted to have a new dress, because times were very hard. We didn't have money for clothes and things like that. There was just something special about this feeling, too. My sister came by one day in the first week of my studying. Her husband was taking her to Northgate Shopping Center to put some things in layaway. She asked if I wanted to go. As she shopped, I went back to look at the dresses. There was one of the most beautiful dresses I think I had ever seen. It was white; it had three quarter length sleeves with little pleats around the sleeves. It was just beautiful. It was $12. That was a lot of money back then. More like fifty dollars now. There was no way I could get it, so we finished shopping and went home. I tried to put the thought of the beautiful dress out of my mind.

"Delight thyself also in the Lord; and he shall give thee the desires of thine heart."—Psalm 37:4

The Key To Power

I was still studying about a week later when my sister and her family came by again on their way to the shopping center and asked if I wanted to go. When we entered the store that day, I thought of the dress. Immediately, a second thought told me, "There is no way it could possibly be cheaper this week." I raised my eyes back toward where the dresses were all hanging. There was a big sign stretched across the store that said, "Your Choice $3.00". I quickly went to the dress rack, and there it was. It was only three dollars. I got my beautiful dress.

I didn't even know at this time, the lesson my Heavenly Father had in store for me about special clothing. I just knew that I wanted special clothes to stand before the people, as I presented God's Word.

"Delight thyself also in the Lord; and he shall give thee the desires of thine heart. Commit thy way unto the Lord; trust also in him; and he shall bring it to pass."—Psalm 37: 4, 5

The Key To Power

The night finally came to share the message at the youth group. As I stood to speak, I was not alone. My message was titled "The Key to Power". I taught how the power is in the blood, and the blood is at the foot of the cross. The key to power is the Cross. This night was an experience I will never forget. As I stood there speaking, it was like I was standing far back and the one who was within me stood in front. He spoke His Words through me. I know now this was His anointing doing the speaking. He was using my body as a vessel.

Definition of Key: a small instrument used for unlocking doors; a symbol of authority.

Used figuratively:

Prophetic authority of Christ - Isaiah 22:22 *"And the key of the house of David will I lay upon his shoulder; so he shall open, and none shall shut; and he shall shut, and none shall open."*

Present - Revelation 1:18 *"I am he that liveth, and was dead; and behold, I am alive for evermore, Amen; and have the keys of hell and of death."*

Plenary authority of Christ's apostles - Matthew 16:19 *"And I will give unto thee the keys of the kingdom of heaven: and whatsoever thou shalt bind on earth shall be bound in heaven: and whatsoever thou shalt loose on earth shall be loosed in heaven."*

What a wonderful experience! I am so thankful for every time He has made Himself real to me. There is nothing in this world that could ever compare to the joy, peace, and blessings He has for us.

I praise Him. He is Wonderful!

Building A Wall Of Faith

Satan seeks to break down the walls of our protection, our faith, and good trust in God. The enemy seeks to break down these walls, so thieves can steal what rightfully belongs to us; the things God Himself has given us.

The walls that Nehemiah was called to rebuild had protected Jerusalem at one time but had been broken down. Bands of thieves were able to enter and steal those things God had blessed them with. Nehemiah's desire was to rebuild the walls of protection around Jerusalem. The Jewish remnant was not prospering because there was no wall of protection. There was an ever-present threat from surrounding nations who could easily come in and rob them of their harvest and their possessions. Repairing the walls took fifty-two days. After the walls were completed, Ezra asked to bring the book of the law of Moses and read it. The Levites caused the people to understand it.

We used to order our Sunday School literature from a place called "Building a wall of Faith." I thought how true this statement is. As we study God's Word, we are building a wall of Faith. Without this wall, the enemy wants to steal, kill, and destroy what God gives us. No wonder Nehemiah was so burdened and had the vision to rebuild the wall.

"So the wall was finished in the twenty and fifth day of the month Elul, in fifty and two days."—Nehemiah 6:15

Nehemiah 8:1, 3, 6

Verse 1: *"And all the people gathered themselves together as one man into the street that was before the water gate; and they spake unto Ezra the scribe to bring the book of the law of Moses, which the Lord had commanded to Israel."*

Verse 3: *"And he read therein before the street that was before the water gate from the morning until midday, before the men and the women, and those that could understand; and the ears of all the people were attentive unto the book of the law."*

Verse 6: *"And Ezra blessed the Lord, the great God. And all the people answered, Amen, Amen, with lifting up their hands: and they bowed their heads, and worshipped the Lord with their faces to the ground."*

The Just Shall Live By Faith

Today, I read about Jacob fleeing from his home and his people. He fled in fear from his home, leaving his mother, father, and brother because of his wrong doing. He laid down to sleep, feeling so very alone and fearful. In the night, God's presence and person became very real to Jacob, not because of his goodness, but because of God's love and mercy for him. God cared for and comforted Jacob in his loneliness with the words, "I will be with you and keep you."

It reminded me of the times in my life when I felt so alone, and He came and made His presence so real to me. When we feel no one cares, He assures us of His love for us. When we feel He is far away, He lets us know in some special way He is so near.

He is Wonderful!

He said in Hebrews 13:5, *"Let your conversation be without covetousness; and be content with such things as ye have: for he hath said, I will never leave thee nor forsake thee."*

"And the Lord, He it is that doth go before thee; he will be with thee, he will not fail thee, neither forsake thee: fear not, neither be dismayed."—Deuteronomy 31:8

Always remember His words.

Keep Your Joy

Satan seeks to draw us away from God and away from God's Word where we're fed and made strong in the Lord. He wants to draw us away from our place of prayer; away from our habits of consecration; away from the joy of stepping out for God. The enemy knows that in drawing us away, he can break our faith down, cause us to feel condemnation, and keep us from God.

Thanks to the Father, Son, and His Holy Spirit! We should remember that we have an advocate with the Father, Jesus Christ, the Righteous one. We can run to Him, ask forgiveness for our failures, and He restores our faith and joy. We need to always be watchful and realize that satan's intentions are to dull our faith and consequently, cause us to drift away from God and His perfect will.

My prayer is that God will always keep us awake and alert, conscious of the enemy's tactics.

Keep the Joy!
Jesus
Others
Yourself

"My little children, these things write I unto you, that ye sin not. And if any man sin, we have an advocate with the Father, Jesus Christ the righteous: and he is the propitiation for our sins: and not for ours only, but also for the sins of the whole world. And hereby we do know that we know him, if we keep his commandments."—I John 2:1-3

What Is The Difference Between Spiritual "Milk" and "Solid Food"?

The writer of Hebrews wrote in the fifth chapter, thirteenth verse, concerning our spiritual maturity. *"For every one that useth milk is unskillful in the word of righteousness: for he is a babe."* The word unskilled in the Greek means "without experience". He that is unskilled is not necessarily ignorant; he may have much great information. He is destined to lose it and need to be taught all over again, unless he can experience it.

What then is "solid food"?

Jesus said in John 4:34 *"My meat (food) is to do the will of Him that sent me, and to finish His work."*

Experience without the Word, and the Word without experience are both inadequate. For us to grow in Christ, we need to know God's Word, and we need to experience it, too.

Fasting And Prayer

I remember our Pastor, Johnny Shepherd, Sr., feeling led to call our church to a month of prayer. We took a certain hour each day or night and prayed at that time each day, like a weekend prayer, except it was to last the entire month. At the same time, I felt led to fast this month along with the hour of prayer. I felt that I was to fast the evening meal each day. I found a blessing in experiencing His presence and walking in it so greatly. My prayer time for the month was 1:00PM to 2:00PM every day. I found that I was led to fast many more times than just the evening meal. It was such a blessing to fast for sometimes days at a time.

After the fast and month of prayer was over, one day I received word that one of my grandchildren had gotten a bad cut to their throat. When I received the official report, I was told that it was so very close to the jugular vein.

The spirit of the Lord suddenly reminded me of the month of fasting and prayer. I praise Him for His wonderful love and for His leading us.

He is Wonderful!

I've never regretted being obedient to God's leading me. I'm so thankful.

"The name of the Lord is a strong tower; the righteous runneth into it, and is safe."—Proverbs 18:10

The Safe Place

We must have a hunger and desire to do what pleases the Father and stay close to Him where there is safety. Satan seeks to draw us away from this safe place because he knows if he can get us away from the Father, he can deceive us and fill our minds and desires with other things. That is his purpose and what he works after.

The word "deceive" means to make a person believe as truth, something that is false; to mislead.

We must trust and depend on God to keep us in His will. This is the safest place we could ever be. He can keep us there if we are obedient to Him and His Word. We rely on His Spirit to lead us, guide us, and teach us.

"But whoso hearkeneth unto me shall dwell safely and shall be quiet from fear of evil."—Proverbs 1:33

God Send A Great Awakening: In Him Is No Darkness

I John 1:5 reads, *"This then is the message which we have heard of him, and declare unto you, that God is light, and in him is no darkness at all."*

"Take heed therefore that the light which is in thee be not darkness."—Luke 11:35

We know from God's Word that God is light, and we understand that there is no darkness in Him at all. As Luke advises us in chapter eleven verse thirty-five, we should take heed that the light which is in us not be made darkness.

The word darkness, here in Luke, if we refer to the root word meaning, comes from the word, skotes; it means "to cover." The word is used literally for darkness that is brought about by shutting out light, and metaphorically for spiritual, moral, and intellectual darkness. The darkness arises from error, ignorance, disobedience, willful blindness, and rebellion. Darkness is an evil system that is absolutely opposed to the light.

Light rejected is light withdrawn. Seek the clear shining of the inner light and remember that it will grow clearer and brighter in proportion as it is obeyed and followed.

"Then spake Jesus again unto them, saying, I am the light of the world: he that followeth me shall not walk in darkness, but shall have the light of life."—John 8:12

God Send A Great Awakening

The world was in gross darkness for thousands of years; then the light of the world came to shine in the darkness. Much like the darkness in our own lives before we come to Christ. I lived in darkness until that same light of the world came and shined in my heart. I began to see things I'd never seen before. My spiritual senses were awakened.

- I tasted, that the Lord, He is good. I Peter 2:3 *"If so be ye have tasted that the Lord is gracious."*

- I could smell. II Corinthians 2:15 *"For we are unto God a sweet savour of Christ, in them that are saved, and in them that perish."*

- He touched my life, I could feel His touch; His peace, His joy, His Love. Zephaniah 3:17 *"The Lord thy God in the midst of thee is mighty; he will save, he will rejoice over thee with joy; he will rest in his love, he will joy over thee with singing."*

- I could see and understand. *"Discretion shall preserve thee, understanding shall keep thee."*—Proverbs 2:11

- I could hear His voice and His Word. *"Doth not wisdom cry? And understanding put forth her voice?"*—Proverbs 8:1

Jesus raised us from a deep sleep.
He is the resurrection and the life!
We are raised from the dead to new life in Him.

Developing Faith

Faith is like film; it is developed in the dark. I heard or read this statement and began to think how it is so true. As I thought on this, I remembered a time when my new grandson developed Respiratory Syncytial Virus. R.S.V. is a breathing problem that affects the lungs. It produces swelling and mucus in the small breathing tubes of an infants' lungs. Anthony was only 1 month old, and we knew that he was going to have to go to the hospital. We knew this was a serious illness.

I sent prayer requests to church, and I began to pray, seeking God about this situation. As I prayed, I had a peace come over me. I recognized this feeling and knew that he was going to be okay. God was going to move.

We took him to the hospital in Richmond, Indiana where they had to send him to Riley Children's Hospital in Indianapolis. He had so much mucus that they had to continually suction it from his lungs so he could breathe. He even had to be put on life support.

Kathy and A.J. began to pray as they saw their baby boy going through all this. We didn't leave the hospital. As we would go to look in on him, it was heart breaking. He attempted to cry but no sound came as he was on the ventilator. As the nurses suctioned, I remember standing there watching this tiny baby go through this. It looked so bad, but when I felt fear start to come I would be reminded of that peace I'd had. I knew that everything was going to be okay. Anthony remained in that condition for three to four weeks. All this time we just held on, knowing he would be alright even though we couldn't see any change for such a long period of time.

Anthony did get better. And that's why I wanted to use this testimony with the statement "Faith is like film; it is developed in the dark". All we can do is hold on and trust God. Have faith in Him in the dark times.

"Now faith, is the substance of things hoped for, the evidence of things not seen."—Hebrews 11:1

Developing Faith

Film: I believe when film is developed, it must be dipped into a mixed solution for processing.

Faith: It also, to be developed, must be dipped into a processing mixture of prayer, hope, faith, and patience.

Film: Must be developed in total darkness; the light would ruin the film.

Faith: Also, is developed with only hope and expectation as we wait for our prayer to be answered. It's a waiting process, and many times we are not able to see any sign that things are any different or better.

"For we are saved by hope: but hope that is seen is not hope: for what a man seeth, why doth he yet hope for?"—Romans 8:24

Film: We know that there is a picture on the film. We just must wait for it to show up.

Faith: We just hold on and trust in God. He does show up. He answers our prayers. Our faith is stronger.

Kathy and A.J. saw this happen as it all unfolded, and their faith was made stronger. Little Anthony had complete healing, and he's been fine ever since. He's a young man now, as I write this. He has graduated from high school, where he played football, and he's currently attending college.

He's a son to be proud of. We're so thankful for God's goodness and thank Him for His Word.

"And let the peace of God rule in your hearts, to the which also ye are called in one body; and be ye thankful."—Colossians 3:15

Let the peace of God rule in your hearts, even when it is in the dark.

Determination

We must learn to believe God's Word.

As we begin to step out by faith on God's Word, we will meet with a giant, who stands arms folded, saying we can't enter this spiritual life. We are to pay no attention to him. Our hunger and desire will make him just disappear and our determination will give us entrance through that door.

Jesus said, "Knock and it shall be opened unto you."

Our job is to believe Him and enter.

"Beareth all things, believeth all things, hopeth all things, endureth all things."—I Corinthians 13:7

Jesus Told Us

Things are speedily changing in our world today. Things we never thought of being in our country. Jesus told us to watch and pray and for us to be ready for His appearing. A few years ago, the news was in our local paper that they were going to remove a large monument of the Ten Commandments from our court house yard. I guess this was something that would not be allowed any longer on public property.

Why?

Well the first few verses of the Ten Commandments speak of "Only one God; the only True God." As we know from the very beginning of God choosing Abraham and the Hebrew nation as His own people, they were to keep God's commandments and obey His laws. He told them when they were obedient, they would be blessed. When they did not obey and keep His commandments, they would face judgement. We can see this over and over in the Old Testament.

The other nations had their own gods. One nation claimed their god or gods and another nation had their own. But that in no way changes the truth. There is still only one true and living God. He gave us His Word, to live by. We can see the examples of belief and unbelief and the effects it brings.

As we walk in the truth of His Word, we can see very plainly that our nation is going in the way of judgement as people live as it pleases them. The laws are becoming more and more corrupt. Thank God for His people who still believe and walk in His ways and follow His Words of truth. It is not His will that any should perish, but that all come to repentance. There is a new birth where we become a part of God's great redemption plan. It prepares us for our meeting with Him. God is a Holy God, and the only way we can stand before Him is in His Son Jesus Christ.

Forgiven and free from sin and guilt.
He is our Wonderful Savior!

"Therefore be ye also ready: for in such an hour as ye think not the Son of man cometh."—Matthew 24:44

The Meaning

Thank you, Father, for the things,
Tragedy so often brings.
May we cease to question why,
We must suffer, but apply,
Truths we learn from it when loss.
Sends us stumbling to the cross.
You can turn the darkest night,
Of the soul to dazzling light.
You can make our weakness strong.
Change our weeping into song.
What we think is tragedy,
Is your opportunity.
With divine forgiveness to,
Bring us back again to you.

Dorothy A Stickell

Soldiers Of God

A Special Call

"Now as he walked by the sea of Galilee, he saw Simon and Andrew his brother casting a net into the sea: for they were fishers. And Jesus said unto them, Come ye after me, and I will make you to become fishers of men. And straightway they forsook their nets, and followed him. And when he had gone a little farther thence, he saw James the son of Zebedee, and John his brother, who also were in the ship mending their nets. And straightway he called them: and they left their father Zebedee in the ship with the hired servants, and went after him."—Mark 1:16-20

Jesus saw the qualities in those He could use. There are also things one must leave behind to follow His call. I noticed how these that Jesus called, didn't even hesitate, but immediately followed Him.

"Who hath saved us, and called us with an holy calling, not according to our works, but according to his own purpose and grace, which was given us in Christ Jesus before the world began."
—II Timothy 1:9

A Special call requires a special training. Jesus walked with the disciples three years. Every day was a special time of training, as they spent time together. Every day they were learning.

You, too, have been called!

Soldiers Of God

A Special Call Requires Special Clothing

This special clothing that we are to wear is the righteousness of God, which simply means that we are in "right standing" with God. We are clothed in the righteousness of God. We, as Christians, are clothed alike. As the Bible reads in Isaiah 64:6, it is not in our own righteousness that we are clothed but in His.

"But we are all as an unclean thing, and all our righteousnesses are as filthy rags; and we all do fade as a leaf; and our iniquities, like the wind, have taken us away."—Isaiah 64:6

When we believe in Jesus, sin is removed from our account and righteousness is deposited. Jesus is perfect; yet He died for our sins, so we could be in right standing with God.

May we wear that special clothing.

"I counsel thee to buy of me gold tried in the fire, that thou mayest be rich; and white raiment, that thou mayest be clothed, and that the shame of thy nakedness do not appear; and anoint thine eyes with eyesalve, that thou mayest see."—Revelation 3:18

Soldiers Of God

A Special Call Requires a Special Commission

"And Jesus came and spake unto them, saying, All power is given unto me in heaven and in earth. Go ye therefore, and teach all nations, baptizing them in the name of the Father, and of the Son, and of the Holy Ghost: Teaching them to observe all things whatsoever I have commanded you: and, lo, I am with you alway, even unto the end of the world. Amen."—Matthew 28:18-20

Also, we read in Mark 16:15, "And he said unto them, (Jesus talking), Go ye into all the world, and preach the gospel to every creature."

This special commission must be obeyed as a commandment. Those receiving this commission are to be witnesses; therefore, they must wait for the power in order to do so. This power will come when the Holy Ghost comes upon you.

Obedience simply means submitting to authority.

"And behold I send the promise of my Father upon you: but tarry ye in the city of Jerusalem, until ye be endued with power from on high."—Luke 24:49

"But ye shall receive power, after that the Holy Ghost is come upon you: and ye shall be witnesses unto me both in Jerusalem, and in all Judea, and in Samaria, and unto the uttermost part of the earth."—Acts 1:8

You have been commissioned.

Soldiers Of God
A Special Call Requires Complete Discipline

Jesus said in Mark 8:34, *"...Whosoever will come after me, let him deny himself and take up his cross, and follow me."*

Paul said in I Corinthians 9:27, *"But I keep under my body, and bring it into subjection: lest that by any means, when I have preached to others, I myself should be a castaway."* (literally rejected)

We must be alert and disciplined, putting God's will first at all times.

"Be sober, be vigilant; because your adversary the devil, as a roaring lion, walketh about, seeking whom he may devour." —I Peter 5:8

Soldiers Of God

Requires a Special Armor

A special call requires one to use his armor expertly.

"Finally, my brethren, be strong in the Lord, and in the power of his might. Put on the whole armour of God, that ye may be able to stand against the wiles of the devil. For we wrestle not against flesh and blood, but against principalities, against powers, against the rulers of the darkness of this world, against spiritual wickedness in high places. Wherefore take unto you the whole armour of God, that ye may be able to withstand in the evil day, and having done all to stand. Stand therefore, having your loins girt about with truth, and having on the breastplate of righteousness; and your feet shod with the preparation of the gospel of peace; Above all, taking the shield of faith, wherewith ye shall be able to quench all the fiery darts of the wicked. And take the helmet of salvation, and the sword of the Spirit, which is the word of God: Praying always with all prayer and supplication in the Spirit, and watching thereunto with all perseverance and supplication for all saints;"—Ephesians 6:10-18

We have an enemy to war against. He seeks to destroy our soul and the souls of our children. He is the enemy of God, and we must fight against him and his army. He has traps set to entangle and destroy. Sin blinds the eyes, so one can't see the dangers ahead; the enemy of our souls is very sly and deceiving.

God has equipped His army with the armor that will withstand the enemy and overcome him and his army.
God has never lost a battle, and He is on our side!
Praise the Lord, He is our strong tower!
We have the Father, and the Son, and the Holy Ghost.

Soldiers Of God

A Special Call Requires Special Courage

Jesus came to destroy the works of the devil!

We can be encouraged because it says in II Timothy 4:18, *"And the Lord shall deliver me from every evil work, and will preserve me unto His heavenly kingdom; to whom be glory for ever and ever. Amen."*

Satan blinds eyes; Jesus opens blind eyes. Satan discourages saying, you can't be forgiven. Jesus says you are forgiven; my blood cleanses from all sins. Repent and believe my Word.

"For God hath not given us the spirit of fear; but of power, and of love, and of a sound mind."—II Timothy 1:7

Jesus came to destroy the works of the devil!

Leaders, Be Strong And Of Good Courage; Go After It

"Now after the death of Moses the servant of the Lord it came to pass, that the Lord spake unto Joshua the son of Nun, Moses' minister, saying, Moses my servant is dead; now therefore arise, go over this Jordan, thou, and all this people, unto the land which I do give to them even to the children of Israel."—Joshua 1:1,2

God is calling His people to step forward as leaders in our homes, our families and our communities, in God's service. He is calling Fathers to lead in the home, and God is calling each of us to a deeper place in Him. It is necessary for leaders to move ahead of the people and to depend upon God for direction. The actions of a leader must be mixed with faith and courage.

In the first chapter of Joshua, God spoke several times the words to Joshua "Be strong and of good courage." God told Joshua, "I will be with you, I will not leave you, nor forsake you."

God's instructions to the people in Joshua 3:3 were, "When ye see the ark of the covenant of the Lord your God, and the priests and Levites bearing it, then ye shall remove from your place, and go after it."

Timing is a vital lesson for the 20th century church. When the Holy Ghost moves among us, it is time for us to yield, to move ahead, to press in, to receive power for service and to serve. Not in every church service, nor in every private prayer time, does the Spirit move in a special way upon us, but we need to be sensitive and expectant so that when He does come to us with direction, we may respond with all our hearts. Whether it is in giving us a burden for the lost, anointing us to witness, or impressing upon our hearts the urgency of some task, timing is an important element in God's Kingdom.

**When the direction is clear,
we need to go after it with all our hearts.**

Going Into Battle

Jesus said, "Abide in me." He also said, "Without me, ye can do nothing."

If we go into battle on our own, we are sure to lose the battle. But if we prepare ahead of time to go into the battle in the name of the Lord, we will most certainly win. Someone may say, "How can I ever prepare?" We prepare in the presence of the Lord. We declare war on Satan. We must pray and seek for spiritual strength in the presence of the Lord and stand in faith toward God. We will win this war.

If we were chosen to go to military war in the natural, and we just stood still and failed to move when the call came, the enemy would just keep closing in on us. We would surely be defeated. We must move forward when God says go. We must learn to be obedient to the call of God and His direction.

There is a battle to be won.
Take your position where God has placed you.

"Then said David to the Philistine, thou comest to me with a sword, and with a spear, and with a shield: but I come to thee in the name of the Lord of hosts, the God of the armies of Israel, whom thou hast defied."—I Samuel 17:45

Going Into Battle

Our Place Of Safety

When our enemy is out to get us, what should we do?

When trouble comes, remember:

"He that dwelleth in the secret place of the most High shall abide under the shadow of the Almighty."—Psalm 91:1

No harm can come to us there, for we can trust in Him.

"I will say of the Lord, He is my refuge and my fortress: my God; in him will I trust."—Psalm 91:2

"For in the time of trouble he shall hide me in his pavilion: in the secret of his tabernacle shall he hide me; he shall set me up upon a rock."—Psalm 27:5

"Thou shalt hide them in the secret of thy presence from the pride of man: thou shalt keep them secretly in a pavilion from the strife of tongues."—Psalm 31:20

"Thou art my hiding place; thou shalt preserve me from trouble; thou shalt compass me about with songs of deliverance. Selah."—Psalm 32:7

In I Samuel 19:2, Jonathan tells David, whom he loves, that there may be danger, so he tells David to "take heed to thyself until the morning, and abide in a secret place, and hide thyself." He told David, I will go and see how things are with my father, and I'll let you know.

David was to stay in that "secret place" until he knew what to do.

He is our place of safety!

Going Into Battle

The mission of Jesus Christ is to win hearts back to God, to set our chained spirits free from sin and self. The message we get from Andrew Murray, like a telegram from the front line is this. Fight to bring the rule of God over your own heart. That's the first training needed if you want to survive and win the spiritual war.

"Finally, my brethren, be strong in the Lord, and in the power of his might. Put on the whole armour of God, that ye may be able to stand against the wiles of the devil. For we wrestle not against flesh and blood, but against principalities, against powers, against the rulers of the darkness of this world, against spiritual wickedness in high places."—Ephesians 6:10-12

Keep Your Eye On Jesus

At times when we feel ourselves getting farther away from that rest in the Lord, we cry out, Lord save me, I want to be closer to you. I need my thoughts and my heart to be centered on you and not on the things around me.

When Peter walked on the water and took his eyes off Jesus, he saw the wind boisterous all around him. We can get our eyes on things around us also. Too much of this or that, whatever it might be causes us to take our eyes off the Lord. When we realize and come to our spiritual senses, We cry out, "Lord, save me." That's when Jesus reaches out His hand and pulls us back to safety.

"And Peter answered him and said, Lord, if it be thou, bid me come unto thee on the water. And he said, "Come". And when Peter was come down out of the ship, he walked on the water, to go to Jesus. But when he saw the wind boisterous, he was afraid; and beginning to sink, he cried, saying, Lord, save me. And immediately Jesus stretched forth his hand, and caught him, and said unto him, "O thou of little faith, wherefore didst thou doubt?"—Matthew 14: 28-31

The Teachers Inventory Sheet; To Be Checked Daily

Daily
Study for lesson

___Mon ___Tues ___Wed ___Thurs ___Fri ___Sat ___Sun

Pray and ask God for His help.

___Mon ___Tues ___Wed ___Thurs ___Fri ___Sat ___Sun

Pray for class

___Mon ___Tues ___Wed ___Thurs ___Fri ___Sat ___Sun

Sunday

Was I on time?　　　　　____ Yes　　____ No

Was I early?　　　　　　____ Yes　　____ No

Did I greet each student?　____ Yes　　____ No

You need to ask yourself these questions about your teaching assignment.
- Is this something I feel like God has called me to do?
- Do I really enjoy teaching this class?
- Do I realize that I am doing a very important job?
- Do I realize that I am planting seed (God's Word) in hearts that will produce Life? There are others that will also have a part in the results, but my part is to plant.

Jesus Wants Us To Know Him, Not Just Know About Him

Paul wrote in Galatians 1:11-12, *"But I certify (assure) you brethren, that the gospel which was preached of me is not after man. (derived from any human source) For I neither received it of man, neither was I taught it, but by the revelation of Jesus Christ."*

Jesus asked Peter in Matthew 16:15-17, *"But whom say ye that I am?" Peter said, "Thou art the Christ, the son of the living God." Jesus answered and said unto him, "Blessed art thou Simon Bar-jona: for flesh and blood hath not revealed it unto thee, but my Father which is in heaven."*

This was divine revelation.
Jesus wants us to know Him, not just about Him.

Revelation 1:1a reads; *"The Revelation of Jesus Christ, which God gave unto him, to shew unto his servants things which must shortly come to pass......"*

"I John, who also am your brother, and companion in tribulation, and in the kingdom and patience of Jesus Christ, was in the isle that is called Patmos, for the word of God, and for the testimony of Jesus Christ."—Revelation 1:9

**It is when we seek to know Him,
He reveals Himself to us.**

Anointed To Share The Burden

We need a compassion for hurting people, to share the burden for lost souls. To do the work that Jesus said was His meat. What did God send Jesus to do? He sent Him to seek and to save the lost and give His life.

When we seek and ask for the Holy Ghost, what are we asking? Do we understand what we ask? Jesus asked His disciples, "Are ye able to drink of the cup and be baptized with the baptism I am baptized with?

We need to be emptied of self, if we are to be filled with Him, His love, compassion, and burden. That's what we are asking. If we are too full of the flesh, we don't run very well. We need to be emptied of ourselves and filled with His Spirit. If someone comes in need, we will be able to help that someone. If we are emptied of self, God's Spirit will begin to move in us. He has a burden for the lost and hurting souls.

To be like Him and share His life means much. To live His life or allow Him to live through and in us, we must give up our lives. We must die to self. We must be emptied to be filled. We must be crucified with Him, partake of His suffering, and we will reign with Him.

"Wherefore be ye not unwise, but understanding what the will of the Lord is. And be not drunk with wine wherein is excess; but be filled with the Spirit."—Ephesians 5:17,18

Putting First Things First

I want to talk to you about family and the importance of demonstrating family care, establishing family relationships, and developing family faith. I feel like it's important, and I want to stress the necessity of taking family responsibilities seriously.

Because of our need for people and relationships, the family unit forms the most important community in the world.

I'd like to ask you, "What does the ideal home consist of?" This is not an exhaustive list, but some of the things that come to mind are love, responsibility, sense of humor, discipline, communication, recreation, acceptance, forgiveness, the list could go on and on.

Family is something that God takes seriously.

"And he said, A certain man had two sons: And the younger of them said to his father, Father, give me the portion of goods that falleth to me. And he divided unto them his living. And not many days after the younger son gathered all together, and took his journey into a far country, and there wasted his substance with riotous living. And when he had spent all, there arose a mighty famine in that land; and he began to be in want. And he went and joined himself to a citizen of that country; and he sent him into his fields to feed swine. And he would fain have filled his belly with the husks that the swine did eat: and no man gave unto him. And when he came to himself, he said How many hired servants of my father's have bread enough and to spare, and I perish with hunger! I will arise and go to my father, and will say unto him, Father, I have sinned against heaven, and before thee, And am no more worthy to be called thy son: make me as one of thy hired servants. And he arose, and came to his father. But when he was yet a great way off, his father saw him, and had compassion, and ran, and fell on his neck, and kissed him."—Luke 15:11-20

There was something this young man had experienced in his father's house and with his family that not only caused him to return, he knew he could return.

Putting First Things First

Community

The family is a small community; a miniature society of its own. The word community comes from the day of ancient cities when the wall around the city was the principle means of protection. Each citizen was given the responsibility of maintaining a certain part of the wall. If even one person neglected his duty, the whole city was vulnerable to attack at the weak place in the wall. This same idea of care and responsibility in the family community should be put first in our lives.

"And thou shalt love the Lord thy God with all thine heart, and with all thy soul, and with all thy might. And these words, which I command thee this day, shall be in thine heart: And thou shalt teach them diligently unto thy children, and shalt talk of them when thou sittest in thine house, and when thou walkest by the way and when thou liest down, and when thou risest up. And thou shalt bind them for a sign upon thine hand, and they shall be as frontlets between thine eyes. And thou shalt write them upon the posts of thy house, and on thy gates."—Deuteronomy 6:5-9

Putting First Things First

What Do We Owe Our Children?

As parents, we are to admonish our children. As the scripture says in Deuteronomy 6:7, we are to teach our children diligently the ways and Word of God. We are to talk of Him and His ways when we sit in our house and we walk by the way, when we lie down and when we rise up.

As parents, we are to train up our children. Proverbs 22:6 reads, *"Train up a child in the way he should go: and when he is old, he will not depart from it."*

As parents, we are to provide for our children. II Corinthians 12:14 says, *"Behold, the third time I am ready to come to you; and I will not be burdensome to you: for I seek not yours, but you: for the children ought not to lay up for the parents, but the parents for the children."*

As parents, we are to nurture our children. Ephesians 6:4, *"And ye fathers, provoke not your children to wrath: but bring them up in the nurture and admonition of the Lord."*

We are to avoid anger and harshness when it comes time to correct.

As parents, we should keep our children under control. I Timothy 3:4, *"One that ruleth well his own house, having his children in subjection with all gravity (honesty)."*

As parents, we should love our children. Titus 2:4 tells us, *"That they may teach the young women to be sober, to love their husbands, to love their children."*

Living In The Present

Let us remember as each day dawns, *"This is the day which the Lord hath made, we will rejoice and be glad in it."* (Psalm 118:24)

We should never dwell on yesterdays, unless they can do something for our todays. Neither should we dream about the future unless we do something in the present to help make that dream a reality.

We may plan to memorize hundreds of Bible verses and fail to learn one truth today. If we are constantly living in the future, we are weakening our spiritual stature.

Maybe we dream of winning hundreds of people to Christ, but unless we speak to one person today about his soul, it's only idle dreaming.

For us to desire a deep knowledge of the Word and then study faithfully every day, this is living in the present.

Let The Word Be Made Flesh

Let the Word be made flesh by hearing the Word of God with faith. Hebrews 4:2, *"For unto us was the gospel preached, as well as unto them: but the word preached did not profit them, not being mixed with faith in them that heard it."*

Let the Word be made flesh by reading God's Word. I Timothy 4:13-16, *"Till I come, give attendance to reading, to exhortation, to doctrine. Neglect not the gift that is in thee, which was given thee by prophecy, with the laying on of the hands of the presbytery. Meditate upon these things; give thyself wholly to them; that thy profiting may appear to all. Take heed unto thyself, and unto the doctrine; continue in them: for in doing this thou shalt both save thyself, and them that hear thee."*

Let the Word be made flesh by studying God's Word. II Timothy 2:15, *"Study to show thyself approved unto God, a workman that needeth not to be ashamed, rightly dividing the word of truth."*

Let the word be made flesh in action. Colossians 3:16, *"Let the Word of Christ dwell in you richly in all wisdom; teaching and admonishing one another in psalms and hymns and spiritual songs, singing with grace in your hearts to the Lord."*

Let The Word Be Made Flesh

A generous man was walking along a busy street. He noticed a street child standing with bare feet on the cold sidewalk. The little girl's eager face was pressed against the glass window of the shoe store. The story was easily read. She was longing for a pair of socks and new shoes. The gentleman took the child into the store. The clerk fitted her with shoes and socks. The bill was paid. The small girl and gentleman were soon out on the sidewalk again. Half shocked the child suddenly desired to express her thanks. In so doing she merely said, "Say mister, is your name Jesus?"

Someday, when we are filled with God's love and God's Word, may it be said of us, The Word was made flesh.

Author unknown

"Then shall the king say unto them on his right hand, Come, ye blessed of my Father, inherit thy kingdom prepared for you from the foundation of the world: For I was an hungered, and ye gave me meat: I was thirsty, and ye gave me drink: I was a stranger, and ye took me in: Naked, and ye clothed me: I was sick, and ye visited me: I was in prison, and ye came unto me. Then shall the righteous answer him, saying Lord, when saw we thee an hungered, and fed thee? Or thirsty, and gave thee drink? When saw we thee a stranger and took thee in? or naked, and clothed thee? Or when saw we thee sick, or in prison, and came unto thee? And the King shall answer and say unto them, Verily I say unto you, inasmuch as ye have done it unto one of the least of these my brethren, ye have done it unto me." —Matthew 25:34-40

Grace

Grace is something that God imparts to the hearts of believers. The phrase "Grace be unto you" in I Corinthians 1:3 means a blessing from God that enables the believer to do God's will gladly and willingly. The desire to do the will of God does not come naturally. Man's natural disposition is to do what he wants to do. Have you ever noticed what a child does when about to be led across a street? The child will naturally pull away, not wanting to be led. That is human nature in action. We lack the inward strength to do what we should even when we understand what it is. We, in the natural sense, are "palsied" or paralyzed; meaning, we can see and hear, but cannot move.

When Paul writes "Grace be unto you", he is praying that these believers be given grace; that inward capacity which enables believers to do the will of God. First, to receive the grace of God, we must receive Jesus Christ as Savior and trust Him with our sins. Next, the Holy Spirit, will give us the inward strength and desire and enable us to do God's will.

That is the Grace of God.

Grace is "unmerited favor"; it is a gift of God. Any good thing within a person comes to him from the Grace of God in his heart. Peace is that blessed gift from God which enables the believer to have full and complete confidence in God. Peace is something God gives the believer when he yields himself to God's will.

The Word

It's good to recall things concerning God's Word and to remember them over and over. In II Peter 3: 1-2, he writes, "*This second epistle, beloved, I now write unto you; in both which I stir up your pure minds by way of remembrance: That ye may be mindful of the words which were spoken before by the holy prophets, and of the commandment of us the apostles of the Lord and Savior.*"

Peter is saying that it is good for us to be reminded of things we already know. That's why I want to talk to you about God's Word. We need to know God's word and have His Word hidden in our hearts. We all go through trials and temptations. Only one thing will help us to be overcomers, and that is God's Word. Often in scripture Jesus said, "It is written". He was reminding listeners of things they already knew.

Remember: The Word of God is the authority.

"*But continue thou in the things which thou hast learned and hast been assured of, knowing of whom thou hast learned them; and that from a child thou hast known the holy scriptures, which are able to make thee wise unto salvation through faith which is in Christ Jesus. All scripture is given by inspiration of God, and is profitable for doctrine, for reproof, for correction, for instruction in righteousness: That the man of God may be perfect, thoroughly furnished unto all good works.*"—II Timothy 3:14-17

The Path To Greatness Is Goodness

What comes from heaven as a promise should be sent back to heaven in a prayer.

Humility is the great preserver of peace and order in all Christian societies. Consequently, pride is the great disturber of them. Humbling ourselves to God under His hand is the way to deliverance and exaltation. God has always remembered His people. When we go to church, a place that has been dedicated to God, we are to reverence and remember the One who has never forgotten us. We meet there and worship Him. He meets there with us and will bless us.

**He still remembers His people.
Praise His Wonderful Name forever!**

"Likewise ye younger, submit yourselves unto the elder. Yea, all of you be subject one to another, and be clothed with humility: for God resisteth the proud, and giveth grace to the humble. Humble yourselves therefore under the mighty hand of God, that he may exalt you in due time: Casting all your care upon him; for he careth for you."—I Peter 5:5-7

What Causes Lukewarmness?

When we make our coffee in the morning, if the coffee maker becomes disconnected, the coffee soon becomes lukewarm. As individuals, or even the church body, we can become lukewarm if we fail to stay connected to Christ, through Bible study (God's Word) and prayer. A coffee maker may not keep the coffee hot if the heating elements get dirty or corroded. Likewise, we must never become morally corrupt and corroded.

The battery in our cars is the same way. If the cables or connections to the battery become corroded or disconnected, the battery cannot do its job. It must be cleaned and maintained. It will corrode if it is not cleaned from time to time.

Any object being plugged into a power source, must remain connected, clean, and maintained.

"I know thy works, that thou art neither cold nor hot: I would thou wert cold or hot. So then because thou art lukewarm, and neither cold nor hot, I will spue thee out of my mouth. Because thou sayest, I am rich, and increased with goods, and have need of nothing; and knowest not that thou art wretched, and miserable, and poor, and blind, and naked: I counsel thee to buy of me gold tried in the fire, that thou mayest be rich; and white raiment, that thou mayest be clothed, and that the shame of thy nakedness do not appear; and anoint thine eyes with eyesalve, that thou mayest see. As many as I love, I rebuke and chasten: be zealous therefore, and repent. Behold, I stand at the door and knock: if any man hear my voice, and open the door, I will come in to him, and will sup with him, and he with me. To him that overcometh will I grant to sit with me in my throne, even as I also overcame, and am set down with my Father in his throne."—Revelation 3:15-21

The Deep Makes A Difference

Jesus wants us to become "Soul Winners";
catchers of men.

Luke 5: 1-11 *"And it came to pass, that, as the people pressed upon him to hear the word of God, he stood by the lake of Gennesaret, And saw two ships standing by the lake: but the fishermen were gone out of them, and were washing their nets. And he entered into one of the ships, which was Simon's, and prayed him that he would thrust out a little from the land. And he sat down, and taught the people out of the ship. Now when he had left speaking, he said unto Simon, Launch out into the deep, and let down your nets for a draught. And Simon answering said unto him, Master, we have toiled all the night, and have taken nothing: nevertheless at thy word I will let down the net. And when they had this done, they enclosed a great multitude of fishes: and their net brake. And they beckoned unto their partners, which were in the other ship, that they should come and help them. And they came, and filled both the ships, so that they began to sink. When Simon Peter saw it, he fell down at Jesus' knees, saying Depart from me; for I am a sinful man, O Lord. For he was astonished, and all that were with him, at the draught of the fishes which they had taken: And so was also, James, and John, the sons of Zebedee, which were partners with Simon. And Jesus said unto Simon, Fear not; from henceforth thou shalt catch men. And when they had brought their ships to land, they forsook all, and followed him."*

The people pressed upon Him in verse one, to hear the Word of God. His words have life. These people pressed in like the woman with the issue of blood. She said, "I must touch him, or I die."

These fishermen were washing their nets after having been fishing all night. Jesus told Simon (Peter) to launch out a little from the land, then Jesus sat down and began to teach the people from the ship. The word launch means to start, set out, to cause to slide into the water, set afloat. For Jesus to use Simon's vessel to teach from, he had to thrust or launch out a little from the land. He had to get away from the bank. I must wonder just how Simon felt to have Jesus teaching from his ship.

The Deep Makes A Difference

Jesus wants us to become "Soul Winners";
catchers of men.

Jesus tells Peter to not only launch out into the deep, but also to let down his nets for a draught or (a haul), meaning what is drawn. In verse five, Peter addresses Jesus as Master. Master is a person who rules or commands; he's a director. Also, Master, can be defined as a male teacher, or an expert, who knows all there is to know about his work.

We know that they had fished all night without Jesus, and they'd caught nothing. Simon may have been thinking, "We're fishermen; we know how to fish! We've been doing this for years." But he said, "Nevertheless, at thy word, I will let down the net."

Simon was obedient to what Jesus told him to do. No matter what he thought, He obeyed the Masters' word.

It's not about what we think, it's about what He knows.

It was after they had obeyed, they were able to see the results.

In verse seven, they beckoned to their partners which were on the other ship to come and help them. "And they came and filled both the ships." We must be able to see, they were working together in unity. No jealousy; no strife; just unity; working together.

It is under the leadership and direction of Jesus,
that we will see great results.
They were in the deep!

The Deep Makes A Difference

Jesus wants us to become "Soul Winners"; catchers of men.

Peter realized that he had just witnessed a miracle. He was aware that he was in the presence of the Lord. Suddenly, Peter became aware of his own sinfulness. Overwhelmed with the events he'd seen unfold before him, Peter fell down at Jesus' knees and said, "Depart from me; for I am a sinful man, O Lord."

Peter and those with him were astonished. The Scripture says he was amazed; he was greatly surprised.

It's overwhelming when we see what God can do. We begin to see ourselves differently, for who we really are and in a completely different light. The realization brings confession.

Isaiah had a similar realization in Isaiah 6:5, 8, *"Then said I, woe is me! For I am undone; because I am a man of unclean lips, and I dwell in the midst of a people of unclean lips: for mine eyes have seen the King, the Lord of hosts."*

"Also I heard the voice of the Lord, saying, Whom shall I send and who will go for us? Then said I, Here am I; send me."

A vision and a commission!
Jesus told Peter in verse ten,
"Fear not, from henceforth thou shalt catch men."
From this time on, you'll be catching men!

The Deep Makes A Difference

Jesus wants us to become "Soul Winners";
catchers of men.

After launching out into the deep and then returning to land, they forsook all and followed Him. "Full-Time Service with Him." Maybe this "all" included their ideas, their ways, and their service to Him."

We read later in Luke 18:28, "Then Peter said, Lo, we have left all, and followed thee." Jesus answered Peter in verses twenty-nine and thirty, "Verily, I say unto you, there is no man that hath left house, or parents, or brethren, or wife, or children, for the kingdom of God's sake, Who shall not receive manifold more in this present time, and in the world to come life everlasting."

The Deep Makes A Difference

Jesus wants us to become "Soul Winners";
catchers of men.

A CALL…A CALL…A CALL
God is calling for us to launch out into the deep.

There are so many needing help; so many just needing someone to point them to Jesus. Little children, hungry, lost, and cold, who need help to find the way. Children whose hearts are ready; they just need brought in. It makes me think of my own Sunday School experiences as a small girl. I'm so thankful for the people who came to take us to church.

My question is this: What are we doing today?

I had a dream on Saturday, August 17th, 1991. I was worried about my children. I pulled a curtain back it seemed everything was red and like fire. In the dream, I told someone beside me, "We will just have to wet ourselves down." (before we could go in to get them out.)

**We must be covered in God's Spirit and
His anointing before we can pull them out.
We are laborers together with God.**

"Go ye therefore, and teach all nations, baptizing them in the name of the Father, and of the Son, and of the Holy Ghost: Teaching them to observe all things whatsoever I have commanded you: and, lo, I am with you always, even unto the end of the world. Amen."—Matthew 28:19,20

Praying God's Word

It was in a desperate time that I prayed these words.

"Ask, and it shall be given you; seek, and ye shall find; knock, and it shall be opened unto you. For everyone that asketh receiveth, and he that seeketh findeth; and to him that knocketh it shall be opened."— Matthew 7:7-8

As I prayed these words back to God, I reminded Him.
"You said to ask; Father, I am asking.
You said to seek; I am seeking
You said to knock; Lord, I'm knocking"

He did open unto me. I came into His Wonderful presence and there the need was met.

Praise His Wonderful Name!

The Call Of Wisdom

Proverbs 8 speaks of wisdom and tells us what wisdom has to offer. The writer refers to wisdom as she or her. As I read this chapter in God's Word, the following verses describing wisdom seemed especially rich to me. I want to share my thoughts with you.

Verse 1: Wisdom's fame: *"Doth not wisdom cry? And understanding put forth her voice?"*

Verse 10: Wisdom's excellency: *"Receive my instruction, and not silver; and knowledge rather than choice gold."*

Verse 12: Wisdom's nature: *"I, wisdom, dwell with prudence, and find out knowledge of witty inventions."*

Verse 15: Wisdom's power: *"By me kings reign, and princes decree justice."*

Verse 18: Wisdom's riches: *"Riches and Honour are with me; yea, durable riches and righteousness."*

Verse 22: Wisdom's everlastingness: *"The Lord possessed me in the beginning of His way, before His works of old."*

Verse 32: Wisdom's blessing to those who follow her: *"Now therefore hearken unto me, O ye children: for blessed are they that keep my ways."*

There are always two ways; two voices; good and evil. These two voices utter. Wisdom utters her voice. The second voice is compared to the voice of a strange woman. She and her ways are addressed in Chapter 7:5-25. If you will read these verses, you will quickly notice how the voices differ and the goal to which they lead their followers.

This strange woman is constantly pushing us toward the ways of death; she's loud and stubborn. As we cry out for wisdom, the voice of good becomes our nurse and our help. She nourishes us to health and rescues us. As we listen to her, she shows us the truth, giving us understanding and compassion. We then become laborers together with her helping those yet without wisdom and understanding.

Wisdom will overcome all!

In Jesus' Name

Many years ago, when I married my husband, I took his name. I no longer was my own; my name had been changed. I had joined myself to him, and we were now one. When we give up our own lives and accept Jesus, we become one with Him. We take His name. His name is His character. Only when we are one with Him and clothed in His Righteousness and in His Love, do we have a right to use His Name.

As I prayed one day entering His presence, I asked the Father for something in particular. He revealed to me the meaning of asking in Jesus' name. As I sat there before the Father, I was in Jesus, and it was He that was asking the Father, revealing our oneness.

If a wife is not true to her husband, she has no right to use her husband's name.

We, as the church, must be faithful to the beloved!

"And whatsoever ye shall ask in my name, that will I do, that the Father may be glorified in the Son. If ye shall ask any thing in my name, I will do it."—John 14:13,14

Open Eyes

God has a set time for all things. We can see this all through the Bible. In Acts chapter ten we read where the time came; God had chosen to open the door to the Gentiles. As we read through the Old Testament, the Jews were God's chosen people. All other nations, by Jewish law, were not even to come unto the Jewish people. They weren't to enter their houses, and they weren't even to eat with them.

We see things change though the New Testament. In Acts, chapters nine and ten we meet Cornelius. He was a devout man who feared God with all his house and prayed to God always. Cornelius was a Gentile, and he did much for the people in giving much alms. Cornelius saw in a vision an angel of God coming unto him and telling him what to do. Remember what kind of man Cornelius was. We can only know and understand, as God opens the way for us.

In Chapter ten, God had to reveal His will to Peter regarding Cornelius, his family and ultimately all Gentiles. Peter was a Jew, keeping the law and didn't understand what this all meant. God opened the way for Peter, and he said, "I perceive". His eyes were opened to the truth of God's Word. As he told Cornelius and the others in Acts 10:34-35 *"Then Peter opened his mouth, and said, Of a truth I perceive that God is no respecter of persons: But in every nation he that feareth him, and worketh righteousness, is accepted with him."*

Open Eyes

We must understand what happens to us when we receive Jesus Christ as our savior. Our eyes of understanding are opened. I remember very well how old things were passed away; all things became new that day when I received "New Life" in Him. It was March 29th, 1963. That was the day I was born again. When I left the church that night, I felt the whole world was cleansed. It was my heart that was now clean. The next morning when I looked at the sky, it appeared bluer and the clouds whiter than I'd ever seen. The trees looked greener; everything was just beautiful. The way I felt was a wonderful peace purer than I'd ever known. I had the windows open the following morning, and a fresh breeze was blowing in. I could hear the birds singing, and it seemed like it was the first time I'd ever heard them. I had new eyes and new ears. I was no longer lame, but now my walk was also healed. I walked a straight and narrow way now. I no longer walked in the ways of the flesh. I had been quickened by His Spirit, to walk in the newness of life.

"And you hath he quickened, who were dead in trespasses and sins; Wherein in time past ye walked according to the course of this world, according to the prince of the power of the air, the spirit that now worketh in the children of disobedience: Among whom also we all had our conversation in times past in the lust of our flesh fulfilling the desires of the flesh and of the mind; and were by nature the children of wrath, even as others. But God, who is rich in mercy, for his great love wherewith he loved us, Even when we were dead in sins, hath quickened us together with Christ, by grace ye are saved."—Ephesians 2:1-5

Open Eyes

Today, I think of Cornelius and Peter along with others throughout the New Testament whose "eyes" were opened by God. We only know the things which God opens our eyes to and our ears to. God sent Peter to preach the Word to Cornelius and his house.

"But Peter rehearsed the matter from the beginning, and expounded it by order unto them, saying, I was in the city of Joppa praying: and in a trance I saw a vision, A certain vessel descend, as it had been a great sheet, let down from heaven by four corners; and it came even to me: Upon the which when I had fastened mine eyes, I considered, and saw fourfooted beasts of the earth, and wild beasts, and creeping things, and fowls of the air. And I heard a voice saying unto me, Arise, Peter; slay and eat. But I said, Not so, Lord: for nothing common or unclean hath at any time entered into my mouth. But the voice answered me again from heaven, What God hath cleansed, that call not thou common. And this was done three times: and all were drawn up again into heaven. And, behold, immediately there were three men already come unto the house where I was, sent from Caesarea unto me. And the Spirit bade me go with them, nothing doubting. Moreover these six brethren accompanied me, and we entered into the man's house: And he shewed us how he had seen an angel in his house, which stood and said unto him, Send men to Joppa, and call for Simon, whose surname is Peter; Who shall tell thee words, whereby thou and all thy house shall be saved."—Acts 11: 4 – 14

If it could be our daily prayer, "Lord, help me to see and know your ways and your will. Help me to be able to let go of my ways and my own will."

Trusting In Ourselves

So many times throughout my life, when I have failed to speak the right word or handle a matter in the right way, I've made a mess. So, I cry to my Father, "Oh Father, give me more Grace. Help me to be like you made me when I first received you and everything was new. It was your holiness that I was so content with. You are the perfect one."

When we're confronted with different circumstances, we don't like what we see in ourselves. Why is it like this? Are we trusting in ourselves and our righteousness?

We must remember how easy it is to think we're doing ok then. Oh my!

Moses tried on his own to deliver the children of Israel from bondage, and he failed.

"And it came to pass in those days, when Moses was grown, that he went out unto his brethren, and looked on their burdens: and he spied an Egyptian smiting an Hebrew, one of his brethren. And he looked this way and that way, and when he saw that there was no man, he slew the Egyptian, and hid him in the sand. And when he went out the second day, behold, two men of the Hebrews strove together: and he said to him that did the wrong, Wherefore smitest thou thy fellow? And he said, Who made thee a prince and a judge over us? Intendest thou to kill me, as thou killedst the Egyptian? And Moses feared and said, Surely this thing is known."—Exodus 2:11-14

Then God, forty years later, showed Moses His holy ground.

We must remember it is all in Jesus. We must abide in Him and trust in Him. He is the perfect one.

Only in Him are we holy!

Genuine Love

As a new Christian, I had a lot of opposition from my husband who hadn't given his heart to the Lord when I did. God filled my heart with love! So many times, I Corinthians 13:7 came to me. It says those who have genuine love for others will *"Beareth all things, believeth all things, hopeth all things, endureth all things."*

I am so thankful for God's Word. He will lead us day by day. We just need to follow Him. He is saying we will bear all things, believe all things, hope all things, and endure all things. We will Love by defending and holding other people up. We will believe the best about others, continually crediting them with good intentions. We will hope all things and never give up on people but affirm their future. Lastly, we will endure all things; we will persevere and remain loyal to the end.

Genuine love is all that will stand. There are many things that will come to separate us from the love of God, but many waters cannot quench love. There is nothing that shall be able to separate us from the love of God.

A marriage will be destroyed without love because something will come to cause it to fail. Genuine love will keep it together; genuine love keeps holding on; genuine love cannot turn lose.

Higher Heights; Deeper Depths

First, We Are A Disciple

A disciple is a follower or pupil; a learner. Jesus told the disciples, as He called them; "Come follow me, I will make you to become fishers of men." The disciples learned many things as they walked with Jesus. They listened to His every Word and watched the things He did. As their faith grew, they had to exercise it. Like the time Jesus was asleep in the storm, their faith was weak. On other occasions, He sent them out and they came back all excited because the devils were subject unto them. They were learning. Later, as Jesus was nearing His departure, He told them to go to Jerusalem and wait for the promise of the Father.

Acts 1:4 *"And being assembled together with them, commanded them that they should not depart from Jerusalem, but wait for the promise of the Father, which, saith he, ye have heard of me."*

Chapters thirteen through seventeen in the book of John show us a very precious time that Jesus spent with His disciples. The chapters share His last moments instructing His disciples and telling them about things to expect.

In John 17:18, Jesus said; *"As thou hast sent me into the world, even so have I also sent them into the world."*

The disciples were to go and wait for the Holy Ghost as it occurred in Acts 1:8 *"But ye shall receive power after that the Holy Ghost is come upon you and ye shall be witnesses unto me both in Jerusalem, and in all Judaea, and in Samaria, and unto the uttermost part of the earth."*

We too must wait; we too will be witnesses. We must wait to be sent as the first apostles were sent.

Higher Heights; Deeper Depths

Preparing For God's Revelations

There came a second part of my experience, as a child of God; a revelation he opened to me. Up to this time, all the experiences I had were making me strong in love and building my faith. I think of the three years the disciples had with Jesus and how they came to know Him. At His departure, He told them to wait for the promise of the Father. He knew they had more to experience.

Jesus told His disciples in Matthew 20:22,23, *"...Ye know not what ye ask. Are ye able to drink of the cup that I shall drink of, and to be baptized with the baptism that I am baptized with? They say unto Him we are able. And he saith unto them, Ye shall drink indeed of my cup, and be baptized with the baptism that I am baptized with: but to sit on my right hand, and on my left, is not mine to give, but it shall be given to them for whom it is prepared of my Father."*

Jesus did indeed drink this cup of suffering. As Luke 22:42 shares, Jesus prayed, *"...Father, if thou be willing, remove this cup from me: nevertheless not my will, but thine, be done."*

Jesus had asked, *"Are ye able to drink this cup and be baptized?"* These very thoughts caused me to remember a time that I was led of His Spirit to fast; I didn't even realize that I was fasting. During the fast, I remembered Moses and how he went up into the thick darkness where God was. *"And the Lord came down upon mount Sinai, on the top of the mount: and the Lord called Moses up to the top of the mount; and Moses went up."* (Exodus 19:20)

I mention Moses because of the Lord telling him to come to the top of the mount. When we are lifted or we enter that cloud, God has things to reveal to you there.

Higher Heights; Deeper Depths

On The Mount Of God

As I fasted for many days, I realized that God has a time for preparing us for the things He wants to reveal to us. Moses not only received God's commandments, but God had more to reveal to Moses.

"And Moses went up unto God, and the LORD called unto him out of the mountain saying, Thus shalt thou say to the house of Jacob, and tell the children of Israel; ye have seen what I did unto the Egyptians, and how I bare you on eagles' wings, and brought you unto myself. Now therefore, if ye will obey my voice indeed, and keep my covenant, then ye shall be a peculiar treasure unto me above all people: for all the earth is mine: And ye shall be unto me a kingdom of priests, and an holy nation. These are the words which thou shalt speak unto the children of Israel."—Exodus 19:3-6

Verse 9, *"And the LORD said unto Moses, Lo, I come unto thee in a thick cloud, that the people may hear when I speak with thee, and believe thee forever. And Moses told the words of the people unto the LORD."*

Verse 16; *"And it came to pass on the third day in the morning, that there were thunders and lightnings, and a thick cloud upon the mount, and the voice of the trumpet exceeding loud; so that all the people that was in the camp trembled."*

Verse 19,20; *"And when the voice of the trumpet sounded long, and waxed louder and louder, Moses spake, and God answered him by a voice. And the Lord came down upon mount Sinai, on the top of the mount: and the Lord called Moses up to the top of the mount; and Moses went up."*

Exodus 20:21 *"And the people stood afar off, and Moses drew near unto the thick darkness where God was."*

Higher Heights; Deeper Depths

On The Mount Of God

"And Moses rose up, and his minister Joshua: and Moses went up into the mount of God. And he said unto the elders, Tarry ye here for us, until we come again unto you: and, behold, Aaron and Hur are with you: if any man have any matters to do, let him come unto them. And Moses went up into the mount, and a cloud covered the mount. And the glory of the Lord abode upon mount Sinai, and the cloud covered it six days: and the seventh day he called unto Moses out of the midst of the cloud. And the sight of the glory of the Lord was like devouring fire on the top of the mount in the eyes of the children of Israel. And Moses went into the midst of the cloud, and gat him up into the mount: and Moses was in the mount forty days and forty nights."— Exodus 24:13-18

Moses remained on the mountain in the midst of the Glory of God for forty days. God revealed to him the ten commandments, and the building pattern for the tabernacle and the furnishings thereof, leaving nothing out. God revealed to Moses the Priesthood and even the garments for the priests to wear during this time on the Mount.

"And Moses said unto the children of Israel, See, the Lord hath called by name Bezaleel the son of Uri, the son of Hur, of the tribe of Judah; And he hath filled him with the spirit of God, in wisdom, in understanding and in knowledge, and in all manner of workmanship;"—Exodus 35:30-31

"Thus did Moses: according to all that the Lord commanded him, so did he."—Exodus 40:16

Higher Heights; Deeper Depths

On The Mount Of God

The time had come in my life for deeper things of God. I was going through very difficult times, but I didn't understand at the time all these things were also working for my good. Like He said in Romans 8:28, *"And we know that all things work together for good to them that love God, to them who are the called according to his purpose"*.

Early one morning as I awoke, I heard a voice. It was like it filled and shook the room. He spoke seven words to me. I have never told anyone what these words were, but it started a journey that was new to me. Like the priests that entered the Jordan to cross in Joshua 3:4, I had never been this way before. (Jordan symbolizes death.)

I've written before about how I would read the Word while the children were winding down, getting ready for their nap. When it was quiet, and they were all asleep, I took that special time to pray and get in His presence.

Those were wonderful times. Then one day, it was very painful as God took me in the Spirit to an experience that was so real to me. I was asked to give my son; the one I had asked Him for. I said, "I will give him back to you." It was so hard, because I didn't know what this all meant and what would happen as a result. I was given a glimpse of the Father's sacrifice He had made for me.

As I wept before Him and didn't know how it would be, I said, "Yes." Then He gave me the scriptures about Abraham, when he offered Isaac and the provision He made and pointed to my Savior, His son. This was so real; a revelation, making His Word real to me.

> *"And Abraham called the name of that place Jehovah-jireh: as it is said to this day. In the mount of the Lord it shall be seen."*
> — Genesis 22:14

Highest Heights; Deepest Depths

Making Us A Witness

Acts 1:8 says *"But ye shall receive power, after that the Holy Ghost is come upon you: and ye shall be witnesses unto me both in Jerusalem, and in all Judea, and in Samaria, and unto the uttermost part of the earth."*

We too must wait; then we will receive the Holy Spirit; that's what makes us a witness. It is only in the Spirit, we receive what God reveals to us.

As I was praying one day, these words came out of my mouth, "I am the Alpha and the Omega; the first and the last." I was so startled, I began telling God how sorry I was. I didn't mean to say that. He then let me know He was speaking through me. He was in me, and I in Him; One with Him. He was teaching me. Then He went further in revelation, taking me places I'd never been before.

These things come only as we spend time in His presence. In the secret place of His presence, does He reveal His secrets.

"And he said unto me, It is done. I am Alpha and Omega, the beginning and the end. I will give unto him that is athirst of the fountain of the water of life freely."—Revelation 21:6

Ask; Seek; Knock

There are times when we come to the Lord in prayer, and it seems we don't enter in or don't feel His presence like we need to. I remember one of those times, and I felt desperate as I began crying out to Him. I remember telling Him, "Lord, you said ask, and you shall receive; I am asking. You said seek and ye shall find, and I am seeking. You said knock, and it shall be opened unto you. Lord, I am knocking."

Since that time, I have thought of Mary so many times, as she knelt in His presence, and washed His feet with her tears.

How Wonderful He is!

"Ask, and it shall be given you; seek, and ye shall find; knock, and it shall be opened unto you: For everyone that asketh receiveth; and he that seeketh findeth; and to him that knocketh it shall be opened."—Matthew 7:7,8

There Must Be A Desire To Know Him

After I came to know the Lord, I would leave every church service with a desire to live a life that would please God. There was a deep desire; a deep hunger. Then when Jesus touched me, I desired for Him to touch me again. Oh, how my heart hungered after Him. I longed for Him. I seemingly had lost interest in the things of the world. I came to Him and surrendered my life to Him. It was such a joyous time, words can't describe.

I Peter 2:2 took precedence in my heart. *"As newborn babes, desire the sincere milk of the word, that ye may grow thereby."*

As a newborn babe, I now desired the sincere milk of the Word. My desire was to know all about Him. We cannot know much about Him without the Word!

Jesus said in Mark 11:24, *"Therefore I say unto you, What things soever ye desire, when ye pray, believe that ye receive them, and ye shall have them."*

My desire was to know about the Holy Ghost, I wanted to know about speaking in tongues. His answer to me was so very real.

"Blessed are they which do hunger and thirst after righteousness: for they shall be filled."—Matthew 5: 6

"If ye then, being evil, know how to give good gifts unto your children: how much more shall your heavenly Father give the Holy Spirit to them that ask Him?"—Luke 11:13

"Follow after charity, and desire spiritual gifts, but rather that ye may prophesy."—I Corinthians 14:1

"For in this we groan, earnestly desiring to be clothed upon with our house which is from heaven:"—II Corinthians 5:2

My First Fast

Being a young Christian, not knowing the Word, I was like a baby desiring the milk of the Word. I was anxious to grow. I was so hungry for the Word. I wanted to know all about Him. One night at church the preacher gave a message about fasting. I didn't know anything about fasting, so I wanted to know more about it. When we got home from church that night, I was going to read my Bible to find out more. As we went through the kitchen, I saw a bag of potato chips open on the table. I got a handful. As I started to my mouth with one, I suddenly felt an odd feeling in my jaws. I didn't want to take a bite. So, I put them back. I didn't understand, but I just followed what I felt. I picked up my Bible and began to read. I read and read that night.

The next morning, I cooked breakfast for the family. I still felt that same feeling, so I didn't eat. All day it was like that. The next day I felt the same; the third day the feeling continued. It was a beautiful day, so Paul, my husband, took us for a picnic by a big bridge. I fixed a big picnic basket of food and our time as a family was so enjoyable. I still didn't eat. It was like I was totally full. I realized later that I was full of the joy and peace of the Lord

He was teaching me, and I was learning about fasting. He is a personal Savior, knowing our desires, knowing our heart.

He is Wonderful, and He is the Best Teacher!
None other is like Him.
He teaches by His Word and by His Spirit.

"Shew me thy ways, O Lord; teach me thy paths. Lead me in thy truth, and teach me: for thou art the God of my salvation; on thee do I wait all the day. Remember, O Lord, thy tender mercies and thy loving kindness; for they have been ever of old."—Psalm 25:4-6

Blind Man's Bluff

Have you ever heard of or played a game called "Blind Man's Bluff"?

You are blindfolded and entirely dependent upon the instructions of your playmates. You cannot see the ground or the objects in your path or who is standing close to you. All you do is listen for the next direction and follow it to the letter. If you do what you are told, trusting your friends to steer you in the right direction, then you get the thrill of making it to the decided destination.

As we follow Jesus Christ, we are also taking a step by step walk of faith, not knowing everything that lies ahead. Only He knows how to get you where He wants you to be. As we follow His directions, He takes responsibility for the outcome of your obedience.

When we let Him be in control, we don't have to worry or fear the consequences. With faith in His all-knowing-ever present-completely reliable guidance, we don't have to stumble around in confusion.

"And Jesus, walking by the sea of Galilee, saw two brethren, Simon called Peter, and Andrew his brother, casting a net into the sea: for they were fishers. And he saith unto them, Follow me, and I will make you fishers of men. And they straightway left their nets, and followed him. And going on from thence he saw other two brethren, James the son of Zebedee, and John his brother, in a ship with Zebedee their father, mending their nets; and he called them. And they immediately left the ship and their father, and followed him."—Matthew 4:18-22

Jesus says to us all, "Follow me."

What Is Speaking In Tongues?

As a young Christian, there was so much I didn't know. Another night while at church, I was hearing things about "Receiving the Baptism of the Holy Ghost", and "Speaking in tongues." I had never heard about these things before, so I desired to know more. We were again visiting another church, and a friend we had ridden to church with that night made the statement on the way home, "When you receive the Holy Ghost, you will speak in other tongues."

As I said, I was a new Christian. I had been born again; all things were new to me. I felt wonderful and so full of joy and peace and love. I didn't see how I could ever feel more wonderful than this. I didn't doubt these things that I was being introduced to; I just didn't understand. I was already so full. I went home that night and began to read everything I could find in the Bible about speaking in tongues.

Then, I went to Pray.

Psalm 105:4 *"Seek the Lord, and his strength: seek his face evermore."*

What Is Speaking In Tongues?

I took it all to Him.

Part of my prayer went something like this. "Lord, Paul said he would that we all speak with tongues, but rather that we prophesied; for greater is he that prophesies than he that speaks with tongues, except he interprets that the church may receive edifying." As I knelt there in His presence, I said, "Lord, I just want everything you have for me." His presence was so great. A spirit of praise came over me as I began to just praise, worship and Love Him. It was so wonderful as I worshiped Him. As I praised Him, suddenly a word came out of my mouth. Following this, I said "Hallelujah." God spoke to my heart and said, "That is what you just said, in another language." He again had heard and known my desire to know Him; to know His Word. He was teaching me that "speaking in tongues" is very real.

"But the anointing which ye have received of him abideth in you, and ye need not that any man teach you: but as the same anointing teacheth you all things, and is truth, and is no lie, and even as it hath taught you, ye shall abide in Him."—I John 2:27

"Henceforth I call you not servants; for the servant knoweth not what his lord doeth: but I have called you friends; for all things that I have heard of my Father I have made known unto you." —John 15:15

He said, "I will teach you all things."

There came a time later, at the baptizing with The Holy Ghost, that He spoke more than one word. I will speak of this later!

Heavenly Breezes

Early one morning as my husband, Paul, was heading out the door to go to work, I noticed a picture hanging by the door was crooked. I reached up to straighten it. As I did, I grabbed my chest in pain. It was the worst pain I had ever had as it shot down my arm. Our daughter, Ruth, was up, so I had her to wake the others to get ready for school. I couldn't even turn myself over or move. Ruth had to help me to even move.

I went to sleep and dreamed this dream.

I was in a house, and I was standing over a baby in a baby bed. Everything was so white. The purest white, almost like clouds. The baby was wet, so I changed its diaper. The baby looked pleasant all the while, never crying or fussing. Then it seemed there were two rooms joined. Teresa, another one of our daughters, was standing there when suddenly the best breeze began blowing. I said to Teresa, "Keep those windows open; it will always continue blowing." It was such a fresh and wholesome breeze. The very rooms were pure white, like clouds filled them beautifully. It was as if this fresh breeze was relieving pressure. It seems like I may have even spoken those words. It was a heavenly breeze, and I felt so good. When I awoke, all my pain was gone!!

As I told my mom and dad about this dream, Dad told me that he too had had a similar dream a long time ago. He said he was having trouble with his kidneys and heart. He was only about 12 years old. He had stood up in the bed and passed out. While he was unconscious, he had a dream. He was lying under a big shade tree with the best breeze blowing on him. When he awoke, he was fine as far as he can remember. He lived to be eighty-three years old.

"Now when Daniel knew that the writing was signed, he went into his house; and his windows being open in his chamber toward Jerusalem, he kneeled upon his knees three times a day, and prayed, and gave thanks before his God, as he did aforetime."—Daniel 6:10

When Daniel was in danger, he went into his house, opened his windows, and prayed.

God heard his prayer.

Heavenly Breezes

The Lord reminded me this morning it was my prayer time. I looked at the clock, and it was 9:00AM. As I entered into a spirit of prayer, I began to see how, by keeping our senses open to Him, a heavenly breeze will always flow through us. The pure breeze of His Spirit flows. It heals and brings deliverance. My prayer is that our Heavenly Father will always help us to keep all our senses open to Him, so He can flow through us to this world we're in. That pure flow of His Spirit is Life.

Jesus said, "Freely ye have received; freely give." God has put a precious gift inside of us. We must take care as we would a most precious jewel, tender and pure.

We must be sure to tend to the spiritual needs.
Love as Jesus loves!

"Praise ye the Lord. Praise ye the name of the Lord; praise him, O ye servants of the Lord. Ye that stand in the house of the Lord, in the courts of the house of our God. Praise the Lord; for the Lord is good: sing praises unto his name; for it is pleasant. For the Lord hath chosen Jacob unto himself and Israel for his peculiar treasure. For I know that the Lord is great, and that our Lord is above all gods. Whatsoever the Lord pleased, that did He in heaven, and in earth, in the seas, and all deep places. He causeth the vapors to ascend from the ends of the earth; he maketh lightnings for the rain; he bringeth the wind out of his treasuries."—Psalm 135:1-7

We Are Not Alone

Jesus said in John 8:12-16 *"I am the light of the world, he that followeth me shall not walk in darkness, but shall have the light of life. The Pharisees therefore said unto him, Thou bearest record of thyself; thy record is not true. Jesus answered and said unto them, Though I bear record of myself, yet my record is true: for I know whence I came, and whither I go; but ye cannot tell whence I come, and whither I go. Ye judge after the flesh; I judge no man. And yet if I judge, my judgement is true: for I am not alone, but I and the Father that sent me."*

The Father sent His son Jesus into the world to give light and truth unto the world.

Verse 29 in the same chapter says, *"And he that sent me is with me: the Father hath not left me alone; for I do always those things that please Him."*

Jesus is saying that He is in loving fellowship with the Father; He is in oneness with Him. Jesus was sent into the world to do the Father's will. Jesus said to His followers, "Deny yourself, take up your cross and follow me."

When Jesus went away, (died, arose, and ascended) He said, I will not leave you comfortless (orphans). I will send you another comforter.

"And I will pray the Father, and he shall give you another Comforter, that he may abide with you forever; Even the Spirit of truth; whom the world cannot receive, because it seeth him not, neither knoweth him: but ye know him; for he dwelleth with you, and shall be in you."—John 14:16, 17

A Safe Place

Hebrews 9:1 reads, *"Then verily the first covenant had also ordinances of divine service, and a worldly sanctuary."* The Old Testament sanctuary did not fully reveal God's presence. At that time, we were not able to fully enter God's presence.

Jesus is our pattern; our perfect example. He shows us the way into the full presence of God. Then, we will be able to enjoy the place that Jesus has gone to prepare for us.

The word Shekinah comes from Judaic writings, meaning the abiding presence of Almighty God.

John 10:27-30, tells us there is a place of safety where we are placed and kept in God's hand: *"My sheep hear my voice, and I know them, and they follow me: And I give unto them eternal life; and they shall never perish, neither shall any man pluck them out of my hand. My Father, which gave them me, is greater than all; and no man is able to pluck them out of my Father's hand. I and my Father are one."*

"He that dwelleth in the secret place of the most High shall abide under the shadow of the Almighty. I will say of the Lord, He is my refuge and my fortress: my God; in him will I trust. Surely he shall deliver thee from the snare of the fowler, and from the noisome pestilence. He shall cover thee with his feathers, and under his wings shalt thou trust: his truth shall be thy shield and buckler."—Psalm 91:1-4

We are placed by the Father in that safe place; the Son's hand and covered by his wings.

A Safe Place

It took Moses a long time to get to this place of safety. He experienced many hard times and trials, even failures; he had lessons to learn. Moses had a desire to know God. He dad a desire to dwell in Him, and he esteemed God's presence highly. How do we get to this place?

Moses prayed to God in Exodus 33:15 *"….If thy presence go not with me, carry us not up hence. For wherein shall it be known here that I and thy people have found grace in thy sight? Is it not in that thou goest with us? So shall we be separated, I and thy people, from all the people that are upon the face of the earth."*

It is God's presence with us and in us that separates of from all other peoples. It's His presence that sets us apart; we are a sanctified people!

In Exodus 33:18, Moses prayed to God, *"I beseech thee, shew me thy glory."* Moses was asking God to show him His splendor; His honor; His fullness of Perfection.

"And the Lord said, Behold, there is a place by me, and thou shalt stand upon a rock: And it shall come to pass, while my glory passeth by, that I will put thee in a clift of the rock, and will cover thee with my hand while I pass by:"—Exodus 33:21, 22

God told Moses, "There is a place by me; there's a clift in the rock."

A Safe Place

When you are overwhelmed, run to the rock. He is a safe retreat by night.

As we go through things in this life, we don't have to fear. If we can just seek that safe place of God's presence, there is safety there.

It doesn't matter how dark or how thick the darkness. It doesn't matter how long it goes on. Be obedient. Have a desire to enter that place of safety.

> I can tell you there is rest there.
> **He is our wonderful Father and Savior!**

I can remember a few words of a song that says, "He's our rock of strength, salvation and defense. Jesus is our light. We'll see a glimmer of light in the darkness and all will be well."

"For ye are dead, and your life is hid with Christ in God."
— Colossians 3:3

Garden Times

How I love the memories of the spring times gone by. Gardening always brings a smile to my face. I can recall the times when the dirt clots flew through the air from one garden row to another. It was a fun time for even that one too small to hoe or pull the weeds.

Then came the harvest time. Picking the beans was a big job, so you invited your friends to come along to help. In poured the baskets full. Then, another big job of breaking them for the canning; another job for friends to help. So, help they did. Tomatoes, oh so many.

I can still remember the playhouse in the backyard. Full of baskets of beans for the breaking. We brought out one basket at a time. Each child had a friend or two. So, invite them they did; you've never heard so much laughter.

What a joyful time!
What a wonderful time to remember.

Lean Thou On Me

If there's no other way, except through pain and loss,
To stamp Christ's image on my soul.
No other way, except the cross,
And then a vail stills all my soul.

As stills the waves on Galilee,
Canst thou not bear the furnace?
If mid the flame, I walk with thee.
I bare the cross; I know its weight.

I drank the cup I held for thee.
Canst thou not follow where I lead?
I'll give thee strength. **Lean thou on me!**

Author Unknown

God Is Truth

Living a holy life, means living above the standard of the world, while still in the world. We can only do this as we give our lives totally to Jesus.

The New Testament tells us that the scribes and Pharisees, who were the writers and interpreters of the laws of God, had developed all kinds of interpretations that were misleading and confusing to the people. Jesus condemned those leaders and compared them to blind people leading blind people in Matthew 15:14.

Everything Jesus spoke came directly from the Father.

John 14:10 *"Believest thou not that I am in the Father, and the Father in me? The words that I speak unto you I speak not of myself: but the Father that dwelleth in me, he doeth the works."*

John 17:6 *"I have manifested thy name unto the men which thou gavest me out of the world: thine they were, and thou gavest them me; and they have kept thy word."*

So many don't comprehend the Bible's spiritual significance because they have not submitted to its guidance.

The concept of many of the scribes and Pharisees in the days of our Lord is that they were secure in their religious position and refused to give up their own authority.

Because of unrestrained speech (constant careless talk), the effectiveness of many Christians carries very little impact.

An obligation rests upon every Christian to let His words be an overflow of the Spirit-filled life.

Our hearts are revealed by what we say.

Matthew 12:34 *"O generation of vipers, how can ye, being evil, speak good things? For out of the abundance of the heart the mouth speaketh."*

God's People Are A Special People

His will is for us to teach our children of His ways and not the ways of the world.

The time will come when He will draw them to Him. But if they are so much in the pleasures of the world, they will have a harder time hearing His voice. He gave us a promise in Proverbs 22:6 *"Train up a child in the way he should go: and when he is old, he will not depart from it."*

We are a special people, separated unto the Lord. Our children must also realize how special they are and loved of God. They must realize that God has a plan for each of their lives. This will help keep them separated from the pleasures of the world and allow them to be a light to others.

As parents, God will give us wisdom
and help us guide them in His ways.
They have been, they are, and they will be blessed.
He is a wonderful Father!

"And these words, which I command thee this day, shall be in thine heart: And thou shalt teach them diligently unto thy children, and shalt talk of them when thou sittest in thine house, and when thou walkest by the way, and when thou liest down, and when thou risest up. And thou shalt bind them for a sign upon thine hand, and they shall be as frontlets between thine eyes. And thou shalt write them upon the posts of thy house, and on thy gates."—Deuteronomy 6:6-9

An Encouraging Word

As my dad was getting ready for surgery, I asked God for something from His Word to help encourage him. This was the scripture He gave me.

"They that trust in the Lord shall be as mount Zion, which cannot be removed, but abideth for ever. As the mountains are round about Jerusalem, so the Lord is round about his people from henceforth even for ever."—Psalm 125:1-2

God will encourage us through His Word. Dad was encouraged that day as I read to him. He lived many years after.

Special Moments

I was thinking about Joseph as he embraced and kissed his brethren. As they talked with him, their fears left. A special touch from the Lord removes our fears. It lets us realize His love as we talk with Him.

Others also need to know our love for them. Our children, our grandchildren, great grandchildren, and others need that special loving touch in a hug or a pat.

Years ago, at church one night, no one knew the heavy load I felt, but a sister during the service touched my hand. As she patted me on the hand, she said, "It's going to be alright." As she did that, the heavy feeling just lifted from me and was gone. I thank our precious Lord and His children that encourage each other with a loving touch.

In the book of Genesis, Joseph sent all the others from the room, so he could be alone with his brothers when he made himself known to them. This was a special moment. I remembered when I came to Jesus that night at Mt. Zion Church. As He was calling me to Him, He said "Come" with His arms outstretched towards me. It was like there was no one in that little church house but the two of us, as He personally revealed Himself to me by His Spirit.

> I realized how real and how near and
> how Wonderful He truly is.
> There is nothing in this world that
> can compare to His presence.
> **He is Wonderful!**

"Then Joseph could not refrain himself before all them that stood by him; and he cried, Cause every man to go out from me. And there stood no man with him, while Joseph made himself known unto his brethren."—Genesis 45:1

Be Focused

For us to be focused, we have to block out many other things and continually concentrate on our goal.

"If any of you lack wisdom, let him ask of God, that giveth to all men liberally, and upbraideth not; and it shall be given him. But let him ask in faith, nothing wavering. For he that wavereth is like a wave of the sea driven with the wind and tossed. For let not that man think that he shall receive anything of the Lord. A double minded man is unstable in all his ways."—James 1:5-8

Jesus said in Matthew 6:22, *"The light of the body is the eye: if therefore thine eye be single, thy whole body shall be full of light."*

Any distraction can hinder us, and Jesus is asking that our eye be single or focused.

We need to stay focused on spiritual matters.

God's Word instructs us to renew our mind in God's Word and train it (our mind) to bring every thought captive to the obedience of Christ.

In II Corinthians 10:5, *"Casting down imaginations, and every high thing that exalteth itself against the knowledge of God, and bringing into captivity every thought to the obedience of Christ;"*

Peter instructs us to be vigilant, alert, and watchful. There's not a single moment we can drop our guard.

I Peter 5:8 *"Be sober, be vigilant; because your adversary the devil, as a roaring lion, walketh about, seeking whom he may devour."*

The Lord wants your full attention all the time. When your focus is fixed on Him, He will build your faith in the quiet moments.

Let us set *Him* before our eyes.

Who Are You Pleasing?

"And he that sent me is with me: The Father hath not left me alone; for I do always those things that please Him."—John 8:29

We either feed the flesh or we feed the spirit. We must ask ourselves the question; Which one is stronger in my life?

Do we lose control? The flesh is seen; ourselves.

Do we keep control completely? If we can answer, "yes", then the spirit is in control and we obey Him. He is the one who is seen.

Prayer is major. We will not be able to maintain control under pressure without prayer. We need Him, His Word, His Spirit controlling us, if we are to be obedient.

"Then said Jesus to those Jews which believed on Him, if ye continue in my word, then are ye my disciples indeed;"—John 8:31

Abide in Him. He abides in us.

Our Prayer Closet

"But thou, when thou prayest, enter into thy closet, and when thou hast shut thy door, pray to thy Father which is in secret; and thy Father which seeth in secret shall reward thee openly."
—Matthew 6:6

As we spend time in our closet of prayer, do we realize how valuable this time is? Do we realize what it cost for us to be able to spend time here? When we enter and shut the door, let us worship and remember what a privilege it is to be here.

What did it cost for us to be able to enter here?
Jesus hung between heaven and earth until it was finished.

"When Jesus therefore had received the vinegar, he said, It is finished: and he bowed his head, and gave up the ghost."
—John 19:30

"Having therefore, brethren, boldness to enter into the holiest by the blood of Jesus, By a new and living way, which he hath consecrated for us, through the veil, that is to say, his flesh;"—Hebrews 10: 19,20

Our Prayer Closet

Remember the setting up of the Tabernacle in the Old Testament. It was the Old Covenant. Moses followed God's pattern as God had instructed him. Moses had set up the golden altar; Exodus 40:26,27. Moses also set up the altar of incense to burn sweet incense upon, and he placed a veil before the entrance into the Holy of Holies.

"And behold, the veil of the temple was rent in twain from the top to the bottom; and the earth did quake, and the rocks rent;" —Matthew 27:51

That same veil we read about in Exodus put in place by way of the Old Covenant we find in Matthew is being rent in twain or torn in two pieces. The veil was torn giving us access into God's presence. All this was made possible by Christ's sacrifice.

"And after the second veil, the tabernacle which is called the Holiest of all; which had the golden censer, and the ark of the covenant overlaid round about with gold, wherein was the golden pot that had manna, and Aaron's rod that budded, and the tables of the covenant;"—Hebrews 9:3,4

Our Prayer Closet; Your Secret Place

Your secret closet or secret place, whatever you want to name it, is a special space to get alone with God.

"Oh Father, draw us to that place with you. You will reveal things to us we would otherwise never know or think about. Your presence is Wonderful Father. I Love you, and I thank you for everything you do for us. Everything you reveal to us is so precious; so good!"

- The Greek word for closet used in Matthew 6:6 means a private room.

- Jesus found a mountain top; Peter found a rooftop; the prophets found a wilderness.

- If you love someone, you will find a place, you will find the time to be alone with that person.

- There are many benefits to that secret place; there are resources found there and a daily replenishing.

"For which cause we faint not; but though our outward man perish, yet the inward man is renewed day by day. For our light affliction, which is but for a moment, worketh for us a far more exceeding and eternal weight of glory; While we look not at the things which are seen, but at the things which are not seen: for the things which are seen are temporal; but the things which are not seen are eternal."—II Corinthians 4:16-18

The Miracle Of Prayer

God gave us sunshine, birds, and trees,
The star filled sky above.
He gave us beauty, flowers and friends,
And special folks to love.

And then because each life would bring.
Its share of stress and care.
He gave to us a wonderful gift,
The Miracle of Prayer.

He knew the sun would sometimes hide,
Behind a cloud of gray.
And we'd have need of faith and love,
And strength for each new day.

How comforting it is to know,
His love is always there.
To comfort, help and guide us,
Through the Miracle of Prayer.

Author unknown

"And God saw everything that he had made, and, behold, it was very good. And the evening and the morning were the sixth day."
—Genesis 1:31

Spiritual Application To Salvation

By nature, we are sinners. We are in the Egypt of this world which is ruled by Satan. Under Satan's regime, men became slaves and are doomed to eternal destruction. In our helpless condition, God sent His son to become the Lamb of God. As the Lamb, He died at Calvary that through the shedding of His blood salvation might come to all men.

**This was God's plan,
and there is no alternative.**

Man must take the blood of the lamb and apply it to his own house with the promise; "When I see the blood, I will pass over you." Nothing else is sufficient. There must be a personal acceptance of the blood of Jesus Christ, applied to the heart and life. An individual must understand that Christ died for my sin. As individuals, we must understand that His blood accepted can wash away my sin. In so doing, the condemnation of death which is my due, can be removed.

**This act, whereby we accept
in simple Faith and Obedience,
is called Salvation!**

"For God so loved the world, that he gave his only begotten Son, that whosoever believeth in him should not perish, but have everlasting life."—John 3:16

Spiritual Application To Salvation

It is through Salvation that man passes from death unto life; from bondage unto liberty; from darkness to light. We leave an old life for a brand new one, entering an entirely new experience. Through the initial experience of Salvation, we walk to God through sacrifice. Now through the acceptance of His sacrifice, we walk with God through separation.

Salvation is a new beginning!

"This month shall be unto you the beginning of months: it shall be the first month of the year to you."—Exodus 12:2

Through the spiritual life, we should know growth, develop character, and experience maturity.

"Praise ye the Lord. Praise, O ye servants of the Lord, praise the name of the Lord. Blessed be the name of the Lord from this time forth and for evermore. From the rising of the sun unto the going down of the same the Lord's name is to be praised. The Lord is high above all nations, and his glory above the heavens. Who is like unto the Lord our God, who dwelleth on high, Who humbleth himself to behold the things that are in heaven, and in the earth! He raiseth up the poor out of the dust, and lifteth the needy out of the dunghill; That he may set him with princes, even with the princes of his people. He maketh the barren woman to keep house, and to be a joyful mother of children. Praise ye the Lord."— Psalm 113

The Church

I see a group of people standing with a man of God. Standing before them an Elijah, if you would, and they are doing God's will. The group becomes an army with God's Spirit moving in their hearts. He now becomes no more alone in his laboring. The spirit moves, and each member is doing his part and taking his place. They are moving as one to accomplish God's will to win the battle. Each service is a battle; the enemy seeking to destroy and hinder God's work in our lives.

We are laborers together with God, and the battle is His.

We need to be prepared for each church service; there is work to be done. People need God; they need healing. Spiritually blinded eyes need to be opened. Spiritually deafened ears need to be unstopped. The lame need to walk. Those that are bound need to be set free. The church needs to develop self-discipline through God's leadership and prepare for battle. All these things God can accomplish through the Church as one.

"Fulfil ye my joy, that ye be likeminded, having the same love, being of one accord, of one mind."—Philippians 2:2

Five Senses

In the natural, we have five senses. Our eyes give us sight; we can see. Our ears give us hearing and the ability to know sound. Through taste, we can relish flavor. By our sense of smell, we can detect odors or scents in the atmosphere. Lastly, we have a sense of touch; it enables us to feel objects.

At our new birth awakening, all these senses, miraculously awaken spiritually. At our new birth, we suddenly realize "Oh, I can see". We can understand and comprehend the things of God through His spirit.

"The eyes of your understanding being enlightened; that ye may know what is the hope of his calling, and what the riches of the glory of his inheritance in the saints,"—Ephesians 1:18

- At our new birth, our spiritual ears are opened. Now we can hear, spiritually. Jesus said, "My sheep hear my voice."

Galatians 3:2 *"This only would I learn of you, Received ye the Spirit by the works of the law, or by the hearing of faith?"*

- When we are born again, we are able to; *"O taste and see that the Lord is good; Blessed is the man that trusteth in Him."* —Psalm 34:8

"How sweet are thy words unto my taste! Yea, sweeter than honey to my mouth."—Psalm 119:103

- When we are awakened at our new birth, we can sense His sweet savor; His pure aroma.
- At our new birth awakening, we can feel His touch. There is nothing else like His touch…..His touch of compassion.

Five Senses

I think of the time when the world was in gross darkness; *"And God said, let there be light: and there was light."* (Genesis 1:3)

I'm reminded of a time when the spiritual darkness was just as real as that gross darkness, until God sent His Son into the world. *"In Him was life; and the life was the light of men."* (John 1:4)

My life; my world was all in darkness. I wasn't aware of anything except for my life doing whatever I pleased. I fit in with the world. Until God's set time, He began to draw me by His spirit to Him as in John 1:5. *"And the light shineth in darkness; and the darkness comprehended it not."*

> I began to see, understand, and comprehend
> things I never had before.
> My spiritual senses were awakened.

"For God who commanded the light to shine out of darkness, hath shined in our hearts, to give the light of the knowledge of the glory of God in the face of Jesus Christ."—II Corinthians 4:6

"We have also a more sure word of prophecy; whereunto ye do well that ye take heed, as unto a light that shineth in a dark place, until the day dawn, and the day star arise in your hearts:"—II Peter 1:19

My Heart Is Fixed

"My heart is fixed, O God, my heart is fixed: I will sing and give praise."—Psalm 57:7

He who shoots an arrow at a mark directs it and with a fixed eye and steady hand, takes aim. He who takes aim with one eye, shuts the other. If we direct a prayer to God, we must also direct our eye on Him. We must gather in our wandering thoughts and summon them all to draw near to fix our hearts on Him.

When one generation passes and the children are not taught of God and His works for His children, the children grow away from God. How many generations have passed without the little one being taught in the home? They have no knowledge of God or His ways.

Where are we now?
Who do they serve?
Teach your children!

"And also all that generation were gathered unto their fathers: and there arose another generation after them, which knew not the Lord, nor yet the works which he had done for Israel. And the children of Israel did evil in the sight of the Lord, and served Baalim: And they forsook the Lord God of their fathers, which brought them out of the land of Egypt, and followed other gods, of the gods of the people that were round about them, and bowed themselves unto them, and provoked the Lord to anger." "And it came to pass, when the judge was dead, that they returned and corrupted themselves more than their fathers, in following other gods to serve them, and to bow down unto them; they ceased not from their own doings, not from their stubborn way."—Judges 2:10-12, 19

We must teach our children of God and His ways.

Daily

We must enter daily into that place of rest; we must enter into the Spirit of God. This is where we are kept from the spirit of the world. We must come determined to enter in because we know this is our place of safety. Morning and evening we must come; not in a hurry nor carelessly but knowing this is God's will and the place of our safety.

"But thou, when thou prayest, enter into thy closet, and when thou hast shut thy door, pray to thy Father which is in secret; and thy Father which seeth in secret shall reward thee openly. But when ye pray, use not vain repetitions, as the heathen do: for they think that they shall be heard for their much speaking. Be not ye therefore like unto them: for your Father knoweth what things ye have need of, before ye ask him. After this manner therefore pray ye: Our Father which art in heaven, Hallowed be thy name. Thy kingdom come. Thy will be done in earth, as it is in heaven. Give us this day our daily bread. And forgive us our debts, as we forgive our debtors. And lead us not into temptation, but deliver us from evil: For thine is the kingdom, and the power, and the glory, forever. Amen."—Matthew 6:6-13

Do We Truly Know Him?

Do we feel a desire and a need for a deeper commitment to Him? Is it our desire to live a consecrated life unto Him and to do His will in this life? Are we members of His Church; this body of believers in the earth that have been commissioned by Him to point other souls to Him?

Jesus said, *"Go ye therefore, and teach all nations, baptizing them in the name of the Father, and of the Son, and of the Holy Ghost: Teaching them to observe all things whatsoever I have commanded you: and lo I am with you always, even unto the end of the world."* (Matthew 28:19-20) Amen.

> God has given us a commission;
> a work to do while we remain on this earth.
> **We are His people;**
> **we are His church on the earth.**

"But ye are a chosen generation, a royal priesthood, an holy nation, a peculiar people; that ye should shew forth the praises of him who hath called you out of darkness into his marvelous light:"
—I Peter 2:9

Do We Truly Know Him?

Jesus said, "I am the way, the truth, and the life."

"And this is life eternal, that they might know thee the only true God, and Jesus Christ whom thou hast sent."—John 17:3

"And we know that the Son of God is come, and hath given us an understanding, that we may know him that is true, and we are in him that is true, even in his Son Jesus Christ. This is the true God, and eternal life."—I John 5:20

Jesus wants us to know Him!

He said, "Ye must be born again." This is the beginning of our relationship with Him. We will begin to grow in Him. Jesus said, "Take my yoke upon you and learn of me."

It was not possible for man to find his way back to God, without Jesus the Son making the way. Neither is it possible for man to do God's work or God's will in man's own strength and power.

God sent His son!

The Son prayed the Father, and He sent the Holy Ghost back to be to us what Jesus was to the disciples in the flesh. Now His Spirit abides with us and in us. There is much work to be done, and the enemy of our soul wants to hinder us. But Jesus said, "I have all power in heaven and in earth."

He is our help!

Dwelling Place

What is a dwelling place? It is where you live; it's your home. The tabernacle was a dwelling place for God; a dwelling place among His people. The Lord spake unto Moses; "….let them make me a sanctuary; that I might dwell among them." God had always desired to dwell among His people. He gave Moses a pattern to build a sanctuary to make this possible.

Jesus was the next dwelling place. He (Jesus) was made flesh and tabernacled among us. John wrote in John 1:14, *"And the Word was made flesh, and dwelt among us, (and we beheld his glory), the glory as of the only begotten of the Father,) full of grace and truth."*

"Jesus saith unto him, Have I been so long time with you, and yet hast thou not known me, Phillip? He that hath seen me hath seen the Father; and how sayest thou then, Shew us the Father?"— John 14:9

"I and my Father are one."—John 10:30

Where does God dwell today?
In His people.

"What? Know ye not that your body is the temple of the Holy Ghost which is in you, which ye have of God, and ye are not your own?"—I Corinthians 6:19

He dwells in us today!

Glorifying God

How do we glorify God? Praise!

"Whoso offereth praise glorifieth me: and to him that ordereth his conversation aright will I shew the salvation of God."—Psalm 50:23

"And Jesus said unto him, Receive thy sight: thy faith hath saved thee. And immediately he received his sight, and followed him, glorifying God: and all the people, when they saw it, gave praise unto God."—Luke 18: 42, 43

"But ye are a chosen generation, a royal priesthood, an holy nation, a peculiar people that ye should shew forth the praises of Him who hath called you out of darkness into His marvelous light."—I Peter 2:9

How do we glorify God? By calling on Him!

"And call upon me in the day of trouble: I will deliver thee, and thou shalt glorify me."—Psalm 50:15

Glorifying God

How do we glorify God? Through Fruitfulness

"Herein is my Father glorified, that ye bear much fruit; so shall ye be my disciples."—John 15:8

"Being filled with the fruits of righteousness, which are by Jesus Christ, unto the glory and praise of God."—Philippians 1:11

How do we glorify God? By Doing God's will; Service

"Ye are the light of the world. A city that is set on a hill cannot be hid. Neither do men light a candle, and put it under a bushel, but on a candlestick; and it giveth light unto all that are in the house. Let your light so shine before men, that they may see your good works, and glorify your Father which is in heaven."—Matthew 5:14-16

"Having your conversation honest among the Gentiles: that, whereas they speak against you as evildoers, they may by your good works, which they shall behold, glorify God in the day of visitation."—I Peter 2:12

"If any man speak, let him speak as the oracles of God; if any man minister, let him do it as of the ability which God giveth: that God in all things may be glorified through Jesus Christ, to whom be praise and dominion for ever and ever, Amen."—I Peter 4:11

"I have glorified thee on the earth: I have finished the work which thou gavest me to do."—John 17:4

Jesus revealed the Father's will; He gave us the Father's Words in John 17:3. *"And this is life eternal, that they might know thee the only true God, and Jesus Christ, whom thou hast sent."*

What do we see when we see Jesus?
Remember; He glorified God.

What do others see when they see us? Are we One with Him that others can see Him in us, bringing Glory to God?

Discipline

There is a discipline that does not come easy to many.

- The battle of the flesh
- The battle of the schedule
- The battle with interruptions

I can assure you that cultivating these disciplines through our relationship with Christ is worth fighting for.

We wonder, why such a battle? The enemy of our soul knows if he can defeat us here, he will be able to defeat us in every other area of our spiritual lives.

**Our devotions, or our Quiet Time,
should not be so much duty, as it is delight.**

Mary chose that good part in Luke 10:38-42 *"Now it came to pass, as they went, that he entered into a certain village: and a certain woman named Martha received him into her house. And she had a sister called Mary, which also sat at Jesus' feet, and heard his word. But Martha was cumbered about much serving, and came to him, and said, Lord, dost thou not care that my sister hath left me to serve alone? Bid her therefore that she help me. And Jesus answered and said unto her, Martha, Martha, thou art careful and troubled about many things: But one thing is needful: and Mary hath chosen that good part, which shall not be taken away from her."*

It is a privilege that we should not take lightly; the privilege of sharing union and communion with our Lord. It involves:

- Discipline
- Obedience
- Desire

It Is The Humbled Soul That Has Power With God

Before faith can be fully exercised, we must take the right attitude toward Christ.

"And, behold, a woman of Canaan came out of the same coasts, and cried unto him, saying, Have mercy on me, O Lord, thou Son of David; my daughter is grievously vexed with a devil. But he answered her not a word. And his disciples came and besought him, saying, Send her away; for she crieth after us. But he answered and said, I am not sent but unto the lost sheep of the house of Israel. Then came she and worshipped him, saying, Lord, help me. But he answered and said, It is not meet to take the children's bread, and to cast it to dogs. And she said, Truth, Lord: yet the dogs eat of the crumbs which fall from their masters' table. Then Jesus answered and said unto her, O woman, great is thy faith: be it unto thee even as thou wilt. And her daughter was made whole from that very hour."—Matthew 15:22-28

At the time, His mission was to the Jewish people; they were the children. This woman had no claim as a child, and the question was whether she was prepared to take the lower place. It is the humbled soul that has power with God. This woman showed herself prepared to put Jesus in His proper place as Lord and to take her own proper place. As she announced, "I don't want to take the children's food." She demonstrated her willingness to accept even the crumbs that might fall from a master's table; the portion that only a lowly dog would receive. Through her humility, the Lord was able to grant her heart's desire.

May God Give You Wisdom

Church Body

In Exodus 18, Jethro, the father-in-law of Moses, saw a problem and the need for a change in the way Moses was leading. Moses responded by showing the people the truth. He showed them the will of God, not the law, as the commands had not yet been given.

Jethro counseled Moses in a gentle but firm way. Exodus 18: 14, 17-18 *"And when Moses' father in law saw all that he did to the people, he said, what is this thing that thou doest to the people? Why sittest thou thyself alone, and all the people stand by thee from morning unto even? Moses' father-in-law said unto him, 'The thing that thou doest is not good. Thou wilt surely wear away, both thou, and this people that is with thee: for this thing is too heavy for thee; thou are not able to perform it thyself alone.' "*

Jethro basically told Moses to be the teacher and explain to the people what God expected of them. He advised Moses to choose wise, honest men to help him. The result of listening to wise counsel was that Moses' load was lightened and the people were satisfied.

Let our prayer be that not just one would have to do it all; let us be a part of the support system. Ask God where He wants you to be involved in the church. The body has many parts, yet it is in perfect balance when everyone shares the load.

The Key

A key is used as an instrument for fastening or unfastening a lock. Figuratively speaking, because of its power to open or to exclude from all treasures of a city or a house, the key is often used in scripture as a symbol of power and authority.

"And the key of the house of David will I lay upon his shoulder; so he shall open, and none shall shut; and he shall shut, and none shall open."—Isaiah 22:22

The power of the keys consisted not only in the supervision of the royal chambers, but also in deciding who was and who was not to be received in the kings' service.

Our Lord is represented as having the key of David. Revelation 3:7 *"And to the angel of the church in Philadelphia write: These things saith he that is holy, he that is true, he that hath the key of David, he that openeth, and no man shutteth; and shutteth, and no man openeth."*

God, receiving and excluding whom he pleases and committing to his apostles; to Peter first, as the most prominent member of the apostolic body, the keys of the kingdom.

"And I will give unto thee the keys of the kingdom of heaven: and whatsoever thou shalt bind on earth shall be bound in heaven: and whatsoever thou shalt loose on earth shall be loosed in heaven."
—Matthew 16:19

The key of knowledge pertaining to all spiritual things is in the scriptures that the scribes reserved exclusively to themselves. The figure used by our Lord is that of knowledge being a temple into which the scribes should have led the people, but whose gate they closed and held the key with jealous care, even their commentaries, hiding, rather than revealing knowledge.

"Woe unto you, lawyers! For ye have taken away the key of knowledge: ye entered not in yourselves, and them that were entering in ye hindered."—Luke 11:52

Up On The Mount

Mark 9:1-9 says *"Then he (Jesus) said unto them, Verily I say unto you, That there be some of them that stand here, which shall not taste of death, till they have seen the kingdom of God come with power. And after six days Jesus taketh with him Peter, and James, and John, and leadeth them up into an high mountain apart by themselves: and he was transfigured before them. And his raiment became shining, exceeding white as snow; so as no fuller on earth can white them. And there appeared unto them Elias with Moses: and they were talking with Jesus. And Peter answered and said to Jesus, Master, it is good for us to be here: and let us make three tabernacles; one for thee, and one for Moses, and one for Elias. For he wist not what so say; for they were sore afraid. And there was a cloud that overshadowed them: and a voice came out of the cloud, saying, This is my beloved Son: hear him. And suddenly, when they had looked round about, they saw no man any more, save Jesus only with themselves. And as they came down from the mountain, he charged them that they should tell no man what things they had seen til the Son of man were risen from the dead."*

Jesus took the three closest to Him, Peter, James, and John, and led them up into a high mountain apart by themselves. Jesus said that some who stood there with Him should not taste of death until they had seen the kingdom of God come with power. There, He (Jesus) was transfigured before them; a visible experience of Kingdom power, revealing the glory of Jesus the Messiah. His clothes became shining exceeding white as snow; so as no fuller on earth can white them. There appeared unto them Elias (Elijah) and Moses talking with Jesus. This signified that the law and the Prophets supported Jesus in His redemptive mission. Another thing for us to take note of is that there was a cloud that overshadowed them, and they heard a voice come out of the cloud saying, "This is my beloved Son, hear Him."

When one is taken up on the mountain with Jesus, there is much to be revealed there; much to be seen and heard. Do we desire to be so close to Him that He takes us upon the mountain to reveal to us the things we can witness afterwards?

Up On The Mount

All of you that would gladly believe all that the Lord says cherish every whisper of the conscience and the Spirit that convicts of sin, whatever it is. Whether it's a hasty temper, a sharp word, or an unloving or impatient thought, cherish that which condemns it in you as part of the schooling that is to bring you to Christ and full possession of His Salvation.

The new covenant is meant to meet the need for the power to keep us from sin which the old covenant could not give. Come with that need. It will prepare and open your heart for all the everlasting covenant frees you from.

"But now hath he obtained a more excellent ministry, by how much also he is the mediator of a better covenant, which was established upon better promises."—Hebrews 8:6

"For if that first covenant had been faultless, then should no place have been sought for the second. For finding fault with them, he saith, Behold the days come, saith the Lord, when I will make a new covenant with the house of Israel and with the house of Judah: Not according to the covenant that I made with their fathers in the day when I took them by the hand to lead them out of the land of Egypt; because they continued not in my covenant, and I regarded them not saith the Lord. For this is the covenant that I will make with the house of Israel after those days, saith the Lord; I will put my laws into their mind, and write them in their hearts: and I will be to them a God, and they shall be to me a people: And they shall not teach every man his neighbor, and every man his brother, saying, Know the Lord: for all shall know me, from the least to the greatest. For I will be merciful to their unrighteousness, and their sins and their iniquities will I remember no more. In that he saith, A new covenant, he hath made the first old, Now that which decayeth and waxeth old is ready to vanish away."—Hebrews 8:7-13

Let Us Encourage One Another

It is true that discouragement is one of Satan's greatest weapons against the children of God, but encouragement is God's answer to it.

When Moses came to the end of his career and was about to turn his responsibilities over to Joshua, the Lord told Moses to encourage and strengthen Joshua.

"But Joshua the son of Nun, which standeth before thee, he shall go in thither: encourage him: for he shall cause Israel to inherit it."—Deuteronomy 1:38

"But charge Joshua, and encourage him, and strengthen him: for he shall go over before this people, and he shall cause them to inherit the land which thou shalt see."—Deuteronomy 3:28

All of us; young and old; rich and poor; strong and weak need to be encouraged from time to time. How little we may know of the battles, fears and frustrations that struggle in the breast of people all around us. What a privilege it is that each of us can be God's instrument of encouragement to troubled hearts, if only we will.

"And this is the commandment, That we should believe on the name of his Son Jesus Christ, and love one another, as he gave us commandment."—I John 3:23

"For, brethren, ye have been called unto liberty; only use not liberty for an occasion to the flesh, but by love serve one another." —Galatians 5:13

The Family Fortune

A Family that has love for one another; a mutual compassion, care, and concern is fortunate. A family that is filled with joy and happiness; a home where there is singing and peace and confidence; where faith in God is real, and their trust is not only taught and talked about, but is a part of everyday living, these families have great security. Some families have lost the art and joy of family worship, but family is where this fortune is found. Worship and Bible reading can become as much a part of family life as eating and playing. The parents themselves are responsible to God first and then to his family. Parents' responsibilities are to point out by precept, then practice and show a pattern of example where the true riches are found.

"And thou shalt love the Lord thy God with all thine heart, and with all thy soul, and with all thy might. And these words, which I command thee this day, shall be in thine heart: And thou shalt teach them diligently unto thy children, and shalt talk of them when thou sittest in thine house, and when thou walkest by the way, and when thou liest down, and when thou risest up. And thou shalt bind them for a sign upon thine hand, and they shall be as frontlets between thine eyes. And thou shalt write them upon the posts of thy house, and on thy gates."—Deuteronomy 6:5-9

"Train up a child in the way he should go: and when he is old, he will not depart from it."—Proverbs 22:6

"And ye fathers, provoke not your children to wrath: but bring them up in the nurture and admonition of the Lord."—Ephesians 6:4

The Family Fortune

"And God heard their groaning, and God remembered his covenant with Abraham, with Isaac, and with Jacob. And God looked upon the children of Israel, and God had respect unto them."
—Exodus 2:24,25

God called Moses to lead His people from Egyptian bondage. Moses went to Pharaoh and said, "Let my people go." Pharaoh was not willing to let them go. He made things even harder for them and gave them more work to do, accusing them of being idle, and having too much time to think about their God. After a few of the plagues, he even tried to get Moses to compromise. He told Moses, "Okay, go! Just don't go very far away." Then; "Okay, go! Just the men should go." On and on; until finally, when all was accomplished in God's plans, Moses led them out. "The Egyptians shall know I am the Lord," and the children of Israel will know He is the Lord that bought them out of Egypt by a strong hand."

Satan has always tried to separate us and keep us apart from God and His plan for us. Satan works hard to keep us too busy to think on these things. Giving more work; harder work; his strategies are constant. Satan even tries to get us to compromise. His purpose is, don't get too involved or go too far, or don't make it a family thing - just you men go. None of these things work. God sends His Holy Spirit to lead us out of "Egypt" and the bondage of sin unto Him. He brings us out to bring us in.

**God is still at work in our hearts
giving us a desire to live a good life.**

God, by his Holy Spirit leads us out of the world
and the system of the world's thinking.

**He separates us. We become His people,
and He becomes our God.**

"And I will take you to me for a people, and I will be to you a God: and ye shall know that I am the Lord your God, which bringeth you out from under the burdens of the Egyptians. And I will bring you in unto the land, concerning the which I did swear to give it to Abraham, to Isaac, and to Jacob; and I will give it you for an heritage: I am the Lord."—Exodus 6:7,8

Trusting In The Lord

"Jesus said unto him, "Verily I say unto thee, That this night before the cock crow, thou shalt deny me thrice."—Matthew 26:34

Jesus knew that Simon's fallen human nature would fail under this test. Simon did not realize his own weakness. Simon was Peter's former name, in contrast to his new name and new character. Jesus said in Luke 22:31, *"Simon, Simon, behold, Satan hath desired to have you, that he may sift you as wheat: But I have prayed for thee, that thy faith fail not, and when thou are converted, strengthen thy brethren."*

Jesus prayed for Simon and knew that Simon's faith would not fail; the seed of eternal life was truly within him. Simon's failure would result in a complete "conversion". No longer would Simon trust in himself, but he would trust in the Lord completely. Peter's entire personality would be transformed "converted"; then Simon Peter would know exactly how to help others who would be tempted as he was. He became Peter; a strength and "rock" for others' lives.

Being More Aware

Naturally, whatever a person does a lot, they become more conscience of. If one is a painter of houses, he notices the houses that need painting even if he's not looking for them. A tree trimmer notices the trees that need trimmed. One that paints cars or pulls dents or does body work, he notices every dent. A person that cleans houses notices dust that no one else notices. On and on it goes.

I've noticed Paul, my husband's work so many times, through the extra jobs that he has done. Once he worked on a motorhome that needed lots of work; hard work. He tackled it with no complaints. There were rotten boards and beams to be replaced. He had to measure so everything fit just right. Lots of work! He put up drywall and painted by himself. When he finished, and all the work was done, all that anyone saw was the finished product. It appeared all new and well done. Beautiful! However, no one saw the work that went into it. Paul has never complained about the hard work. He is always satisfied to have a finished product.

Spiritually, are we as conscious and aware of our Heavenly Father's will like we should be. When I gave my heart to God, that was a new direction in my life. It was a new birth and it changed my life. My thoughts were different. I remember as we (our family) traveled, I would see a factory with hundreds of cars and think, "How many of those people are alive in God or how many are lost?" On the Sunday School bus on Sunday mornings, I would see little children playing or going to the store and know that they needed to be taught of God's love. They just need someone to bring them in. Are we aware of these things? God needs laborers to work. Are we conscious of these needs?

We need to be more conscious of the Father's will.
This is our work.

Do we see the people that need the Lord?

"Then saith he (Jesus) unto his disciples, The harvest truly is plenteous, but the laborers are few; Pray ye therefore the Lord of the harvest, that he will send forth laborers into his harvest."
—Matthew 9:37,38

Jesus Came To Do His Father's Will

Jesus was always aware of the needs. In John chapter four, He was tired and sat down on a well to rest. He was conscious of why He was there when a certain woman came to draw water from the well. He was aware of this soul's need. He gave her what she needed – "living" water. When His disciples came with food to eat, they said, "Master, eat." But Jesus said, "I have meat to eat that ye know not of." Then He said, "My meat is to do the will of Him that sent me and to finish His work."

He was doing the Father's will.

"Then cometh he to a city of Samaria, which is called Sychar, near to the parcel of ground that Jacob gave to his son Joseph."—John 4: 5

"Jesus saith unto them, My meat is to do the will of him that sent me, and to finish his work."— John 4: 34

Our Testimony Is Important

There was a woman in John chapter four who, after meeting Jesus, had left her water pot and gone back into the city and began to tell the men, "Come and see a man which told me all things that I ever did, is not this the Christ?"

Like the woman, they too knew the Messiah would come. They had heard of Christ no doubt and were waiting for Him to come. These people had lived in darkness for all these years, waiting for Christ to come. He would be the Savior, the light of the world. He would come to save from sin.

People today are in the same condition. If they have not met and received the Savior, they are still in darkness. The harvest is great; the laborers are few.

Many believed because of the woman's testimony; they came to Jesus for themselves. They believed because of His words. They heard Him personally.

Our testimony is important. Tell them about Jesus.

"And many of the Samaritans of that city believed on him for the saying of the woman, which testified, He told me all that ever I did. So when the Samaritans were come unto him, they besought him that he would tarry with them: and he abode there two days. And many more believed because of his own word; And said unto the woman, Now we believe, not because of thy saying for we have heard him ourselves, and know that this is indeed the Christ, the Savior of the world."—John 4:39-42

Consider The Lilies

We enjoy a lily's beauty and fragrance even though we cannot understand the miraculous transformation it represents. Why not do the same regarding God's miracles in the spiritual realm? God speaks to us through His wondrous works in the natural realm. He is saying: See what I can do with you if you will go the way I have planned for you. I desire to plant you too if you are willing. I will take you just as you are; ugly, marred by sin, polluted by this world, and held captive by Satan. As you accept My remedy for sin, and as the blood of Jesus Christ cleanses you, I will put my life within you. I will plant you with my Son in His death and change you into the image of His resurrection glory.

Jesus said to consider the lilies of the field. How they grow! Do they struggle to obtain life? No, they receive life as a gift from the creator. Do they strive to grow? No, they simply yield to nature's laws governing growth. Neither do they get their beauty because of their self-efforts. They are beautiful because it is their nature to be beautiful. How well they illustrate spiritual life and growth! Divine life is a gift given by God to each person who repents of his sins and accepts Christ as his personal Savior. Spiritual growth will come to each child of God who yields to spiritual laws.

Keep yourselves in the soil of the love of God.

Drink of the rain of the Spirit.

**Draw nourishment from the exceeding
great and precious promises.**

"*That by these ye might be partakers of the divine nature, having escaped the corruption that is in the world through lust.*"
—2 Peter 1:4

Consider The Lilies

There may come stormy days and sunny days; dark nights and rainy nights; times of heat and times of cold. If you are planted deeply in Him, resting continually in His love, yielding to His Spirit in every way, you will grow in strength and beauty far surpassing that of Solomon. The purity and fragrance of Christ you will shed forth and others will be attracted to Him, and He will say:

"My beloved spake, and said unto me, Rise up, my love, my fair one, and come away."—Song of Solomon 2:2

Words Giving Rest

Sometimes we see loved ones hurt deeply; nothing hurts more than when we see our children hurt. I remember once seeing one of mine hurt deeply, and it was from someone I never expected it. It was so hard seeing this. When I went to pray about this, God's Spirit spoke to me these words; "These things must needs be."

I understood then. Sometimes when hurt comes to us, it is for our growth, because it makes us stronger and we learn to forgive those that hurt us. This is one of the most needful lessons we will ever learn.

Forgiveness and Love overcome all.

"For if ye forgive men their trespasses, your heavenly Father will also forgive you."—Matthew 6:14

"Put on therefore, as the elect of God, holy and beloved bowels of mercies, kindness, humbleness of mind, meekness, longsuffering; Forbearing one another, and forgiving one another, if any man have a quarrel against any: even as Christ forgave you, so also do ye."
—Colossians 3:12, 13

My Special Place

When I first got saved in the spring of 1963, I had a special prayer room in an old storage room. The storage room adjoined the empty grocery store where we lived in three small rooms in the back. This storage room was the darkest room I had ever seen. It was all closed; no windows; no light coming in at all. This was my prayer room. I had a small foot stool in the center of the room I used as my altar. After I closed the door, I had to feel with my feet to the center of the room until I found the stool. I then knelt and entered the presence of my Father, and His glory filled the room until the darkness no longer existed. It was Wonderful. When our visit was done, I would open my eyes and would be so shocked at how dark the room was.

As I left my prayer room one day after praying, I hesitated at the little window just outside the room. Looking up at the sky, I saw a vision of a beautiful city, all aglow way up in the sky. It was a huge city, and it was bright and glowing with light. The words on my heart were "New Jerusalem".

For years, I remembered this vision but didn't really know exactly why I had seen the image or what its meaning was. That was about 55 years ago. This morning, January 4, 2018, I was reading the scriptures and remembered my Bible reading for the past couple days. I had been thinking of studying about being clothed in His Righteousness. I started reading in 2 Corinthians. I thought about it again as I read chapter 5:1,2. *"For we know that if our earthly house of this tabernacle were dissolved, we have a building of God, an house not made with hands, eternal in the heavens. For in this we groan, earnestly desiring to be clothed upon with our house which is from heaven."*

As I began running reference on these verses, it led me to Revelation 21:1,2, where it says, *"And I saw a new heaven and a new earth: for the first heaven and the first earth were passed away; and there was no more sea. And I John saw the holy city, new Jerusalem, coming down from God out of heaven, prepared as a bride adorned for her husband."*

The word prepared, was darker in print than the rest of the words. As I was dwelling on this, my thoughts went back to the day I came out of my prayer room, looked out the window and saw the vision.

My Special Place

I believe our special place, where we come into the presence and glory of God our Heavenly Father, is where we are prepared to be the Bride of Christ. As the Church, we must spend special time here. His glory will show through us, His body. He said, *"Ye are the light of the world. A city that is set on a hill cannot be hid. Neither do men light a candle, and put it under a bushel, but on a candlestick; and it giveth light unto all that are in the house. Let your light so shine before men, that they may see your good works, and glorify your Father which is in heaven."*—Matthew 5:14-16

As we spend our time in this special place, we will see God's will done in our churches and in our families. Jesus said, *"Our Father which art in heaven, Hallowed be thy name, Thy kingdom come, thy will be done in earth as it is in heaven."*—Matthew 6:9,10

What a wonderful Father and Savior we have with His Spirit to guide us.

"And I saw a new heaven and a new earth: for the first heaven and the first earth were passed away; and there was no more sea. And I John saw the holy city, new Jerusalem, coming down from God out of heaven, prepared as a bride adorned for her husband. And I heard a great voice out of heaven saying, Behold, the tabernacle of God is with men, and he will dwell with them, and they shall be his people, and God himself shall be with them, and be their God. And God shall wipe away all tears from their eyes; and there shall be no more death, neither sorrow, nor crying, neither shall there be any more pain: for the former things are passed away. And he that sat upon the throne said, Behold, I make all things new. And he said unto me, Write: For these words are true and faithful. And he said unto me, It is done, I am Alpha and Omega, the beginning and the end. I will give unto him that is athirst of the fountain of the water of life freely." — Revelation 21:1-6

A Commission And A Revelation

God has dealt with me in dreams many times. In one of these dreams, I had a vision of someone knocking at the door. When I went to the door, it seemed the whole front was glass. When I opened the door, there was a man standing there. His hair was white, and I had no fear or mistrust. I had a feeling of complete peace. He handed me a piece of paper and said, "If you know any children without a father."

That part of the dream ended, and then there was a second part.

In the dream, I heard a knock at the back door and went to answer it. When I opened the door, a man stood there and said, "I came after the children." I kept looking at him with mistrust with a troubled feeling. As I stared at him, suddenly, a mask fell from his face.

I felt this was a commission to bring the fatherless to Him.

Those without Him are fatherless and need Him. The man at the back door in the dream was a revelation of discernment. He only pretended to be the same one who had been at the front door. God's Spirit gives discernment, so we can know the difference.

Temptation And Sin

The temptation of Eve was threefold:

1. Lust of the flesh; physical appetite; the tree good for food.
2. Lust of the eyes; sensitive to beauty; looks good
3. Pride of life; ambition; a desire to become wise;

Sin is more than an act; it is also an attitude of unbelief which eventually produces indifference and disobedience to the Word of God.

"Submit yourselves therefore to God. Resist the devil and he will flee from you."—James 4:7

Because Adam and Eve did not submit to God, they were both unable to resist the devil. The sin of our first parents (Adam and Eve) was rebellion against the expressed will of God, as indeed is all sin. Sin is crossing God's will.

Let us be faithful to God's will, keeping His word.

"But be ye doers of the word, and not hearers only, deceiving your own selves."—James 1:22

The Cross

God lifts us with Himself. With those arms outstretched, He reaches out to lift to that terrible vantage point. All who would be saved He shows the view from the Cross. Only from here are you able to see things as they really are.

- From the cross, you will see how terrible our sin is; that it would do this to the pure Son of God.

- From the cross, you will see how great Christ's sufferings were; that He should go through all this for us.

- From the cross, you will see how great God's love is; that He should choose this way to save us when there was no other.

If you would be saved, you must open your eyes to a view of yourself, the world, and the Savior that the flesh naturally shrinks from.

In looking, you will live!

Author unknown

Temptation And Sin

The temptation of Eve was threefold:

1. Lust of the flesh; physical appetite; the tree good for food.
2. Lust of the eyes; sensitive to beauty; looks good
3. Pride of life; ambition; a desire to become wise;

Sin is more than an act; it is also an attitude of unbelief which eventually produces indifference and disobedience to the Word of God.

"Submit yourselves therefore to God. Resist the devil and he will flee from you."—James 4:7

Because Adam and Eve did not submit to God, they were both unable to resist the devil. The sin of our first parents (Adam and Eve) was rebellion against the expressed will of God, as indeed is all sin. Sin is crossing God's will.

Let us be faithful to God's will, keeping His word.

"But be ye doers of the word, and not hearers only, deceiving your own selves."—James 1:22

The Cross

God lifts us with Himself. With those arms outstretched, He reaches out to lift to that terrible vantage point. All who would be saved He shows the view from the Cross. Only from here are you able to see things as they really are.

- From the cross, you will see how terrible our sin is; that it would do this to the pure Son of God.

- From the cross, you will see how great Christ's sufferings were; that He should go through all this for us.

- From the cross, you will see how great God's love is; that He should choose this way to save us when there was no other.

If you would be saved, you must open your eyes to a view of yourself, the world, and the Savior that the flesh naturally shrinks from.

In looking, you will live!

Author unknown

God Always Keeps His Promise

God always keeps His promises, even though it may be years sometimes before we see the promise come to pass. It will come, just as He has said.

In Genesis 15:4, God promised Abraham a son. It was twenty-five years before Abraham and Sarah had this promised son Isaac. It did come to pass, "at the set time", in Genesis 21:2, just as God said.

God gave me a promise years ago. It was in 1964. I had received Jesus into my life and had been born again in 1963. My husband, Paul, had not gone to the altar the night I did and was still unsaved when I had the dream. In this dream, I was pleading with my husband. I told him, "God said; My Spirit shall not always strive with man." That was all of the dream. As I awoke, I heard a voice speak loudly, "In the eleventh hour."

So many years had gone by. Somewhere around 1993, I had another dream. I dreamed of a cloudy white room, and Paul was passing out gifts. As I looked at his hand, he was wearing a ring. The ring had the face of a clock or watch on top of it. As I awoke, I started to pray, "Lord, are you showing me it is time?"

Things began to change.

Paul had always loved wood working and making things. He began making things for the grandchildren and children. He made book cases, cedar chests, and several other things for me. Paul did beautiful work. One day he came home and went through the house. I was reading and as he went through the room, the Lord spoke to my heart and said; "He won't be here long." As soon as Paul was through the room, I hurried to the bedroom, got on my knees and began to weep before the Lord. I asked Him; "Lord can I stand that?" He began to take me through the scriptures as I entered into His presence. He took me to the place where Moses asked to see God's glory in Exodus. 33:21,22 *"And the Lord said, Behold, there is a place by me and thou shalt stand upon a rock… I will put thee in a clift of the rock, and will cover thee with my hand while I pass by."* I knew He would hide me in Him and I could stand through this.

Soon we found out that Paul had lung cancer in the fourth stage. We grew closer together, and Paul began going with me to God's house. He continued making the wooden shelves and chests and things for the children. He would go to the altar and pray at church, but he would come back looking so sad. Then one night he prayed, and it was all different. He had tears running down his face and a smile of joy and a peace. He said, "I felt something tonight I was afraid I would never feel again." I knew God had answered the promise and answered Paul's prayer.

Paul was so happy and so changed. I was so thankful for all God's goodness and mercies to us all.

He is our Wonderful Savior and our Wonderful Father.

After all is passed, we see His glory!

Special Times With Little Ones

Before children start to school, there are special times you just enjoy being with them telling them about Jesus and sharing His love with them. I remember such a morning as I sat with Stephen our youngest one. Stephen was about four years old. We were reading and talking about Abraham and Isaac going up to Mt. Moriah in obedience to God. He had asked Abraham to take Isaac his beloved son and offer him as a sacrifice. No words could have expressed what Abraham must have felt. But he immediately obeyed. In the morning, he rose up early. It was a three-day journey. Isaac asked his father, "Where is the lamb for a burnt offering?" As they went on to the place God had shown Abraham, Abraham answered and said, "My son, God will provide himself a lamb for a burnt offering." They went; both together. The Bible says as they came to the place which God had told him, Abraham built an altar there, laid the wood in order, bound Isaac his son and laid him on the altar upon the wood. Abraham stretched forth his hand and took the knife to slay his son. The angel of the Lord called unto him out of heaven, and said, "Abraham, Abraham." Abraham answered, "Here am I." The angel of the Lord told him, "Lay not thine hand upon the lad, neither do anything unto him; for now I know that thou fearest God, seeing thou hast not withheld thy son, thine only son from me." (Genesis 22:12)

And Abraham lifted his eyes and looked and behold behind him a ram caught in a thicket by his horns: and Abraham went and took the ram and offered him up for a burnt offering in the stead of his son.—Gen 22:13

As we read and talked about this Bible story that day, Stephen's eyes were filled with tears, and he said, "God gave His son."

We knew this was the One provided; Jehovah-Jireh meaning God will provide. This was also the same mountain that God would some years later give His son as a sacrifice for our sins.

A Separate People

Have you ever been in a crowd of people or just noticed a person that stood out and you thought, "There is something different about that person; something outstanding?" What makes a people separate from all people? What makes that difference? I believe we find the answer to this in Exodus 33:13

"Now therefore, I pray thee, if I have found grace in thy sight, shew me now thy way, that I may know thee, that I may find grace in thy sight: and consider that this nation is thy people." "And God said, My presence shall go with thee, and I will give thee rest."—Exodus 33:13,14

Moses didn't want to go except God's presence go with him. He said, *"For wherein shall it be known here that I and thy people have found grace in thy sight? Is it not in that thou goest with us? So shall we be separated, I and thy people from all the people that are upon the face of the earth. And the Lord said unto Moses, I will do this thing also that thou hast spoken; for thou hast found grace in my sight, and I know thee by name."*—Exodus 33:16,17

**God's presence with and in His people,
makes the difference.**

Waiting For God's Time

God has a set time for all things,
and we must wait for it.

Although Moses was trained in Egypt, he never forgot his nurse, who was his mother, or his heritage. He no doubt, knew and felt God's call was upon his life. Exodus 2:11 says, *"And it came to pass in those days, when Moses was grown, that he went out unto his brethren and looked on their burdens: and he spied an Egyptian smiting an Hebrew one of his brethren."*

Moses did what he thought he should do. As the result, he had to flee for his life.

We find where he fled to Midian and kept his father-in-law's sheep. He had been at the back side of the desert for about 40 years when God came to reveal His will to Moses.

Waiting For God's Time And Revelation

"But when it pleased God, who separated me from my mother's womb, and called me by his grace, To reveal his Son in me, that I might preach him among the heathen; immediately I conferred not with flesh and blood: "Neither went I up to Jerusalem to them which were apostles before me; but I went into Arabia, and returned again unto Damascus."—Galatians 1:15-17

Paul perceived no human instruction following his conversion but withdrew to Arabia where God revealed to him the substance of the Gospel.

Paul said in Galatians 1: 11,12 *"But I certify (assure) you brethren, that the gospel which was preached of me is not after man (derived from any human source), For I neither received it of man, neither was I taught it, but by the revelation of Jesus Christ."*

May we all wait on God's timing.

"Shew me thy ways, O LORD; teach me thy paths. Lead me in thy truth, and teach me: for thou art the God of my salvation; on thee do I wait all the day."—Psalm 25:4,5

It Is God's Will For Us To Praise Him And His Works

"I will praise thee, O LORD, with my whole heart; I will shew forth all thy marvelous works."—Psalm 9:1

"I will extol thee, my God, O King; and I will bless thy name for ever and ever. Every day will I bless thee: and I will praise thy name for ever and ever. Great is the LORD, and greatly to be praised; and his greatness is unsearchable. One generation shall praise thy works to another, and shall declare thy mighty acts. I will speak of the glorious honor of thy majesty, and of thy wondrous works. And men shall speak of the might of thy terrible acts: and I will declare thy greatness. They shall abundantly utter the memory of thy great goodness, and shall sing of thy righteousness. The LORD is gracious, and full of compassion; slow to anger, and of great mercy. The LORD is good to all: and his tender mercies are over all his works. All thy works shall praise thee, O LORD; and thy saints shall bless thee. They shall speak of the glory of thy kingdom, and talk of thy power; To make known to the sons of men his mighty acts, and the glorious majesty of his kingdom. Thy kingdom is an everlasting kingdom, and thy dominion endureth throughout all generations. The LORD upholdeth all that fall, and raiseth up all those that be bowed down. The eyes of all wait upon thee; and thou givest them their meat in due season. Thou openest thine hand, and satisfiest the desire of every living thing. The LORD is righteous in all his ways, and

holy in all his works. The LORD is nigh unto all them that call upon him, to all that call upon him in truth. He will fulfill the desire of them that fear him: he also will hear their cry, and will save them. The LORD preserveth all them that love him: but all the wicked will he destroy. My mouth shall speak the praise of the LORD: and let all flesh bless his holy name for ever and ever." —Psalm 145:1-21

There is a true praise in the thankful telling forth to others of our Heavenly Father's dealings with us.

One generation shall praise thy works to another and declare thy mighty acts.

Conduct

The decisions we make in this world is much like living in a countryside where each road and each path leads in a different direction. One highway may lead North to Canada and another to Chicago, Illinois. One road leads to New York and another to Florida. All such highways have destinations. They all lead somewhere. Country backroads lead somewhere; one to Smith's farm and another to the Brown's farm. Even paths in a yard lead to the garden or the barn or to the house.

Likewise, a man's conduct leads to certain consequences. The laws of harvest never change. Just so in the wisdom of God; the laws of nature do not change. Action may take time to arrive at its consequence, but God knows from the beginning when I act in a certain way where my conduct will lead me.

The flowers and plants have certain needs to prosper, such as the proper soil, ample water, and adequate sunshine. As far as our soul is concerned, it too needs certain conditions under which to prosper. One of these things is the favor of God. This I receive through obedience to Him. Another thing we must have is the Word of God. It will show us which way to go and let us know if we have taken a wrong path, and if so, how to get back on the right one.

Reflections

If our spiritual lives were to be shown in some special mirror with all of our inner thoughts, feelings, and motives revealed, would the way we look to God be a shock to us? The Lord has given us mirrors which reflect our inner selves, if we have the courage to look. A place where spirit-filled believers are gathered is an excellent climate in which to come face to face with our real selves. A person who has neglected his spiritual life is not comfortable around those who are truly filled with God's spirit. Another way the Lord lets us see ourselves is through the constructive criticism of those who love us. Are we able to bear this? Still another way is to examine our communication with the Lord. Do we share all our plans and problems freely with Him? Do we hold back some things; those personal plans we cherish, for instance, and would not want Him to change? Do we avoid the sacred solitude of His presence, or do we enjoy the hour of prayer? Finally, God's Word is a faithful mirror of the spirit. Can we read and truly apply it to our lives?

Oh, to be like Him! Every Christian wants this more than anything. What blessings the Lord has in store for us who are willing to see ourselves as God sees us and to pattern our lives after His. Not only will our outward appearance show our consecration, but our words and deeds will be His, not our own. Our faces will shine with His presence; our eyes will see with His eyes; His compassion will replace our own quick and unfeeling criticism. His divine love will radiate from our lives and the precious fruit of the Spirit will be ours.

We beautify ourselves in many ways, but physical loveliness must fade at last. The truly beautiful are those who look into the mirrors of the Spirit and pray earnestly.

Let the beauty of the Lord our God be upon us.

Old Things Are Past Away

Matthew 9: 16,17 *"No man putteth a piece of new cloth unto an old garment, for that which is put in to fill it up taketh from the garment, and the rent is made worse. Neither do men put new wine into old bottles: else the bottles break and the wine runneth out and the bottles perish: but they put new wine into new bottles, and both are preserved."*

The old forms of Judaism could not contain the spiritual freshness of the gospel. Grace cannot be sewn onto or poured into the system of legalism. His Grace did not come to patch up a brittle, worn out, and obsolete system.

Jesus came to offer a new life imparted by faith in Him.
Behold, all things are new.
Old things are passed away.

I Am Not Ashamed

"For I am not ashamed of the gospel of Christ: for it is the power of God unto Salvation to everyone that believeth…"—Romans 1:16

What does it mean to share your faith?
How can you begin?

Phillip was eager to preach about Christ
wherever he journeyed.
Are you as bold in your witnessing?

Studying the Bible, praying, supporting relationships with other Christians in difficult situations, and depending on the Holy Spirit are all essential to growth. However, we also grow by sharing our faith with the world.

Jesus said in Matthew 5:13 that we are the salt of the earth. He meant we belong out in the world sharing His love with others. The gospel can change the lives of the people to whom we witness. We are the world's salt when we make other people aware of our faith on the job, in our home, and at school.

By reflecting Christlike qualities in our relationships and by introducing friends to Jesus, we bring out the best in life just as salt brings out the best in food.

Sitting At Jesus' Feet

"Now a certain man was sick named Lazarus, of Bethany, the town of Mary and her sister Martha."—John 11:1

I thought about Mary, the sister of Martha and Lazarus; the same Mary that anointed Jesus' feet with fragrant ointment and wiped them with her hair.

Luke records the same occasion.

"Now it came to pass, as they went, that he entered into a certain village: and a certain woman named Martha received him into her house. And she had a sister called Mary, which also sat at Jesus' feet, and heard his word."—Luke 10: 38,39

Jesus commented to Martha who was careful or worried about many things that one thing was needful. Mary had chosen that good part; to sit and learn at the feet of Jesus. Many things in life are important, but we must choose each day to sit at Jesus' feet, humbly, and hear His words.

Learning "at the feet" of Jesus is the most important thing!

The Spirit Of The World And The Spirit Of God

The world has a way of its own. Jesus' coming gives us the true way.

Jesus said in John 14:6 *"I am the Way, the Truth, and the Life, no man cometh unto the father, but by me."*

We must learn to follow Jesus if we are to know the Father. Jesus said, I will pray the Father, and He shall give us another Comforter, that He may abide with you forever.

"Even the Spirit of Truth; whom the world cannot receive, because it seeth him not, neither knoweth him: but ye know him; for he dwelleth with you, and shall be in you."—John 14:17

Jesus said this to His disciples at their last meeting before He went to the cross. Jesus said that the world cannot receive the Spirit of Truth. The spirit of the world knows only the visible and lives by that.

God calls us, by His Spirit, out from the world to live a separate life. A Way of Life and a truth that only God, by His Spirit can do.

"But the Comforter, which is the Holy Ghost, whom the Father will send in my name, he shall teach you all things, and bring all things to your remembrance, whatsoever I have said unto you."
— John 14:26

The Comforter teaches us and shows us all things. He reminds us of His Words and His works. He gives us peace; not the kind the world gives, but His peace.

By What Power Do You Do This?

"And it came to pass on the morrow, that their rulers, and elders, and scribes, And Annas, the high priest, and Caiaphas, and John, and Alexander, and as many as were of the kindred of the high priest, were gathered together at Jerusalem. And when they had set them in the midst, they asked, By what power, or by what name, have ye done this?"—Acts 4:5-7

The leaders couldn't understand how such a thing could be done by men of this standing. They perceived these men, Peter and John, were uneducated and to their thinking, ignorant.

"Then Peter, filled with the Holy Ghost, said unto them, Ye rulers of the people, and elders of Israel, If we this day be examined of the good deed done to the impotent man, by what means he is made whole; Be it known unto you all, and to all the people of Israel, that by the name of Jesus Christ of Nazareth, whom ye crucified, whom God raised from the dead, even by him doth this man stand here before you whole."—Acts 4:8-10

When we look at the helpless man who had laid all these years, we can also see the helplessness of all mankind until Jesus came and set us free.

"This is the stone which was set at nought of you builders, which is become the head of the corner. Neither is there salvation in any other: For there is none other name under heaven given among

men, whereby we must be saved. Now when they saw the boldness of Peter and John, and perceived that they were unlearned and ignorant men, they marveled; and they took knowledge of them, that they had been with Jesus. And beholding the man which was healed standing with them, they could say nothing against it."—Acts 4:11-14

One thing they marveled at was the fact that they realized they had been with Jesus.

Man was hopeless and helpless to do anything about his condition; he was lost and sinful. The sentence of death was upon him until Jesus came, died, raised from the dead, and ascended, conquering Satan, Hell, and the Grave. It is only through Him and faith in His name and what He has done, we are no longer helpless or hopeless.

The Anointed Savior Is Worthy Of All Praise!

Today when a miracle is done, people wonder at this. Two people may observe, and one say, "Oh that is Wonderful!" and the other may question, "By what authority do you do this?" The answer is the same; "Why marvel ye at this or why look ye so intently (earnestly) on us, as though by our own power or holiness we had done this miracle?" Healing is by Faith in the name of Jesus.

In the cultural setting of the Bible, a name could not be separated from the person bearing that name. The very name "Jesus Christ" means "Anointed Savior".

Years ago, I had a dream very much like this. I was dreaming of praying for people and one sister said, "Oh, it must be wonderful!" Another sister's eyes asked me the question, "By what authority do you do this?" I answered her, "You know, Jesus, with the white robe."

It is by His Power, His Holiness, and His Righteousness. His Name is that Authority.

The Search For Happiness

"The woman (at the well) saith unto him, I know that Messias cometh, which is called Christ: when he is come, he will tell us all things." (John 4:25) Just as Jesus talked to the woman at the well, God's word talks to us, showing us our sins.

Jesus is the Word!

"And the Word was made flesh, and dwelt among us, (and we beheld his glory, the glory as of the only begotten of the Father,) full of Grace and Truth."—John 1:14

The entrance of God's words giveth light.

"The entrance of thy words giveth light; it giveth understanding unto the simple."—Psalm 119:130

"Thy word is a lamp unto my feet, and a light unto my path."—Psalm 119:105

People search for happiness, joy, and peace in a troubled world. They try to satisfy that hunger with many things but can't find it. Like the woman at the well, she no doubt, had that lack of satisfaction in her life. Jesus said the water He gives will satisfy. One would never thirst again because the water He gives shall be in him a well of living water, springing up into everlasting life. One who drinks that water is satisfied and never thirsts again for this water satisfies completely.

Like the song that says; "I searched for Him, but I knew not what I searched for. I longed for Him, but I knew not what I longed for, Then I found Jesus. I knew that I would search no more. He filled that longing down in my soul."

There is a place in our hearts for God alone. Until He fills that place, something is missing. The only thing that can fill all voids and satisfy the thirsting of the soul is the living presence of the indwelling Holy Spirit that we receive when we accept Jesus Christ as Savior and Lord of our lives.

The Search For Happiness

To be mindful of what pleases God, we must be in His presence often.

We can be around a person for a while, and we will notice ourselves picking up that persons' ways, their speech, and even actions. We need to be in prayer much, be in God's presence much to become like Him. We will begin to see Him as He is and begin to be more and more like Him. Jesus said, "I am the Way, the Truth, and the Life." We must live and walk in the way Jesus showed us by His life if we will have life in us.

"Then Jesus said unto them, Verily, verily, I say unto you, Except ye eat the flesh of the Son of man, and drink his blood, ye have no life in you. He that eateth my flesh and drinketh my blood, dwelleth in me and I in him. As the living Father hath sent me and I live by the Father: so he that eateth me, even he shall live by me."
—John 6:53,56,57

Jesus lived by the Word of God; "Man shall not live by bread alone, but by every Word that proceeds out of the mouth of God." Jesus was saying that He lived by the Father. Jesus said, "He that eateth me; even he shall live by me."

There is only "One" way.
There is only "One" door we must enter.
There is only "One" bread of life.
Jesus said, "I am the Way. I am the bread of life."

A Prayer Was Prayed; God Heard

"And this is the confidence that we have in him, that, if we ask any thing according to his will, he heareth us: And if we know that he hear us, whatsoever we ask, we know that we have the petitions that we desire of him."—I John 5:14, 15

This prayer was according to God's will. Things began to move, for the worse seemingly. Upon remembering my prayer, I took new courage.

God sometimes must change or rearrange things. Through faith, we must keep holding on through the storms knowing after a while it will be done.

"Now the just shall live by faith: but if any man draw back, my soul shall have no pleasure in him."—Hebrews 10:38

We must put our confidence in him.
We also need patience.

"For ye have need of patience, that after ye have done the will of God, ye might receive the promise."—Hebrews 10:36

We must continually trust God.

The Meaning Of Meekness

The word "meekness" is often associated with the idea of being hesitant or subdued. Meekness is one of the fruit of the Spirit. It is a form of expression not a negative quality. Moses was called the meekest of all men by God Himself. He was not indifferent to the charges of Miriam nor the complaints of the Israelites. He certainly held strong under provocation. Meekness is action, not inaction. It closes a mouth in time of temper. It forgives an insult; it restores the erring. It exercises patience in opposition.

The Spirit works in you; fruit comes from His working. You work together with Him and the activity produces growth. If you must do something, act.

"Bless them that curse you, do good to them that hate you, and pray for them which despitefully use you and persecute you." That is action in the highest order.

That was the way of Christ when He was reviled; He reviled not again but blessed.

"The meek will he guide in judgment: and the meek will he teach his way."—Psalm 25:9

Symbols Of The Word Of God

1. A hammer – To convict
   Jeremiah 23:29 *"Is not my Word like as a fire? saith the Lord; and like a hammer that breaketh the rock in pieces?"*

2. A Fire – to refine
   Jeremiah 23:29 *"Is not my Word like as a fire? saith the Lord; and like a hammer that breaketh the rock in pieces?"*

3. A Mirror – to reflect
   James 1:23, 24 *"For if any be a hearer of the word, and not a doer, he is like unto a man beholding his natural face in a glass: For he beholdeth himself, and goeth his way, and straightway forgetteth what manner of man he was."*

4. A seed – to multiply
   I Peter 1:23 *"Being born again, not of corruptible seed, but of incorruptible, by the word of God, which liveth and abideth for ever."*

5. A laver – to cleanse
   Ephesians 5:26 *"That he might sanctify and cleanse it with the washing of water by the word."*

6. A Lamp – to guide
   Psalm 119:105 *"Thy word is a lamp unto my feet, and a light unto my path."*

7. Rain and Snow – to refresh
   Isaiah 55:10,11 *"For as the rain cometh down, and the snow from heaven, and returneth not thither, but watereth the earth, and maketh it bring forth and bud, that it may give seed to the sower, and bread to the eater: So shall my word be that goeth forth out of my mouth: it shall not return unto me void, but it shall accomplish that which I please, and it shall prosper in the thing whereto I sent it."*

Symbols Of The Word Of God

8. A Sword – to cut

   Hebrews 4:12 *"For the word of God is quick, and powerful, and sharper than any two-edged sword, piercing even to the dividing asunder of soul and spirit, and of the joints and marrow, and is a discerner of the thoughts and intents of the heart."*

   Ephesians 6:17 *"And take the helmet of Salvation, and the sword of the Spirit, which is the word of God:"*

9. Gold – to enrich

   Psalm 19:7-11 *"The law of the Lord is perfect, converting the soul: the testimony of the Lord is sure, making wise the simple. The statues of the Lord are right, rejoicing the heart: the commandment of the Lord is pure, enlightening the eyes. The fear of the Lord is clean, enduring forever: the judgement of the Lord are true and righteous altogether. More to be desired are they than gold, yea, than much fine gold: sweeter also than honey and the honeycomb. Moreover by them is thy servant warned: and in keeping of them there is great reward."*

10. Power – to create faith and eternal life

    Romans 10:17 *"So then faith cometh by hearing, and hearing by the word of God."*

    I Peter 1:23 *"Being born again, not of corruptible seed, but of incorruptible, by the word of God, which liveth and abideth for ever."*

11. Food – to nourish

12. Milk – for babes.

    I Peter 2:2 *"As newborn babes, desire the sincere milk of the word, that ye may grow thereby."*

13. Bread – for the hungry.

    Matthew 4:4 *"But He (Jesus) answered and said, It is written, Man shall not live by bread alone, but by every word that proceedeth out of the mouth of God."*

14. Meat – for men.

    Hebrews 5:11-14 *"Of whom we have many things to say, and hard to be uttered, seeing ye are dull of hearing. For when for the time ye ought to be teachers, ye have need that one teach you again which be the first principles of the oracles of God; and are become such as have need of milk, and not of strong meat. For every one that useth milk is unskillful in the word of righteousness: for he is a babe. But strong meat belongeth to them that are full age, even those who by reason of use have their senses exercised to discern both good and evil."*

15. Honey – For desert.

    Psalm 19:10 *"More to be desired are they than gold, yea, than much fine gold: sweeter also than honey and the honeycomb."*

Seven Steps In Obtaining Help

1. Recognition of a meeting place with God

   Hebrews 4:16 *"Let us therefore come boldly unto the throne of grace, that we may obtain mercy, and find grace to help in time of need."*

2. Consciousness that this meeting place is made possible through the atoning blood of Christ

   Hebrews 10: 19, 20 *"Having therefore, brethren, boldness to enter into the holiest by the blood of Jesus. By a new and living way, which he hath consecrated for us, through the veil, that is to say, his flesh."*

3. Obedience in coming to this throne

   Hebrews 10: 22 *"Let us draw near with a true heart in full assurance of faith, having our hearts sprinkled from an evil conscience, and our bodies washed with pure water."*

4. Calling upon God for mercy and grace in time of need. To obtain mercy for the past; grace for present and future

   Hebrews 4:16 *"Let us therefore come boldly unto the throne of grace, that we may obtain mercy, and find grace to help in time of need."*

5. Boldness to approach

   Hebrews 4:16 *"Let us therefore come boldly unto the throne of grace, that we may obtain mercy, and find grace to help in time of need."*

6. Fervency and earnestness in presenting needs

   James 5:16 *"Confess your faults one to another, and pray one for another, that ye may be healed. The effectual fervent prayer of a righteous man availeth much."*

   Luke 11:5-13 *"And he (Jesus) said unto them, Which of you shall have a friend, and shall go unto him at midnight, and say unto him, Friend, lend me three loaves. For a friend of mine in his journey is come to me, and I have nothing to set before him. And he from within shall answer and say, Trouble me not: the door is now shut, and my children are with me in bed; I cannot rise and give thee. I say unto you, Though he will not rise and give him, because he is his friend, yet because of his importunity he will rise and give him as many as he needeth. And I say unto you, Ask, and it shall be given you; seek, and ye shall find; knock and it shall be opened unto you. For everyone that asketh receiveth; and he that seeketh findeth; and to him that knocketh it shall be opened. If a son shall ask bread of any of you that is a father, will he give him a stone? Or if he ask a fish, will he for a fish give him a serpent? Or if he shall ask an egg, will he offer him a scorpion? If ye then, being evil, know how to give good gifts unto your children: how much more shall your heavenly Father give the Holy Spirit to them that ask him?"*

7. Faith in the answer

   Hebrews 11:6 *"But without faith it is impossible to please him: for he that cometh to God must believe that he is, and that he is a rewarder of them that diligently seek him."*

   James 1:5-8 *"If any of you lack wisdom, let him ask of God, that giveth to all men liberally, and upbraideth not; and it shall be given him. But let him ask in faith, nothing wavering. For he that wavereth is like a wave of the sea driven with the wind and tossed. For let not that man think that he shall receive anything of the Lord. A double minded man is unstable in all his ways."*

Matthew 17:20 *"And Jesus said unto them, Because of your unbelief: for verily I say unto you, If ye have faith as a grain of mustard seed, ye shall say unto this mountain, Remove hence to yonder place and it shall remove; and nothing shall be impossible unto you."*

Matthew 21:22 *"And all things, whatsoever ye shall ask in prayer, believing, ye shall receive."*

Mark 11:22-24 *"And Jesus answering saith unto them, Have faith in God. For verily I say unto you that whosoever shall say unto this mountain, be thou removed, and be thou cast into the sea; and shall not doubt in his heart, but shall believe that those things which he saith shall come to pass; he shall have whatsoever he saith. Therefore, I say unto you, What things soever ye desire, when ye pray, believe that ye receive them, and ye shall have them."*

When Thou Hast Shut The Door

"But thou, when thou prayest, enter into thy closet, and when thou hast shut thy door, pray to thy Father which is in secret; and thy Father which seeth in secret shall reward thee openly."
—Matthew 6:6

I dreamed I was praying. I was in the Spirit with my head upon my Father's breast, absorbed in His love. Others around could see me and tell I was leaning upon my Father, but they couldn't see Him. There were so many faces around, but those didn't bother me or frighten me. The scripture came to me: Perfect love casteth out all fear.

How do we get this perfect love?
What about this place of love?

Isn't that what Jesus meant when He said in Matthew 6:6? *"But thou when thou prayest, enter into thy closet, and when thou hast shut thy door."*

When we enter and shut the door, we are shutting out all that would hinder us, resting in His complete presence.

There is no fear there.
Spending quality time here will keep us at all times.

We Must Be Changed

When we suffer and struggle, do we believe
the Holy Spirit is doing what He came to do?

He is the ruler bringing us through; making us an overcomer through it, over satan, the flesh, and our molded ways. Believe Him; Lean on Him; Look to Him; Trust Him. This is what He came to do, and He will do it.

So many times we are like the Jews when Jesus came; they hadn't expected Him to come as a babe and grow up as He did. They had expected a king coming to take rulership and to conquer. Yet, that is just what Jesus did in our lives. He conquered death; satan; all things.

What a wonderful Savior He is!
We can trust Him.

So many times in my life, I remembered His word:

"For we know that all things work together for good to them that love God, to them who are the called according to His purpose." — Romans 8:28

Build The Home

The breakdown of the home results in the breakdown of the homeland. The nation is no stronger than its homes and its home life. Give a start in life that includes character, moral integrity, and a spiritual foundation.

**Build a home with care and common sense.
Build it on a spiritual foundation.**

- Build character into the home:

   Instill a sense of honesty and being fair, not giving children everything they want nor doing everything for them. They must be taught to recognize certain responsibilities as their own and to earn their own way.

- Emotional development of a child:

   He must be assured he is loved, not only by God but also by the members of his family. He must have a feeling of "belonging". He has the need for words of commendation for his achievements and of encouragement for his constructive endeavors.

- Mental Development:

   In this modern age of movies, radio, television, comic books, and cluttered magazine stands, there are influences that are not good. Video games that are out today must be limited in time spent and parent approved.

Important Announcement!
Great Event!
What?

The Coming of The Son of God!

"Which also said, Ye men of Galilee, why stand ye gazing up into heaven? This same Jesus, which is taken up from you into heaven, shall so come in like manner as ye have seen him go into heaven." —Acts 1:11

HOW?

"And then shall appear the sign of the Son of man in heaven and then shall all the tribes of the earth mourn, and they shall see the Son of man coming in the clouds of heaven with power and great glory."—Matthew 24:30

WHEN?

"Watch therefore: for ye know not what hour your Lord doth come."—Matthew 24:42

WHAT ARE WE ADVISED TO DO?

"Therefore be ye also ready: for in such an hour as ye think not the Son of man cometh."—Matthew 24:44

WHY IT IS IMPORTANT TO BE READY?

"For we must all appear before the judgment seat of Christ; that everyone may receive the things done in his body, according to that he hath done, whether it be good or bad."—II Corinthians 5:10

HOW CAN WE BE READY?

"If we confess our sins, he is faithful and just to forgive us our sins, and to cleanse us from all unrighteousness."—I John 1:9

Faith – Believing - Doing

I remember a story of an old turpentine worker who's faithful dog died in a great forest fire, because he would not desert his master's dinner pail, which he had been told to watch. With tears on his face, the old man said, "I always had to be careful what I told him to do 'cause I knew he'd do it."

How many of us could the Lord say such a thing?

Love of God makes us obedient unto Him.
What He asks; we give.
Where He sends; we go.
While He leads; we follow.

Love is not cautious; it is very brave and generous.

- It is easy to say we believe in the church and the work of God's kingdom, but the real test is the challenge to believe enough to commit our lives to it.

- It is easy to give a testimony in church when only fellow believers are listening, but the real test is the challenge to testify of God's love at school, at work, or to a neighbor, where it's not quite so popular.

- It is easy to say we believe but another thing to believe enough to do something.

Her Name Is Ruth

When I was due to give birth to our fifth child, we hadn't picked a name yet for a boy or girl. I believe it was the morning before I went to the hospital, I awoke with the name Ruth on my heart so real. I knew this would be the name our little girl would have. Another beautiful little girl.

As she grew up, she reminded me many times of the Ruth in the Bible with so many good qualities. When she was a teenager, she had a terrible headache one day; it just wouldn't go away. She cried and cried in pain. My dad, Ruth's papaw Allen, came by and prayed for her. Her headache instantly stopped. That has been many years ago. She's now 51 years old. This week she told me that she had just thought of that headache she'd had so many years ago and the miracle that had taken place that day.

I Praise the Lord for all His wonderful works to our children and to us.

He is Wonderful!

Repentance

"I tell you, Nay: but, except ye repent, ye shall all likewise perish."
—Luke 13:3

"And he (Jesus) said, A certain man had two sons. And the younger of them said to his father, Father, give me the portion of goods that falleth to me, And he divided unto them his living. And not may days after the younger son gathered all together, and took his journey into a far country, and there wasted his substance with riotous living."
—Luke 15:11-13

What do we mean by repent? The Bible gives us part of the answer in Isaiah 55:7, where it says, "Let the wicked forsake his way."

Unsaved people want to do as they please. They want their own way about things. Repentance means to quit trying to get one's "own way"; to become willing to have God's way about everything. That would mean always doing the right thing, rather than what you might want to do. Of course, you can quit a sin and yet think in your heart, "I can't do that, but it's not so wrong; I wish I could do it." That is not repentance. To repent means to take the same attitude toward every sin that God does; to hate it. People never laugh about or treat lightly any sin of which they have really repented. Repentance also includes a sorrow for sin; not just because sin brought trouble or punishment. A repentant person is sorry because his sin has grieved God.

People can regret having done wrong yet not repent. For instance, a little girl ran away from home. When she saw her mother coming with the switch, she regretted having run off, but she was not repentant. People who repent have a kind of sorrow for sin that causes them to turn from sin, with all their hearts. God says to this man, woman, boy, or girl;

"For all those things hath mine hand made, and all those things have been, saith the Lord: but to this man will I look, even to him that is poor and of a contrite spirit, and trembleth at my word." —Isaiah 66:2

The minute he finds out what God wants him to do, the repentant person does exactly that. Any person who doesn't care about obeying God and keeping His Word, shows that he is still lost. He has not known true repentance.

"The sacrifices of God are a broken spirit: a broken and a contrite heart, O God, thou wilt not despise."—Psalm 51:17

Obedient Because We Know To Be Obedient

The just shall live by faith.

At one time, we may have felt and went by feelings a lot. Then, we must learn that we can't go by feelings but by what we know to do. We choose to read our Bibles, go to church, be quiet when we need to, pray, and so on. These right actions will be our safe guards our strength, our faithfulness, and the girdle to our loins. Righteousness is the girdle of our reins. By doing things we know in our hearts to do and not following the way our feelings lead us, we will grow. God's Word is our protection, our shield, our strength.

Jesus said, "I will never leave you nor forsake you." The disciples were afraid when Jesus was not with them. Jesus asked His disciples, "Where is your faith?"

We need to know God's Word and hide it in our hearts.

"Thy word have I hid in mine heart, that I might not sin against thee."—Psalm 119:11

Out Of The Mouth Of Babes And Sucklings Thou Hast Perfected

Praise

When my daughter Teresa was about four or maybe five years old, she prayed and worshipped daily. One day a neighbor lady who lived next door heard her. The lady came over, thinking she had done something bad. Teresa was praying and shedding tears. I told our neighbor, "No, she is praising the Lord. She loves Jesus". Every day Teresa raised her little hands to tell Jesus how she loved Him.

"And when the chief priests and scribes saw the wonderful things that he (Jesus) did, and the children crying in the temple, and saying Hosanna to the Son of David; they were sore displeased, And said unto him, Hearest thou what these say? And Jesus saith unto them, Yea; have ye never read, Out of the mouth of babes and sucklings thou hast perfected praise?"—Matthew 21: 15,16

Being Made Ready

"Behold I will send by messenger, and he shall prepare the way before me; and the Lord, whom ye seek, shall suddenly come to His temple, even the messenger of the covenant, whom ye delight in: behold He shall come, saith the Lord of Hosts."—Malachi 3:1

"The voice of him that crieth in the wilderness, Prepare ye the way of the Lord, make straight in the desert a highway for our God." — Isaiah 40:3

"Now in the fifteenth year of the reign of Tiberius Caesar, Pontius Pilate being governor of Judea, and Herod being tetrarch of Galilee, and his brother Philip tetrarch of Ituraea and of the region of Trachonitis, and Lysanias the tetrarch of Abilene. Annas and Caiaphas being the high priests, the word of God came unto John the son of Zacharias in the wilderness. And he came into all the country about Jordan, preaching the baptism of repentance for the remission of sins. As it is written in the book of the words of Esaias the prophet, saying, The voice of one crying in the wilderness, Prepare ye the way of the Lord, make his paths straight. Every valley shall be filled, and every mountain and hill shall be brought low; and the crooked shall be made straight, and the rough ways shall be made smooth; And all flesh shall see the salvation of God."—Luke 3:1-6

There was one appointed to prepare the way of the Lord. He would go before Him and his name was John the Baptist. He came preaching repentance. John the Baptist let the people know he was not the promised Messiah, but that Messiah would be coming after him.

"And as the people were in expectation, and all men mused in their hearts of John, whether he were the Christ, or not; John

answered, saying unto them all, I indeed baptize you with water; but one mightier than I cometh, the latchet of whose shoes I am not worthy to unloose: he shall baptize you with the Holy Ghost and with fire: Whose fan is in his hand, and he will thoroughly purge his floor, and will gather the wheat into his garner; but the chaff he will burn with fire unquenchable. And many other things in his exhortation preached he unto the people."—Luke 3:15-18

Notice what John said of the one to come: *"He shall baptize you with the Holy Ghost and with fire."*

Being Made Ready

"What? Know ye not that your body is the temple of the Holy Ghost which is in you, which ye have of God, and ye are not your own?"—I Corinthians 6:19

There are many things in our lives that we may need to change, but everything doesn't happen all at once. As we read God's Word, we begin to see ourselves more clearly. Through the Holy Spirit, we begin to see things that we may not have been aware. Conviction begins to grip our hearts, and we begin to repent of the things we see. The Spirit of God is preparing our hearts for Him. I remember when the Spirit began drawing me to Him, I had to give up some things. It wasn't hard. When I knew He wasn't pleased, and I understood that what I was doing wasn't His will, I asked Him and He delivered me. He set me free completely.

We really don't realize just how much of the ways of the world we have taken hold of, but the Spirit of the Lord lets us know. I am so thankful we know He is the one that has revealed those things to us.

One day as our little family was traveling from Sarasota, Florida to Tampa, Florida, to visit my parents, I had a very real experience. It always seemed to me that the clouds were so near to the earth in Florida. It was such a beautiful day. I noticed how near the clouds appeared. Suddenly, it became so real to me that Jesus could come in this cloud so near right now. I cried in my heart, "Oh, not now." I didn't want Jesus' pure eyes to look on me in the state I was in (I wasn't dressed in a way I should be). Before that moment, I had never even thought about that before.

It was made very real to me that I wasn't prepared in two ways. I was still clothed in my sins and in my unrighteousness; I was naked before Him. I was still being prepared for His coming. After that day, I never dressed again as I was dressed that day.

His Spirit is so real and Wonderful!

"*But the anointing which ye have received of him abideth in you, and ye need not that any man teach you: but as the same anointing teacheth you of all things, and is truth, and is no lie, and even as it hath taught you, ye shall abide in him. And now, little children, abide in him; that, when he shall appear, we may have confidence, and not be ashamed before him at his coming.*"—I John 2:27,28

Light Overcomes Darkness

So many times, I have tried to explain just how my walk with the Lord began; as I would think about it, it seemed one day nothing was different. I lived that same life as I had for many years. Then suddenly something happened or changed. Just in one day, things began to change. Reading God's Word, I realized what had happened.

"Through the tender mercy of our God; whereby the dayspring from on high hath visited us. To give light to them that sit in darkness and in the shadow of death, to guide our feet into the way of peace."
— Luke 1:78, 79

Jesus had come to give light.

He was that light.
I am so thankful for God's set time
that He shined in my heart and
began to draw me to Him.

His Word is our foundation!

We Need a Set Time for Prayer

There is the helpless and lame man at the gate; those needing help. This man had been lame from his mother's womb. We too, were born in need.

"For when we were yet without strength, in due time, Christ died for the ungodly."—Romans 5:6

This man was laid at the gate of the Temple. What better place to come expecting to receive help? When we began searching for God, where did we go? To the place always reminding us of God? The lame man saw Peter and John, and he looked to them for alms (help).

The world is looking for help from us today!

We Are Laborers Together With Him

The Church has a work to do in this world.
We have a responsibility.

"Now Peter and John went up together into the temple at the hour of prayer, being the ninth hour. And a certain man lame from his mother's womb was carried whom they laid daily at the gate of the temple which is called Beautiful, to ask alms of them that entered into the temple; Who seeing Peter and John about to go into the temple asked an alms. And Peter, fastening his eyes upon him with John, said Look on us. And he gave heed unto them, expecting to receive something of them. Then Peter said, Silver and gold have I none; but such as I have, give I thee: In the name of Jesus Christ of Nazareth rise up and walk. And he took him by the right hand, and lifted him up: and immediately his feet and ankle bones received strength. And he leaping up stood, and walked, and entered with them into the temple, walking, and leaping, and praising God. And all the people saw him walking and praising God. And they knew that it was he which sat for alms at the Beautiful gate of the temple: and they were filled with wonder and amazement at that which had happened unto him. And as the lame man which was healed held Peter and John, all the people ran together unto them in the porch that is called Solomon's, greatly wondering." — Acts 3:1-11

In Acts 1 and 2, we see where the Holy Ghost has come as Jesus had promised. In Acts 3, we see Peter and John going up to the temple at the hour of prayer.

We Are Laborers Together With Him

The Church is to be as God purposed it.
We have a responsibility

Jesus taught oneness; John 17:11 "...that they may be one as we are."

"That they all may be one; as thou Father art in me, and I in thee, that they also may be one in us; that the world may believe that thou hast sent me."—John 17:21

**The Church must have one purpose;
To point others to Jesus the Savior of all mankind.**

Peter fastened his eyes upon the lame man in Acts 3, with John. They saw the need. Peter said, "Look on us."

**We see unity and oneness;
the two working together as one.**

This reminds me of the high priest's robe that had on the hem of it a golden bell and a pomegranate, another golden bell and another pomegranate, (See Exodus 28:34). We see harmony; balance; harmony; balance. Were it not for the pomegranates (fruit) between the golden bells, there would have been a clanging of the bells, but we hear the pleasant sound of harmony, with God's design.

This is the way it is when the Church works together as one in love. When the world sees love and harmony in the church, it gets their attention. Like the lame man who gave heed expecting to receive something.

We see in Acts 3:6 that Peter then shifted the attention from the natural (what the man thought to be needful), to the true need. He fixed his attention on Jesus Christ of Nazareth. This lame man had no doubt heard of Jesus and possibly had even seen Him. Notice in verse seven, Peter took the lame man by the right hand and lifted him up. It reminds me of the song that says, "Just to be, His hand extended, reaching out to the oppressed."

We Are Laborers Together With Him

**The Church labors together with Him.
We have a responsibility**

We do our part; He will do the rest; Acts 3:7 *"...Immediately his feet and ankle bones received strength."*

**Results: We see God's Word fulfilled
when we labor together with Him.**

"Then shall the lame man leap as an hart, and the tongue of the dumb sing: for in the wilderness shall waters break out, and streams in the desert."—Isaiah 35:6

In Acts 3:9, the lame man was now a witness to these people who knew him and knew how he had been a cripple from his mother's womb; they are filled with wonder and amazement. They saw the difference and knew something had happened to him. The man held Peter and John in verse eleven; a gratefulness also fills our hearts as we think of the ones that first led us to the Lord and helped us to receive Him.

"And when Peter saw it, he answered unto the people, Ye men of Israel, why marvel ye at this? Or why look ye so earnestly on us, as though by our own power or holiness we had made this man to walk? The God of Abraham, and of Isaac, and of Jacob, the God of our fathers, hath glorified his Son Jesus; whom ye delivered up, and denied him in the presence of Pilate, when he was determined to let him go.

But ye denied the Holy One and the Just, and desired a murderer to be granted unto you; And killed the Prince of life, whom God hath raised from the dead; whereof we are witnesses."—Acts 3:12-15

When Peter saw all the people with their eyes fixed on he and John, he humbly directed the people's attention away from them saying, *"Why marvel ye at this? Or why look ye so earnestly on us, as though by our own power or holiness we had made this man to walk?"*

We, the Church, like Peter must point to Jesus. The Savior.

"And his name through faith in his name hath made this man strong, whom ye see and know: yea, the faith which is by him hath given him this perfect soundness in the presence of you all."
—Acts 3:16

"But those things, which God before had shewed by the mouth of all his prophets, that Christ should suffer, he hath so fulfilled."
—Acts 3:18

Peter pointed them to the fulfilling of God's Word.

In Acts 3:19, Peter told them this was the very thing that Moses had spoken about and the remedy for their sins. *"Repent ye therefore, and be converted, that your sins may be blotted out, when the times of refreshing shall come from the presence of the Lord;"*

God raised up His Son Jesus, sent Him to bless us, in turning every one of us away from our iniquities.

Baptism In The Word

On this journey with the Lord, I remember sitting at the table one day with my Bible reading and absorbed in His Word. I was fasting but didn't really realize I was fasting. For days, I had been studying and praying. I arose from the table where I had been reading; it was as if the heavens opened above me, and I thought of being baptized and coming up out of the water.

One day shortly after, my mother made a remark about the water being the Word. I thought of the scripture in Ephesians 5:26 *"That he might sanctify and cleanse it with the washing of water by the word."* I also thought of John baptizing with water. The Bible says he came in the Spirit of Elijah to baptize unto repentance.

Through this journey, God has helped me realize things I had never known. I thought my mother was mixed up when she said something about the water being the Word. When I read scripture verses like Ephesians 5:26, I know she was exactly right in her interpretation of the scriptures. My mind goes back to coming up from my Bible and what a blessing I felt.

The water (His Word) will cleanse us. We see ourselves as we really are and repent. We are being prepared for the One coming. Our hearts are being prepared for the baptizing in the Holy Ghost.

Strength For Each Day

I knew that tomorrow I had a very busy day ahead of me. I had several appointments to keep. I realized I would need strength from the Lord. As I lay down for the night, I began to pray and ask for God to give me strength for the next day to be able to get everything done. I had been so sick and without strength that day. When I got up the next morning, I knew God had answered my prayer. As I went through the day to each appointment, I kept thanking Him for the strength.

When one is 80 years old, we must ask for strength often; I know my Father doesn't mind. It is His pleasure to give us what we need. He is just disappointed when we don't ask.

Thank you, Father, for your love.

"Hast thou not know? Hast thou not heard, that the everlasting God, the Lord the Creator of the ends of the earth, fainteth not, neither is weary? There is no searching of his understanding. He giveth power to the faint; and to them that have no might he increaseth strength. Even the youths shall faint and be weary, and the young men shall utterly fall: But they that wait upon the Lord shall renew their strength; they shall mount up with wings as eagles; they shall run, and not be weary; and they shall walk and not faint."—Isaiah 40:28-31

God Has Absolute Power

God has absolute power and has given His Son all authority. The Son gives power to those whom He has chosen to represent Him. When one would ask, "By what power or authority do you do this?" We, with confidence in Him, not in ourselves, but in Him, have the power to do whatever He bids us to do.

Like David said to the giant,
"In the name of the Lord I come against you."

Jesus has also given us a commission; "Go, heal the sick and cast out devils; nothing shall by any means harm you."

He has all power in heaven and in earth!
Has He sent you?
Then, Go! In His name.

My Mother's Stories

God uses childhood experiences to teach us along with His Word. He reveals Truths that we can understand when we are still babes in Him. I remember my mother telling us stories of her childhood, and when she got saved. She remembered them afresh. That's when she realized a whole new meaning through the Word of God.

She said that when she was a little girl about five years old, there were a lot of sheep that had died due to a hard and bitterly cold winter. When the baby lambs were born in the spring, many of the ewes died. The lambs were alive but had no mother to feed them. The man who owned the sheep was giving the little lambs away to farms that had ewes that could feed and keep them alive. My mother said she wanted one of those little lambs so bad. The owner said she could have one, but he never did give it to her. She was so disappointed. When she got saved many years later, she had a dream that she had a little lamb in her hand. Oh, she loved it so much and didn't want it to ever go away.

Another childhood memory she had unknowingly involved the "lamb" of God. One day she was running and playing in a field. She had run a pretty good distance from the house when suddenly, she heard her mother call her name. She stopped right then, turned around and ran back home. She asked her mother what she wanted. Her mother answered her, "I didn't call you." Mom said, "Yes, I heard you call." Her mother replied, "No, I didn't call for you." My mother said she'd always wondered why her mom said she hadn't called for her. When she got saved, she was in prayer one day; God brought that experience back to her memory. He let her know that it was He who had called her name. Just beyond the point where she was running was an old abandoned well.

In prayer we receive many wonderful things. We have a very personal and close relationship with our Father.

He is Wonderful!

My mother is now 97 years old, and she can still tell the story.

Need Of Church Today:

To Get In The Place Of His Presence!

What is conscious? Knowing; having experience; aware.

The opposite of conscious is unconscious; unknowing or unaware.

Coma: A prolonged unconsciousness caused by disease, injury, or poison.

In Genesis chapter twenty-eight, we read about Jacob being made "God conscious." Jacob had to flee from his home and leave his mother and father. He had been untruthful, and now he was afraid for his life. His brother had made it known that he was going to kill Jacob. In the place he'd escaped to, he was alone, afraid, and in greater trouble than he had ever been in.

God always knows our need! He sometimes must take us away from ease and comfort or a busy life before He can make us more aware of Him. When it seems all is gone, God is there. We're just getting in a place where God can show us He is near to us.

God knew what Jacob needed that lonely night. As Jacob lay down to sleep, he probably had much on his mind. Jacob had come to this place, alone with God! God began to reveal Himself to Jacob in a dream. Jacob said. "The Lord is in this place."

"And Jacob awaked out of his sleep, and he said, Surely the Lord is in this place; and I knew it not." (Genesis 28:16) Jacob is now aware of God's presence, he had not been aware of before. He said, "I knew it not."

Now that Jacob was aware, he was afraid. He had a new fear; a fear of God. He knew for sure God was real. He was conscious of God's greatness and His Holiness. A great reverence filled his heart. Jacob was awakened to a new sense of mission and he felt a compelling indebtedness to God and His work. Jacob awoke to a new understanding. He now understood that God was with him. Jacob knew for sure that God was real and that he must account to Him for his life.

If we're ever to do anything for God, we must get in this place of His presence. Jacob never fully understood or felt the effects of what he had done until he was in the presence of God.

Having Your Feet Shod

The Bible tells us that we are to have our feet shod with the preparation of the Gospel of peace. To be shod, means to be fitted and securely fastened into place. Our feet must be planted, rooted, and grounded in the foundation of truth. The Gospel is our foundation of truth. The Gospel of peace is that Gospel of truth which brings peace to the soul of man.

"How beautiful upon the mountains are the feet of him that bringeth good tidings, that publisheth peace; that bringeth good tidings of good, that publisheth salvation; that saith unto Zion, Thy God reigneth!"—Isaiah 52:7

"O Zion, that bringest good tidings, get thee up into the high mountain; O Jerusalem, that bringest good tidings, lift up thy voice with strength; lift it up, be not afraid; say unto the cities of Judah, Behold your God!"—Isaiah 40:9

Arise shine; for thy light is come, and the glory of the Lord is risen upon thee."—Isaiah 60:1 "

"And how shall they preach, except they be sent? As it is written, How beautiful are the feet of them that preach the Gospel of peace, and bring glad tidings of good things!"—Romans 10:15

Encounters With God

Times when God comes to us and times we come to God are different.

There are times I have been desperate and needed an answer in prayer; like the experience I wrote about when I really needed to know and feel His presence. I came with His word. "You said ask, and ye shall receive; I'm asking. You said seek and ye shall find; I am seeking. You said knock and it shall be opened unto you; I'm knocking." As I bowed low weeping, suddenly there before me I saw His feet. Truly, His Word never fails. His presence is so precious. I came to Him; He met me there.

Times when He comes to us are precious and few. Even in the Old Testament, men of old had only a few encounters with God as He spoke to them.

I guess the one I remember most is of Abraham in Genesis 17: 1-5; when Abraham was 99 years old. God appeared to Abram and made a covenant with him and changed his name. Abram had fallen on his face, and God talked to him there.

I had one such encounter in my Christian walk. I awoke early one morning from sleep, and the room was full of the presence of God. It was an experience I will never forget. The whole room was filled with His presence as He spoke only a few words to me. Seven words. The scripture that describes it best is found in Revelation 4:1 *"After this I looked, and, behold, a door was opened in heaven: and the first voice which I heard was as it were of a trumpet talking with me; which said, Come up hither, and I will shew thee things which much be hereafter."* I heard as it were a trumpet talking with me.

Behind Closed Doors

The Ark of the Covenant was behind the veil in the tabernacle, where only the High Priest could go once each year on the day of atonement. That was the veil that was torn from the top to bottom, when Jesus was crucified.

"Jesus, when he had cried again with a loud voice, yielded up the ghost. And behold, the veil of the temple was rent in twain from the top to the bottom; and the earth did quake, and the rocks rent."—Matthew 27:50-51

As Jesus yielded up the ghost, He opened the way to direct contact with God. Now, because of what the Son of God did for us, we can enter that holy presence of the Father. Behind closed doors, we can experience His love and care for us.

"Oh Father, help us never to forget this Wonderful Place."

"He that dwelleth in the secret place of the most High shall abide under the shadow of the Almighty."—Psalm 91:1

"Let us therefore come boldly unto the throne of grace that we may obtain mercy and find grace to help in time of need."—Hebrews 4:16

Listen To His Voice

In John 10:27 Jesus spoke these words, *"My sheep hear my voice, and I know them, and they follow me."*

So many times, I have needed direction and prayed, "Lord I don't know what to do." As I cast all my cares upon Him and entered that closeness in His presence, He spoke to my heart. As He has spoken to me, it may have only been a few words; a part of scripture, but I knew; that was my answer.

I have always encouraged others to hide God's Word in their hearts, to memorize scripture. When Jesus speaks to us, He speaks His Word.

Maybe we could ask ourselves, "In those moments in prayer, as I seek His direction, am I able to receive it? Can I hear Him instructing me? What it is that I need to do and when and how I should do it?

Be acquainted with His Word.

His Word is Wonderful!

Sometimes it is a still small voice;
He speaks to our hearts.

Christ In You: The Hope Of Glory

A people corrupted by sin and the natural man cannot see, hear, nor understand God, or His ways, until God opens their eyes, ears, and understanding to spiritual things.

"But the natural man receiveth not the things of the Spirit of God: for they are foolishness unto him: neither can he know them, because they are spiritually discerned."—I Corinthians 2:14

Paul writes in Colossians 1:25-27, *"Whereof I am made a minister, according to the dispensation of God which is given to me for you, to fulfill the Word of God. Even the mystery which hath been hid from ages and from generations, but now is made manifest to His saints. To whom God would make known what is the riches of the glory of this mystery among the Gentiles; which is Christ in you, the hope of glory:"*

Understanding all hope of real glory is in discovering Christ's very life in you. This mystery or hidden truth was hidden but now has been revealed. Only God, through His Holy Spirit reveals these hidden truths.

"And that he might make known the riches of his glory on the vessels of mercy, which he had afore prepared unto glory, Even us, whom he hath called, not of the Jews only, but also of the Gentiles?"
—Romans 9:23,24;

He is the Hope of Glory
to Jews and Gentiles.

Soul Winners

An empty vessel serves little practical purpose.
Only that which a vessel receives can it give.

"Then Peter said, Silver and gold have I none; but such as I have, give I thee: In the name of Jesus Christ of Nazareth rise up and walk."—Acts 3:6

Soul winning often suffers at this point. The would-be soul winner soon discovers that unless he works at it, all he has to offer the thirsting soul is an empty cup.

There are two things with which the vessel must be filled - The Spirit of God and the Word of God.

"He that believeth on me, as the scripture hath said, out of his belly shall flow rivers of living water. (But this spake he of the Spirit, which they that believe on him should receive: for the Holy Ghost was not yet given; because that Jesus was not yet glorified.)"— John 7:38,39

"Let the word of Christ dwell in you richly in all wisdom; teaching and admonishing one another in psalms and hymns and spiritual songs, singing with grace in your hearts to the Lord."— Colossians 3:26

"And take the helmet of salvation, and the sword of the Spirit, which is the word of God."—Ephesians 6:17

As vessels of God, we must be clean, filled with the Spirit of God, and the Word of God if we are to be effective Soul Winners for Christ.

Four Simple Rules

Psalm 37: 4-8 *"Delight thyself also in the Lord; and he shall give thee the desires of thine heart. Commit thy way unto the Lord; trust also in him; and he shall bring it to pass. And he shall bring forth thy righteousness as the light, and thy judgement as the noonday. Rest in the Lord, and wait patiently for him: fret not thyself because of him who prospereth in his way, because of the man who bringeth wicked devices to pass. Cease from anger, and forsake wrath: fret not thyself in any wise to do evil."*

1. "Delight yourself in the Lord."

    We can delight in Him simply because of who He is. He is our God and Father; the Creator of the universe. His wisdom is unlimited and His love unfailing.

2. "Commit your way unto the Lord."

    A true commitment always results in contentment. It becomes unquestioned trust in His Word.

3. "Rest in the Lord and wait patiently for Him."

    Absolute confidence in His Word recognizes that God rules our human affairs and has total trust in the fact that God foresees and controls the most minute details of our lives.

4. "Fret not yourself."

    The fourth requirement needed to experience the most precious enjoyment of life includes freedom - Freedom from all anger, grudges, and frustration by evildoers.

    Proverbs 7:2 *"Keep my commandments, and live; and my law as the apple of thine eye."* The phrase "the apple of thine eye" refers to something as precious as one's eye. It's to be guarded with special care.

Only One Way

Our loved ones seek to get free from their troubles, addictions, and fears. They may even spend time behind bars and plan to go a different way when they get home. Some families encourage them to go to church and do things different. But going to church is just not enough; they must get through to Jesus. Other things or ways do not bring that freedom one has to have. Only Jesus can set us free. So, while going to church is good, it is not enough. All must keep pressing through until they find Jesus is real to their souls. He is the Way; the only Way, the Truth and the Life.

Come to Jesus.
He loves you!

"Come unto me, all ye that labor and are heavy laden, and I will give you rest. Take my yoke upon you, and learn of me; for I am meek and lowly in heart: and ye shall find rest unto your souls. For my yoke is easy and my burden is light."—Matthew 11: 28-30

"The law and the prophets were until John: since that time the kingdom of God is preached, and every man presseth into it." — Luke 16:16

Pressing in is accomplished in prayer warfare, coupled with a will to surrender one's life and self interests to gain God's kingdom goals.

Refusing To Bow

The three Hebrews, Shadrach, Meshach, and Abednego, would not bow to the golden image the King Nebuchadnezzar had commanded that all must fall down and worship when they heard the music. They refused and did not as he commanded. He was outraged and cast them into a burning fiery furnace.

In Daniel chapter 3:17,18, The Hebrews answered the king. *"If it be so, our God whom we serve is able to deliver us from the burning fiery furnace, and He will deliver us out of thine hand, O king. But if not, be it known unto thee O king, that we will not serve thy gods, nor worship the golden image which thou hast set up."*

We find the result in Daniel 3:25. *"He (the king) answered and said, Lo, I see four men loose, walking in the midst of the fire, and they have no hurt; and the form of the fourth is like the Son of God."*

We too, have the same One walking with us, as we refuse to walk (bow to) the ways of Satan and the ways of the world that are not according to God's Word.

We must be prepared as it says in Ephesians 6:10-13. *"Finally, my brethren, be strong in the Lord, and in the power of his might. Put on the whole armor of God, that ye may be able to stand against the wiles of the devil. For we wrestle not against flesh and blood, but against principalities, against powers, against rulers of the darkness of this world, against spiritual wickedness in high places. Wherefore take unto you the whole armor of God that ye may be able to wishstand in the evil day and have done all, to stand."*

We too will be prepared to stand, and He will stand with us.

Think On These Things

"But when it pleased God, who separated me from my mothers womb, and called me by His Grace, to reveal His Son in me..."
— Galatians 1: 15-16a

> **Does that not bring tears to your eyes,**
> **humbleness to your heart,**
> **and thanksgiving to your lips**
> **as you worship and praise**
> **your Heavenly Father?!**

His Words in John 15:16 *"Ye have not chosen me, but I have chosen you, and ordained you, that ye should go and bring forth fruit, and that your fruit should remain: that whatsoever ye shall ask of the Father in my name, he may give it you."*

These words are precious to us and guide our way no matter who we are or where; a mother and housewife living through hard things, as well as a preacher or missionary working on the "battlefield".

The Desires Of Our Heart

I thought of something my older sister, who's only a couple of years older than I am, said to me a few days ago. She talked about the power of prayer. A lot of older people know the experience of physically not being able to get down on their knees to pray, which is hard to get used to. Of course, we can pray walking, sitting, driving, or working. All these are effectual ways in which we can pray, and God hears. In a more special quiet time, there is a desire to get on one's knees in personal times of prayer when we enter in and shut the door to pray to our Father in secret. My sister is no longer able to get on her knees, even though it's a great desire for her to be able to do so. As she began praying, she said, "Lord, I come to you on the knees of my heart."

How wonderful it is that our Heavenly Father knows the desires of our heart, and we can enter that special time with Him "on the knees of our hearts."

"Delight thyself also in the Lord; and he shall give thee the desires of thine heart."—Psalm 37:4

First Behold Then Reflect

Jesus is to be revealed in us
as we are progressively transformed.

*"And not as Moses, which put a **veil** over his face, that the children of Israel could not steadfastly look to the end of that which is abolished: But their minds were blinded: for until this day remaineth the same **vail** untaken away in the reading of the old testament; which veil is done away in Christ. But even unto this day, when Moses is read, the **vail** is upon their heart. Nevertheless when it shall turn to the Lord, the **vail** shall be taken away. Now the Lord is that Spirit: and where the Spirit of the Lord is, there is liberty. But we all, with open face beholding as in a glass the glory of the Lord are changed into the same image from glory to glory, even as by the Spirit of the Lord."* — II Corinthians 3:13-18

"But we all, with open face beholding as in a glass the glory of the Lord are changed into the same image from glory to glory, even as by the Spirit of the Lord."

These words in verse eighteen, cause me to think of the words from a song, The Potter's House; "He said Behold when it was finished, so that all the world could see what God can do! And the sinner changed, clothed in his right mind reflecting the glory of the Lord. Clothed in His Righteousness reflecting His Holiness."

Divine Protection

God has provided us with divine protection and that is the Word of God. As we live by His Words, we have His protection from evil.

I have often thought of this umbrella as a covering we must stay under. Just like children growing up, parents teach the children to be obedient to them. As long as they stay within the godly guidelines the parents set, they are safe under that covering. It is when they decide to do things their own way and be disobedient, that they don't have that protection.

Adam and Eve chose to remove themselves from God's protection. Their way seemed to be a better way to them than God's way. Remember what happened to them. Once they disobeyed God, their innocence was gone; they broke that wonderful fellowship between themselves and God. There was shame, fear, and separation as a result.

God gave parents to guide and love and to protect their children, to train them in God's ways. Children are to be obedient to their parents, and they will be blessed.

God's Word is our protection from the evils of this world.

"The law of the Lord is perfect, converting the soul: the testimony of the Lord is sure, making wise the simple. The statutes of the Lord are right,

rejoicing the heart: the commandment of the Lord is pure, enlightening the eyes. The fear of the Lord is clean, enduring forever: the judgments of the Lord are true and righteous altogether. More to be desired are they than gold, yea, than much fine gold: sweeter also than honey and the honeycomb. Moreover by them is thy servant warned: and in keeping of them there is great reward."—Psalm 19:7-11

Temptations come to try to draw us out; to get us to disobey God's Word. After a while, a person is far away from safety and feels there is no hope, but that is exactly what Satan wants one to believe. Run back as fast as you can, as soon as you realize you've done wrong. Repent; Get back under that protection.

God's Word is His will
His will is His Word.

The Disciple Whom Jesus Loved

John became known as the disciple whom Jesus loved. Do you think Jesus loved him more than all the rest of the disciples? In John 13:23, John was leaning on Jesus' bosom, when Jesus announced that one of them would betray Him. Peter ask John to ask Jesus who it was that would do this. John asked Jesus who it was. Jesus told him it was the one whom He would give the sop to when He had dipped it. We see this one so near to Jesus received the answer he sought. He was confident to ask. Was it because Jesus loved him more or was it because he drew so close and wanted to get as close to Him as He could.

"When Jesus therefore saw his mother, and the disciple standing by, whom he loved, he saith unto his mother, Woman behold thy son! Then saith he to the disciple, Behold thy mother! And from that hour that disciple took her unto his own home." —John 19:26,27

My sister once told me how she had noticed her twin grandsons' greeting when they were small and came to visit. One of the boys would run to play with the others. The other boy would always come and climb up on her lap and love on her first; then he too would run to play with the others.

I think of this when I think of John and his love for Jesus.

He drew as close as he could get. Are we like this?

Do we draw as close to Jesus as we can get?

Omnipotent; Omniscient; Omnipresent

I prayed for my son Alan and his wife Debbie this morning as their flight left for Uganda. I was praying for the work they're doing for our Lord and that His will be accomplished. The Holy Spirit brought to my mind how God has all knowledge. As I prayed for their safety, He reminded me of His always being present everywhere. As my mind went to the plane, He reminded me He has all power. I had never had these words, Omnipresent; Omnipotent; and Omniscient brought so vividly to my mind in prayer before. God was letting me know that all was in His hands.

He is Wonderful!

I am so thankful that we can put our trust in Him.

We can rest in Him.

He is:

Omnipotent: All Powerful.

Omniscient: Knowing everything.

Omnipresent: Present everywhere at the same time.

Daily Grace

When we think of what Jesus accomplished and finished for us, we only have to ask "Give me Grace. You've already done this for me. You gave your life in the flesh, so I could have life in the Spirit. Now, I need daily grace to go through everything I need to, to die in the flesh. You have given me eternal life in you. Lord, now I just need your grace to follow you. Come to the end of myself, so you can be all in all. Your will be done in earth, as it is in heaven. You are the way, the truth, and the life."

"And this is life eternal, that they might know thee the only true God, and Jesus Christ, whom thou hast sent."—John 17:3

Our Good Shepherd

Trusting In Him

The sheep have no concern about their needs. They eat the grass that is provided for the day and drink freely of the water that is before them. They trust the shepherd to provide for their needs. If we could learn to trust the Lord to meet all our needs like the sheep trust their shepherd, our lives would be so different.

No worry; just trust.
Jesus said, "Take no thought, your heavenly Father
knows your needs."
He is concerned about each of us. He is the Good Shepherd.

"I am the good shepherd: the good shepherd giveth his life for the sheep."—John 10:11

Our spiritual needs will also be met. When we have taken the spiritual food that God has provided, we can lie down in green pastures and enjoy what He has provided.

He is the Wonderful Shepherd, and He knows His sheep and their needs.

"The Lord is my shepherd; I shall not want. He maketh me to lie down in green pastures: he leadeth me beside still waters. He restoreth my soul: He leadeth me in the paths of righteousness for his name's sake. Yea, though I walk through the valley of the shadow death, I will fear no evil: for thou art with me; thy rod and thy staff they comfort me. Thou preparest a table before me in the presence of mine enemies: thou anointest my head with oil; my cup runneth over. Surely goodness and mercy shall follow me all the days of my life: and I will dwell in the house of the Lord forever."—Psalm 23: 1-6

What Separates God's People From All Others On Earth?

Occasionally, you see someone and hear them talk or just watch them, and you notice a difference. You think there is just something different about that person.

Moses said in Exodus 33:16 *"For wherein shall it be known here that I and thy people have found grace in thy sight? Is it not in that thou goest with us? So shall we be separated, I and thy people, from all the people that are upon the face of the earth."*

The difference; God was with them.

His presence in us makes the difference. Let your light shine He said. We don't even have to try to make it shine. Jesus said, "Let it shine".

He is the light! Just let him shine!

"Ye are the light of the world. A city that is set on a hill cannot be hid. Neither do men light a candle, and put it under a bushel, but on a candlestick; and it giveth light unto all that are in the house. Let your light so shine before men, that they may see your good works, and glorify your father which is in heaven."—Matthew 5:14-16

God's Set Time

We must not be discouraged or disappointed when God does not move on our time table. Instead, we must continue to put our trust and faith in His knowledge and judgement. Don't complain or run from the place God has put you. Stay true and watch God work on your behalf. God is pleased when we are faithful in service, even in the hard places, whatever they may be; only trust.

**God knows what He is doing
and when He will do it.
Just wait on His timing.**

"To everything there is a season, and a time to every purpose under the heaven."—Ecclesiastes 3:1

Do Our Words Fit Who We Are?

"A man hath joy by the answer of his mouth: and a word spoken in due season, how good is it!"—Proverbs 15:23

"The heart of the righteous studieth to answer: but the mouth of the wicked poureth out evil things."—Proverbs 15:28

"Pleasant words are as an honeycomb, sweet to the soul, and health to the bones."—Proverbs 16:24

"He that keepeth his mouth keepeth his life: but he that openeth wide his lips shall have destruction."—Proverbs 13:3

"A man shall be satisfied with good by the fruit of his mouth: and the recompence of a man's hands shall be rendered unto him."—Proverbs 12:14

"A soft answer turneth away wrath: but grevious words stir up anger."—Proverbs 15:1

"Let the words of my mouth, and the meditation of my heart, be acceptable in thy sight, O Lord, my strength, and my redeemer."—Psalm 19:14

Starting Young

Parents, we must start when our children are really young before they begin to go to school to expose them to God's Word. They can understand and comprehend a lot more than most think. They can even memorize scripture. Alan was one year and one week old when I was born again. He memorized Psalm 119:105 when he was around two years old.

"Thy word is a lamp unto my feet, and a light unto my path."
—Psalm 119:105

I have thought of Moses when he was a baby. Remember when Marion asked the princess if she needed one of the Hebrew women to nurse him? The princess knew he was one of the Hebrew's children. Moses was taught by his mother; loved by her; learned he was one of them.

All this was done while he was a child. He learned of the One True God. When he was weaned, he was taken to the palace to live and be a part of them, learn their ways. He was educated there.

God had already put into him the things that would always be with him.

"O the depth of the riches both of the wisdom and knowledge of God! How unsearchable are his judgements, and his ways past finding out!"—Romans 11:33

Absolute Faith – No Room For Doubt

We must walk in absolute faith
and confidence in God
(No doubting).

Here are some causes for doubting:

1. One's ignorance of the Word of God.
2. Going by feelings instead of what God said in His Word.
3. One's misunderstanding of what God is like.
4. One's focus on the wrong thing (circumstances) rather than focusing on God in whom all things are possible.
5. Sin or guilt in one's life.
6. Previous failures in one's life.

The Consequences of living in doubt:

1. Affects our relationship with God.
2. Affects our prayer life.

   Matthew 21:18-22 *"Now in the morning as he returned into the city, he hungered. And when he saw a fig tree in the way, he came to it, and found nothing thereon, but leaves only, and said unto it, Let no fruit grow on thee henceforward forever. And presently the fig tree withered away. And when the disciples saw it, they marveled, saying, How soon is the fig tree withered away! Jesus answered and said unto them, Verily I say unto you, if ye have faith, and doubt not, ye shall not* *only do this which is done to the fig tree, but also if ye shall say unto this mountain, Be thou removed, and` be thou cast into the sea; it shall be done. And all things whatsoever ye shall ask in prayer, believing, ye shall receive."*

3. Hinders our service to God.

We must not be a doubter.

"But without faith it is impossible to please him: for he that cometh to God must believe that he is, and that he is a rewarder of them that diligently seek him."—Hebrews 11:6

"And straightaway the father of the child cried out and said with tears, Lord, I believe; help thou mine unbelief."—Mark 9:24

We can have absolute faith and believe God.

Words Of Life

"For as the Father raiseth up the dead, and quickeneth them; even so the Son quickeneth whom he will."—John 5:21

Jesus came by the Pool of Bethesda (John 5) and saw a man lying there. He knew the man had been there in that condition a long time; 38 years. Jesus said unto him; "Wilt thou be made whole?" Jesus was asking him, "Do you want to be made whole?" The sick man began to explain why he hadn't gotten into the pool. Then Jesus spoke words of life unto him. Jesus said "Rise, take up thy bed, and walk." And immediately the man was made whole and took up his bed and walked.

The words Jesus spoke, awakened his heart.

"It is the Spirit that quickeneth; the flesh profiteth nothing: the words that I speak unto you, they are Spirit and they are life." —John 6:63

To quicken is to give life. This was a physical resurrection.

God's Word – Our Road Map

The Bible is our road map on our journey through this life. Across the raging seas, we must rely on His Word. He will never fail us. Jesus said, "I will never leave you nor forsake you." He also said, "Follow me." We must keep our eyes fixed on Him.

There are so many things to distract us. Satan wants us to lose our way, so he throws things in our road to try to mislead us and get us off on the wrong road. We are never left alone; we must rely on the Word of God. He will show us the way.

As we read from cover to cover, and study our road map, we will find and stay in the right way.

Jesus said in John 14:6a "I am the way, and the truth, and the life…"

His Word is our strength and our food. We, as individuals, must seek for ourselves. We must read and "eat" the Word for ourselves. Someone else eating a meal won't feed us. We must eat for ourselves.

**The Word is our foundation;
the only foundation that cannot be shaken.**

Jesus Equal With God In Nature

After Jesus healed the impotent man at the pool by speaking words of life to him, the Jews persecuted Jesus and sought to slay Him, because he had done these things on the Sabbath day. But Jesus answered them, "My Father worketh, hitherto, and I work." These Jewish, religious leaders sought the more to kill Him. He not only had broken the Sabbath, but said also that God was His Father, making Himself equal with God. From this point forward, Jesus was on a collision course with the authorities.

"But Jesus answered them, My Father worketh hitherto, and I work. Therefore, the Jews sought the more to kill him, because he not only had broken the Sabbath, but said also that God was His Father, making himself equal with God."—John 5:17,18

Jesus Equal With God In Power

Jesus goes on to tell them in John 5:19 that He can do nothing of Himself but what He sees the Father do. His Father Loves Him and shows Him all things that He Himself does and even greater works they will see Him do. His Father raises up the dead and gives life to them, even so the Son gives life to whom He will. They will come to see this.

Jesus also said in John 9:4 *"I must work the works of Him that sent me, while it is day; the night cometh, when no man can work."*

Jesus Equal With God In Authority

The Father judgeth no man, but hath committed all judgement unto the Son that all men should honor the Son even as they honor the Father that sent Him. All that hear Jesus' words and believe on the Father that sent Him have everlasting life and shall not come into condemnation but are passed from death unto life. The hour is coming and now Jesus said. "The dead shall hear the voice of the Son of God: and they that hear shall live."

We were dead in our sins once. When the word of life was spoken to us, we received life and obeyed. God gave Jesus the Son authority to execute judgement and give life.

"For as the Father hath life in himself, so hath He given to the Son also to have life in himself: and he hath given him authority to execute judgement also, because he is the son of man."—John 5:26,27

Man does not merely need a guide or a teacher; he is dead and needs someone able to resurrect his spirit. This is a spiritual resurrection; a regeneration; a New Birth.

First Love

How was that first love? Remember?
Full of faith; no fear.
First Love is…

- Knowing that God is able; nothing impossible with Him. Knowing that all things work together for our good.
- Prayer time is a joy, meeting with Him, spending precious time in His presence. In quietness with contentment. Enjoying a deep settled peace. Seeing beauty everywhere.
- Being thankful, not complaining. Never judging others.
- Anything that Jesus is not part of, we want no part of.
- Enjoying going to His house, being with our new family.

"Though I speak with the tongues of men and of angels, and have not charity, I am become as sounding brass, or a tinkling cymbal. And though I have the gift of prophecy, and understand all mysteries and all knowledge; and though I have all faith, so that I could remove mountains, and have not charity, I am nothing. And though I bestow all my goods to feed the poor, and though I give my body to be burned, and have not charity, it profiteth me nothing. Charity suffereth long and is kind; charity envieth not; charity vaunteth not itself, is not puffed up, doth not behave itself unseemly, seeketh not her own, is not easily provoked, thinketh no evil; rejoiceth not in iniquity, but rejoiceth in the truth; beareth all things, believeth all things, hopeth all things, endureth all things. Charity never faileth:"—I Corinthians 13:1-8

We Too Must Wait

Making us a witness, we too must wait. It is only in the spirit we receive what He has for us. As I entered the spirit in prayer, the words came; "I am Alpha and the Omega, the First and the Last." The words came out of my mouth, and I was startled. I prayed, "Oh Lord, I'm not saying I am anything." He let me know then that He was speaking through my mouth. He was in me, and I in Him. One with Him. He took me into a deeper revelation as He took Abraham in Genesis 22. He took me to the mount. These things only come as we spend time in His presence. It is time in the secret place of His presence that He reveals His secrets to us.

"And being assembled together with them, commanded them that they should not depart from Jerusalem, but wait for the promise of the Father, which, saith he, ye have heard of me: For John truly baptized with water; but ye shall be baptized with the Holy Ghost not many days hence."—Acts 1:4,5

"And behold, I send the promise of my Father upon you: but tarry ye in the city of Jerusalem, until ye be endued with power from on high."—Luke 24:49

Seeking Treasure

A person cannot understand the spiritual things of God until he has been quickened by God's Spirit and experienced spiritual life in Him (The New Birth). We must dig, as for treasure, seek Him for these truths, and desire Him to open these treasures to us. Then we read and understand with our heart. Jesus came opening the eyes of the blind, so he still opens the blind eyes today. We can see these things and understand. By praying, seeking, and desiring, we can know and understand with our hearts, the things God has given us in His Word, By His Spirit.

As I sat one night in a church service, we opened our Bibles to where the Pastor was going to read. As he read the scriptures, God gave me a vision. As I looked at my Bible on my lap, in it, the passages where deep down between the covers of the Bible, I would find Him. I knew what God was showing me. Not just the top but there was a depth only the Spirit could open to us.

"Blessed be the God of our Lord Jesus Christ, the Father of glory, may give unto you the spirit of wisdom and revelation in the knowledge of him: The eyes of your understanding being enlightened; that ye may know what is the hope of his calling, and what the riches of the glory of his inheritance in the saints, And what is the exceeding greatness of his power to us-ward who believe, according to the working of his mighty power."—Ephesians 1:17-19

For A Purpose

Joseph was truly an example of what we should be as we follow the Lord. All things that happened to him have a lesson for us. There was a purpose in it all. Joseph's challenges were like a school, preparing him for his destiny. All these things were getting him ready for the plan God had for his life. Joseph learned his lesson well, expressing his confidence in God.

**God had His hand in all that happened,
and He can bring good out of evil.**

If we knew and could understand God's reasoning for allowing afflictions in our lives as His children, I believe it would trouble us less.

"To everything there is a season, and a time to every purpose under the heaven."—Ecclesiastes 3:1

Hope In Christ

God can change character!

Joseph's brothers were so unfeeling and cared not for the pleading of Joseph's cry from the pit. Neither did they care for their father who was so broken from what they purposely led him to believe when they brought his son's coat of many colors back to him covered with blood. Fortunately, something had happened to them over the years. Joseph could see this when they were presented to him in Egypt. There had been a change in them.

Yes, there is hope of a character change today.
The power of Christ's Gospel is able to accomplish this.

"But before faith came, we were kept under the law, shut up unto the faith which should afterwards be revealed. Wherefore the law was our schoolmaster to bring us unto Christ, that we might be justified by faith. But after that faith is come, we are no longer under a schoolmaster. For ye are all the children of God by faith in Christ Jesus. For as many of you as have been baptized into Christ have put on Christ."—Galatians 3:23-27

Submission To God's Will

You will notice when reading all about Joseph in the book of Genesis, Joseph never complained or grumbled about his situation. It was repeated several times in different places in scripture, that God was with him. God didn't leave him alone, and neither does Jesus leave us alone. Joseph was submitted to God's will in everything. When he was cast into prison for no fault of his own, God was with him. Joseph was a light to those prisoners all around him.

We too are to be a light in this world. People all around us are prisoners of Satan. Through our kindness and concern and God's love shining through, our lives can give hope to them.

So, put your light to use. Let it shine!

"Ye are the light of the world. A city that is set on a hill cannot be hid."—Matthew 5:14

Wealth That Doesn't Pass Away

Like the man who wins 25 million dollars, everyone rejoices with him. Everyone talks about it; even the news reports it, showing him on the television. Some may say, he's been a hard working man; he deserves it. He literally made a millionaire in one day!

What would it be like to see everyone place this much importance over a poor hardworking (under Satan's bondage) man, when one day he believes and receives the Savior and gets eternal life. Eternal life, which is more than 25 million years of joy, peace and life benefits that make one rich. If his freedom from the clutches of bondage could receive as much attention, just think what it would do. He'd be made a millionaire with just one decision!

**This wealth does not pass away,
and no one can take it away from you.**

"And I give unto them eternal life; and they shall never perish, neither shall any man pluck them out of my hand. My Father, which gave them me, is greater than all; and no man is able to pluck them out of my Father's hand. I and my Father are one."—John 10:28-30

Singers And Singing In Worship

We read in I Chronicles 16 where the musicians were appointed positions. Their assignment was the giving of thanks unto the Lord, calling upon His name, and making known His deeds among the people.

Verse 9 reads *"Sing unto Him, sing psalms unto Him, talk ye of all His Wonderous works."*

We see this is a special God given work. What happens when we worship, lifting our voices as one before Him?

"It came even to pass, as the trumpeters and singers were as one, to make one sound to be heard in praising and thanking the Lord; and when they lifted up their voice with the trumpets and cymbals and instruments of music, and praised the Lord, saying, For he is good; for his mercy endureth forever: that then the house was filled with a cloud, even the house of the Lord; so that the priests could not stand to minister by reason of the cloud: for the glory of the Lord had filled the house of God."—II Chronicles 5:13,14

God's presence and glory can be felt by all.

The War Between The Flesh And Spirit

As we see in Galatians 5:17, the flesh and the Spirit war against each other. *"For the flesh lusteth against the Spirit, and the Spirit against the flesh: and these are contrary the one to the other: so that ye cannot do the things that ye would."*

We can recall that Isaac was the chosen one given by God to Abraham and Sarah as He had promised them. Ishmael was born of the works of the flesh. We saw his true nature after Isaac was born. He began to war against him. It was not an easy thing for Abraham to give up Ishmael. Neither will it be an easy thing for us to break the habits of our flesh. As we put on the new man, which is created after God in righteousness and true holiness, we will be victorious.

The old man must be put off with his deeds.

"And be renewed in the spirit of your mind; and that ye put on the new man, which after God is created in righteousness and true holiness. Wherefore putting away lying, speak every man truth with his neighbor: for we are members one of another. Be ye angry, and sin not: let not the sun go down upon your wrath: Neither give place to the devil."—Ephesians 4:23-27

Obedience

When we need God, we want Him to come now at our desperate moment. What about when He needs us, are we just as available as He is to us?

- If there is someone God is asking us to witness to?
- What about when He needs a temple to stand in to speak to people, are we ready?

Remember, our body is a temple for His use. He will clothe us in Himself. He is to be seen. He is to be heard. His people are who He works through today. If someone comes to mind, do we pray for them or call them to let them know we are thinking about them? There may be a need. If the Lord puts in our heart to go and be a help to someone that needs help, maybe take groceries, do we obey?

How do we move for God?

What about in church service, do we obey? If He lays a song on our hearts or gives us a testimony, do we move instantly?

Let us be obedient to our Father. We will be blessed.

"Give ear, O Lord, unto my prayer; and attend to the voice of my supplications. In the day of my trouble I will call upon thee: for thou wilt answer me. Among the gods there is none like unto thee, O Lord; neither are there any works like unto thy works. All nations whom thou hast made shall come and worship before thee, O Lord; and shall glorify thy name. For thou art great, and doest wondrous things: thou art God alone. Teach me thy way, O Lord; I will walk in thy truth: unite my heart to fear thy name. I will praise thee, O Lord my God, with all my heart: and I will glorify thy name for evermore."— Psalm 86:6-12

Spiritual Warfare – The Whole Armor of God

We are instructed to be strong in the Lord and in the power (authority) of His might. We have no sufficient strength of our own, so we must resist the temptation to try standing in our own strength. We are no match for the enemy on our own. Considering the kind of enemies we have to deal with, we must be well armed. I'm not talking about human enemies. We must be prepared to stand against the powers of darkness. Satan's kingdom is a kingdom of darkness. Christ's kingdom is a kingdom of light. God has given us armor. We must put it on that we may stand against the wiles of the devil. He has many schemes.

We wrestle (to engage actively in a one-on-one combat) against the invisible works of Satan. It will take the whole armor of God, but we will be able to withstand these evil forces. We'll be able to stand for the next battle.

"Finally, my brethren, be strong in the Lord, and in the power of his might. Put on the whole armor of God, that ye may be able to stand against the wiles of the devil. For we wrestle not against flesh and blood, but against principalities, against powers, against the rulers of the darkness of this world, against spiritual wickedness in high places. Wherefore take unto you the whole armor of God, that ye may be able to withstand in the evil day, and having done all, to stand."—Ephesians 6:10-13

Pray In The Spirit

Often when we come before the Lord in prayer, we do not feel like praying. What are we to do in such a case? Cease praying until we feel like praying? No, not at all. Perhaps when we feel least like praying, it is the very time when we need to pray most. We should wait quietly before God and tell Him how we feel. Ask Him to give us a praying spirit and a praying heart. We should let Him know our desire to enter into that place of His presence. Cast all upon Him and praise Him for the opportunity He has made possible for us to come before Him. Soon we will find ourselves in a wonderful place with Him.

Our Wonderful Father,

Thank You!

"Humble yourselves therefore under the mighty hand of God, that he may exalt you in due time: Casting all your care upon him; for he careth for you."—I Peter 5:6,7

"Praying always with all prayer and supplication in the Spirit, and watching thereunto with all perseverance and supplication for all saints."—Ephesians 6:18

Be Not Afraid; Only Believe

When we see a loved one so bound and hopelessly living a life away from God, often the enemy of our soul will say there is no hope. "Why trouble ye the master?" as they said to the man Jairus, concerning his daughter. They told Jairus, "Your daughter is dead!" What were Jesus' words to Jairus? "Be not afraid; only believe."

Keep praying.

It is not hopeless as it may appear to be.

Only believe!

"While he yet spake, there came from the ruler of the synagogue's house certain which said, Thy daughter is dead: why troublest thou the Master any further? As soon as Jesus heard the word that was spoken, he saith unto the ruler of the synagogue, Be not afraid, only believe. "And he (Jesus) charged them straitly that no man should know it; and commanded that something should be given her to eat."—Mark 5:35,36,43

And the peace of God, which passeth all understanding, shall keep your hearts and minds through Christ Jesus."—Phillipians 4:7

Christian Growth

How does a Christian grow? Think of the way your body grows. You don't grow physically by trying. You just grow naturally as you eat healthy food, breathe fresh air, get exercise, and rest (get a good night's sleep). You will just naturally grow. The same is true in the Christian walk. We begin growing as we follow Jesus and practice obedience. God's Word is the Christian's food. What food is for the body, the Word of God is to the soul.

"As newborn babes, desire the sincere milk of the word, that ye may grow thereby."—I Peter 2:2

Read and think about God's Word, put it into practice in your everyday life, and you will grow as a Christian.

Prayer is the Christians' AIR, fresh every day. Naturally, if a person gets no air, he dies. Air is to us physically what prayer is to us spiritually. We will not grow spiritually without prayer; we will die.

Exercise is important to our physical health. We get the exercise we need spiritually by talking about Jesus to others (witnessing). We exercise by telling them what God has done for us and telling others who He is.

Rest is also so important. Jesus said, "Come unto me; I will give you rest." We may labor to be better, but we can take His yoke upon us and learn of Him. He will give us rest unto our souls. As we rest in Him, we will grow in Him.

"But grow in grace, and in the knowledge of our Lord and Savior Jesus Christ. To him be glory both now and for ever. Amen."—II Peter 3:18

Be Not Anxious

There are times we get excited over things and begin to make plans. Suddenly, we begin to think I'd better slow down. This may not even be God's plan for me. As some of the excitement slows down, we begin to wait instead of dreaming on. We think and pray, "Lord, whatever your will is, that is fine with me. You know what your plan is. I trust your judgement and your plan for me."

For many years, I didn't make plans about moving long distances. Lack of work took us one place then another. But I didn't make these plans, my husband did. As I look back now, I can see how even all the moving was part of God's plan. Although our lives were not yielded to Him, He was guiding our paths. It is easy to rest when someone else is making the plans. We just follow. And when we yield to our Heavenly Father's plans and trust Him, there is peace. His Word says to not be anxious and tells us what to do.

"Be careful (anxious) for nothing; but in everything by prayer and supplication with thanksgiving let your requests be made known unto God.
"And the peace of God, which passeth all understanding, shall keep your hearts and minds through Christ Jesus." —Philippians 4:6,7

Trust And Depend On God

How do we let our difficulties affect us? Our trials must come to strengthen and build us. Do we allow the trials to bring us to the place of becoming more and more dependent upon God and our faith to be increased? Do we handle it all by ourselves and let it take us farther and farther away from God, weakening our faith?

We must go through things to learn to trust and depend on God. We must lean on God and draw closer to Him. We must not allow ourselves to be shaken from our steadfastness and love for God by our trials. Trials are permitted to come to our lives in order to try us for our good…..to cause us to come forth as pure gold. God does not tempt us but allows us to be tempted.

Is our love for Him genuine?

Let's follow Him and be strengthened and blessed.

Remember Abraham and his love for God!

"But he knoweth the way that I take: when he hath tried me, I shall come forth as gold."—Job 23:10

What Is Self-Denial

We all know what it means to do what we want to do, to get what we want, to enjoy ourselves as we please. We call this gratifying or pleasing ourselves. Sometimes what we prefer to do, or get, or enjoy, conflicts with what the Lord Jesus wants. If we love Him, we put aside our own wishes and do what pleases Him. Sometimes that will mean giving up what we would have preferred. When we refuse to gratify ourselves, this is self-denial. Jesus said that if anyone wants to be His disciple, he must deny himself and take up his cross and follow Him.

Self-denial involves doing what Jesus wants us to do when we prefer to do something else. Jesus warned, lest we let either the things that worry us or the things we enjoy take such a place in our lives that we fail to be ready for Jesus when He comes.

"Then said Jesus unto his disciples, if any man will come after me, let him deny himself, and take up his cross, and follow me."
— Matthew 16:24

Justification

What does the word justification mean? It is a legal term, describing the act of God as judge by which He declares us to be in a right standing before Him as far as His justice is concerned. We are not justified in ourselves, so the only way by which we can be declared to be in a right standing before God is on the basis of the death of Jesus Christ for our sins. Through Christ bearing our punishment, His righteousness is applied to us by God's grace.

Grace: Unmerited favor

Is justification by faith or by grace? Justification is by the grace of God alone; received through faith alone because of Christ alone.

Justified
Just-as-if- I'd – never sinned

"Being justified freely by his grace through the redemption that is in Christ Jesus."—Romans 3:24

No Need To Worry; Have Faith

When we are going through things, we tend to follow our old habit of worry. We need not worry. Our Heavenly Father knows what we need and He is very aware of our troubles and sufferings. God gave us a wonderful scripture in Philippians that tells us how to overcome these things. As I begin to think on the wonderful times He has given me peace, and experiences of His love and care, I forget the trouble.

Hide His Word in your heart and keep those precious experiences in your mind and heart. If only we can realize, our God can do anything. He is so near to us, even in those times when we don't feel Him as near to us.

He is Wonderful!

"Be careful for nothing; but in everything by prayer and supplication with thanksgiving let your request be made known unto God. And the peace of God, which passeth all understanding, shall keep your hearts and minds through Christ Jesus. Finally, brethren, whatsoever things are true, whatsoever things are honest, whatsoever things are just, whatsoever things are pure, whatsoever things are lovely, whatsoever things are of good report; if there be any virtue, and if there by any praise, think on these things. Those things, which ye have both learned, and received, and heard, and seen in me, do: and the God of peace shall be with you." —Philippians 4:6-9

Baptism In The Holy Spirit

I am so thankful for God's Holy Spirit. I have said so many times "I am so thankful for how God saved me, how He drew me to Him and began to teach me about His ways." It all has truly been a blessing. There is nothing that could ever compare to it. I remember a time so well when I had been saved for some time. It's a time that reminds me of when Jesus was getting ready to be crucified. He spoke precious things in the last hours about the disciples going back to Jerusalem and waiting for the promise of the Father to come. He wanted to baptize them with the Holy Ghost and with fire; after this they would be made a witness unto Him.

I felt like this was the time in my journey with the Lord that it was time for me to dwell and pray and experience the things He had for me. I had contended upon the Lord without distraction, fasting and praying and following Him. Then one night we went to church and the minister asked if anyone wanted or had a need from the Lord to come up and He would pray. I went up. He said, "What do you need the Lord to do for you?" I said, "I want to be baptized in the Holy Ghost." As He looked me in the eye, he said, "Do you believe God is going to do this?" His eyes were like looking into the eyes of Jesus. I thought, "If it's God's will." Then I thought, "This is God's will." I said, "Yes." The minister placed his hands on my head. As I was immersed in God's Spirit, I began speaking in a beautiful language, fluently.

**What a wonderful experience.
He is Wonderful!**

"And, behold, I send the promise of my Father upon you: but tarry ye in the city of Jerusalem, until ye be endued with power from on high."—Luke 24:49

Jesus Our Intercessor

All throughout the book of Numbers, we can see the children of Israel as complainers and murmurers. They were always murmuring against God's chosen leaders, even against God! They were unable to enter the land of Canaan; the land God had promised them. It was a land flowing with milk and honey. Because of their unbelief, only two individuals eventually entered that land of promise. The remainder wandered in the wilderness for thirty-eight years, until their death. They had seen miracles, they had eaten bread from heaven, they'd received water from a rock, and even had the meat that they desired. All that saved them was God's mercy and a leader that prayed and interceded for them.

Jesus is our Intercessor and if we compare our lives today to the journey of the Israelite people, we can see so many parallels. We too came out of Egyptian bondage. We came out of the world and were freed from the bondage of sin. We too were led by the mighty hand of God; by His Spirit. We too saw the miracles. We have eaten the spiritual manna, that bread from above. We too have drunk from that Rock, which is Christ. We've eaten the Meat of His will and experienced divine healings of the Spirit and body.

We have too much to be thankful for to ever complain or look back.

Jesus Our Intercessor

We can make it!
God is our helper!

Have we seen enough of God's Goodness and His Greatness to faithfully press on in the face of hard times and trouble? Are we keeping the faith and giving a good report? Are we depending on our great intercessor, depending on His compassion and guidance to keep us in times of helplessness? We must stay alert and watch. We must set our affections on things above and not on the things in the earth.

Israel's murmurings against God show a lack of faith and trust in God's loving care.

We must take a personal inventory and decide if the circumstances we find ourselves in came from God or by our own actions. Who brought us to the place we find ourselves in? God or our desires and wants. Is God the author of our circumstances? The challenge we face is the old appetite we developed in Egypt. The children of Israel had developed a taste for the onions and garlic of Egypt. The true child of God desires more spiritual experiences and blessings. We never know what we will face tomorrow, but will we be like the Israelites, fearful, unbelieving, complaining, and showing the other nations our fear?

**Our God is able to take care of His children.
We are His people.**

"Let your conversation be without covetousness; and be content with such things as ye have: for he hath said, I will never leave thee, nor forsake thee."—Hebrews 13:5

In Him

I was on my way to surgery when I asked, "Father, should I ask for a Scripture?" The answer that came back to me was, "All My promises are yours." What a wonderful feeling as I went on to surgery. I knew I was not alone. I had asked in times past for a scripture to comfort others going to surgery or other things they were going through. Now He comforts me with these precious Words.

He is so wonderful!

As the days passed I thought on His Word and remembered 2 Corinthians 1:20, 21; *"For all the promises of God in Him are yea, and in Him Amen, unto the glory of God by us. Now He which stablisheth us with you in Christ, and hath anointed us, is God."*

Paul also said in 2 Corinthians 1:3 *"Blessed be God, even the Father of our Lord Jesus Christ, The Father of mercies and the God of all comfort; who comforteth us in all our tribulations, that we may be able to comfort them which are in any trouble, by the comfort wherewith we ourselves are comforted of God."*

Confidence In His Word

The assurance of God's promises brings peace in the middle of the biggest storm.

When God gives the peace and assurance all will be well, we know it will be just as He said!

Think about the shipwreck described in Acts, chapter 27. This was a terrible time to go through; much like some of the storms in our lives. It was a very dark time as those men were tossed on the sea. Verse 20 says they saw neither sun nor stars in many days. As the ship was tossed about, Paul had words of encouragement for them; *"For there stood by me this night the angel of God, whose I am, and whom I serve, saying, fear not Paul..."* (Acts 27:23,24) Although the ship crashed, no one perished. It was just as the Lord said; all men were safe.

We can trust His Words in the darkest times. He will not leave us; He will be with us through it all and bring us through. We will be stronger and able to encourage and comfort others.

"Wherefore, sirs, be of good cheer for I believe God, that it shall be even as it was told me."—Acts 27:25

God Always Has A People

God chose the tribe of Levi to conduct services in the tabernacle. The entire tribe was about God's business.
God always has a people.

I think of John the beloved and how close to the Lord he chose to stay. So many wonderful times he revealed the love and words of God's Spirit in his books. In the book of Revelation, we see how he received the Revelation of Jesus Christ while on the Isle of Patmos.

God always has a people who hunger to be as close and hear everything the Lord has to say.

Are we that people?

Help us, Lord, to be that people who desire

and hunger to be one with you.

"That they all may be one; as thou, Father, art in me, and I in thee, that they also may be one in us: that the world may believe that thou hast sent me."—John 17:21

Thankful For The Lessons

I am so thankful for the lessons The Lord has taught me on my journey with Him.

I remember one day, long ago, I was not thinking about the things I had. Instead, I was thinking about the things I didn't have. Suddenly, I felt like I needed to pray, so I went to my bedroom. As I knelt to pray, these words came to me; "Be content with such things as you have, for have I not said, I will never leave you nor forsake you." Wonderful words I will never forget, and the lesson I am so thankful for. He is always aware of our thoughts. He is always near, and He cares about our every feeling, thought, and need. He will direct us and our thoughts and always supply our every need. We don't have to worry. We have everything we will ever need when we have Him.

He is Wonderful!

"Let your conversation be without covetousness; and be content with such things as ye have: for he hath said, I will never leave thee, nor forsake thee."—Hebrews 13:5

The Anointing Of The Holy Spirit

The anointing of the Holy Spirit is wonderful. He anoints us to do His work. We may sing and testify about Him and what He has done in our lives. We may preach, teach, or speak a word when needed to encourage someone. Everything God does is wonderful and brings life. He just needs those who are willing and obedient to do His will. It's so good to know that we don't have to do all this on our own. When Jesus called us, He also let us know that we would not be alone. He would send us another comforter, which is the Holy Ghost, who would teach us all things, and remind us of the things He had said. He would always be with us and in us.

**As we follow the leading of His Holy Spirit,
and obey, He will be glorified.**

Jesus, speaking of "Living Water", says in John 7:37-39, "*. . . If any man thirst, let him come unto me and drink. He that believeth on me, as the scripture hath said, out of his belly shall flow rivers of living water. (But this spake He of the Spirit, which they that believed on Him should receive: for the Holy Ghost was not yet given; because that Jesus was not yet glorified).*"

As we obey and are led by His Spirit, we find He still blesses and brings life to those we minister to, in song, testimony, preaching, teaching and encouraging, because it is the Holy Spirit. We are only the vessels He uses.

His blessings to us are wonderful!

What A Wonderful Comforter He Is

"The days of our years are threescore years and ten; and if by reason of strength they be fourscore years, yet is their strength labor and sorrow; for it is soon cut off, and we fly away. So teach us to number our days, that we may apply our hearts unto wisdom."—Psalm 90:10, 12

These were such comforting words to me as I was going through a difficult time. I had been in the hospital, and even though the doctors were trying, I was not getting my problem solved. After the third admission, my issue was finally resolved, and I had surgery. I had this scripture on my mind daily; it was a great comfort; it was just so special. I even mentioned it to several people, visitors and nurses. It was especially meaningful to me, since I am now 81 years old. It reminds me that when my earthy life is cut off, that is not all, but we will fly away.

Jesus said in John 14:2,3 *"In my Father's house are many mansions; if it were not so, I would have told you. I go to prepare a place for you. And if I go and prepare a place for you, I will come again, and receive you unto myself; that where I am, there ye may be also."*

We can look forward to flying away with Him one way or another, because He said in I Thessalonians 4:17, *"Then we which are alive and remain shall be caught up together with them in the clouds, to meet the Lord in the air: and so shall we ever be with the Lord."*

We can always believe and rely on His promises.
What a wonderful Comforter and Savior!

For God So Loved The World

We see people imprisoned every day. Some are literally behind bars. Others may not be behind bars but are prisoners just the same to Satan. Bars cannot be seen, but the absence of freedom is the same.

The Blood of Jesus Christ is the price paid for our freedom. You see, all of us were prisoners, without a chance of parole or ever being set free. God, in His love, was willing to give His Son to be the sacrifice for our sin debt and free us. He purchased us back from Satan's power and possession. There was no other way that we could be set free. All man's blood was contaminated with sin because of Adam's sin. He disobeyed God, losing his dominion over all to Satan. Only a blood sacrifice could atone for sin.

In the Old Testament, the blood of bulls and goats was used as a sacrifice. This blood, offered by the High Priest once each year, only covered sins for a time.

The Precious Son of God was man's only hope. So, God sent His only Son. He loved us so much, and the same love was in Jesus. He was willing to give so we could have life. That is the only way we can be free today.

Jesus tells us in John 3:1-16 about a new birth that will give us a whole new life. If you have not received this new life in Him, believe and accept what He has done for you. He died in your place for your sins and was raised from the dead. He ascended back to the Father, and He is now at the right hand of the Father interceding to His Father for you.

"For God so loved the world, that he gave his only begotten Son, that whosoever believeth in him should not perish, but have everlasting life."—John 3:16

WORKS CITED

Myers, F. (1974). *Great Verses Through the Bible*. New York: Harper Collins.

Spurgeon, C. (1997). *Joy in Christ's Presence*. New Kensington: Whitaker House.

Stedman, R. (2006). *The Power of His Presence*. Grand Rapids: Discovery House Publishers.

www.ingramcontent.com/pod-product-compliance
Lightning Source LLC
Chambersburg PA
CBHW071229290426
44108CB00013B/1342